WINNING THE BATTLE FOR RELEVANCE

WINNING
THE **BATTLE** FOR
RELEVANCE

WHY **EVEN THE GREATEST** BECOME OBSOLETE...
AND **HOW TO AVOID THEIR FATE**

MICHAEL McQUEEN

New York

WINNING THE BATTLE FOR RELEVANCE
WHY EVEN THE GREATEST BECOME OBSOLETE...

AND HOW TO AVOID THEIR FATE

Published in New York, New York, by Morgan James Publishing. Morgan James and The Entrepreneurial Publisher are trademarks of Morgan James, LLC. www.MorganJamesPublishing.com

The Morgan James Speakers Group can bring authors to your live event. For more information or to book an event visit The Morgan James Speakers Group at www.TheMorganJamesSpeakersGroup.com.

A **free** eBook edition is available
with the purchase of this print book.

CLEARLY PRINT YOUR NAME ABOVE IN UPPER CASE

Instructions to claim your free eBook edition:
1. Download the Shelfie app for Android or iOS
2. Write your name in **UPPER CASE** above
3. Use the Shelfie app to submit a photo
4. Download your eBook to any device

ISBN 978-1-63047-821-6 paperback
ISBN 978-1-63047-822-3 eBook
ISBN 978-1-63047-823-0 hardcover
Library of Congress Control Number:
2015916058

Cover Design by:
Chris Treccani
www.3dogdesign.net

In an effort to support local communities and raise awareness and funds, Morgan James Publishing donates a percentage of all book sales for the life of each book to Habitat for Humanity Peninsula and Greater Williamsburg.

Get involved today, visit
www.MorganJamesBuilds.com

Habitat
for Humanity®
Peninsula and
Greater Williamsburg
Building Partner

ACKNOWLEDGEMENTS

Like any worthwhile endeavor, this project has required an enormous and largely unseen level of sacrifice. From the years of research to the months of writing and the countless hours of thinking out loud, what you hold in your hand would not have been possible without the unwavering support and encouragement of my beautiful wife, Hailey. Thank you for your steadfast belief in me and longsuffering patience. You are the best running mate a man could hope for.

Thanks also to the many cheerleaders who I am blessed to have in my life. While there are so many names I could list, special mention must go to Kirryn, Toby, Michael, Kirsty, Trevor, Temre, Graham, Sam, Dave and Amber. In your own way, you have each played a key role in my life and the life of this book.

To my wonderful parents on both sides. Your steadfast love and uncanny knack for picking up typos and grammatical errors means more than you could know. There really is nothing like a set of Baby Boomer eyes!

To the fantastic team at Ode Management and to my publishers at Morgan James – you are a joy and privilege to work with.

To my editor Josephine; cover designer Jen; and dinosaur photographers Andrew and Carla. Thank you all so much for helping take my words and turn them into something worth reading.

Finally, to my own Author and sustainer – the one who first gave me the inspiration for this book and then gave me the creativity and strength to see the vision through. Words could never be enough.

CONTENTS

INTRODUCTION:

WELCOME TO THE INFLECTION POINT

On a recent speaking tour, I stopped in a small rural town to grab a bite to eat. As I strolled down the main street looking for anything that might be open, I stumbled across an enormous real estate sign that stopped me in my tracks. What caught my attention was the property being sold.

It was clear the beautiful old church had seen better days. Timber boards covered windows where stained glass once glistened; a trail of stairs leading to the church's giant front doors was overrun with weeds; birds nestled in a broken ceiling on the front porch.

On a side wall of the building a marble plaque with faded gold-leaf inscription read simply, "*This stone was laid by President of the Baptist Union, 20th June 1903. Dedicated to the Glory of God.*"

As I continued down the street, I imagined the many significant moments and memories that had taken place within the walls of the once busy church. I envisaged a small group of committed individuals determined to create something sacred and beautiful, and I imagined the sacrifices they would have made to see their dream fulfilled.

Hosting baptisms, weddings and funerals, the building would have once been central to the life pulse of the town.

And then I wondered: what happened?

At what point did this church cease being core to the rhythms and cycles of this town's residents... and why? Was it a change in the community's values or DNA? Was there a clergy leadership scandal that caused the church's membership to scatter? Did the local economy fall on hard times? Had the congregation aged and eventually died out?

Whatever the cause, the result was clear. Somewhere along the line, this little church had failed to keep pace with the world around it – a predicament in which they are far from alone.

All around the globe, many similar enterprises are struggling to remain relevant to their respective 'communities'. Non-profit groups, religious organizations and entire political systems are grappling with shifting social values. Institutions of all shapes and sizes are trying to figure out what the new 'normal' looks like – and if there even is one.

In the commercial realm too, recent years have seen scores of iconic businesses and brands fall by the wayside, morphing from revolutionary to relic in the space of a few decades. What, for example, happened to Nokia, Borders, Kodak, Nortel, Blockbuster or Blackberry?

As traditional profit models and distribution channels are disrupted or destroyed, corporations, industries and brands are trying to keep pace and remain viable. The lesson is clear: no industry is immune to extinction.

Having dedicated over a decade to tracking the dominant trends shaping business and society, there is no doubt in my mind that we are at a pivotal point in history. We are experiencing an unprecedented convergence of economic, social, technological and geo-political disruptions that are widespread, rapid and fundamental.

WE ARE AT AN INFLECTION POINT IN THE HISTORY OF MANKIND — A POINT AT WHICH THE FUTURE CANNOT BE DISCERNED BY LOOKING TO THE PAST

In short, we are at an inflection point in the history of mankind - a point at which the future cannot be discerned by looking to the past.

Recognizing these shifts in the social landscape, my research in recent years has become focused on three key questions:

1. *How* does the journey from prominence to obsolescence unfold – are there discernible patterns and cycles that organizations and leaders ignore at their peril?
2. *Why* have such a disproportionately large number of companies, institutions or brands faded from the scene in recent years?
3. *What* separates the enduring from the endangered – and what can we learn from those who are prevailing and prospering in the face of disruption?

These three questions have largely informed the structure of this book. In section one, we will examine a cycle of rise and fall evident in every arena of human endeavor.

In section two, we will explore the five roads to irrelevance – the five common reasons why even the greatest become obsolete – and how these offer signposts for us all.

In the third and final section we will look at a series of habits and strategies that have enabled the enduringly relevant to stay ahead of the curve for years or decades at the time.

So get set. Think of this book as a boot camp of sorts – a preparation for the battle we must all fight in the years ahead: *the battle for relevance*.

SECTION 1:
The Cycle of Relevance

CHAPTER 1:

THE RELEVANCE CURVE

Like most things in business and life, relevance follows an incredibly predictable cycle or pattern – one which can be best depicted by a model I call the Relevance Curve.

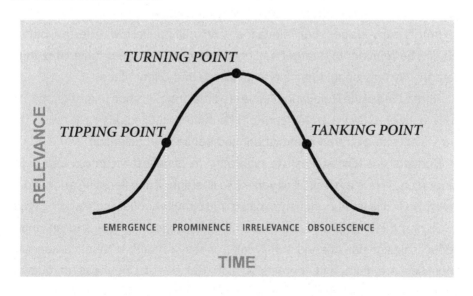

Similar to a lifecycle graph, the Relevance Curve tracks the four sequential phases that products, ideas and organizations naturally go through over time in their journey from emergence to prominence and finally obsolescence.

For simplicity of discussion, in the pages that follow I will use the word *'entity'* as an interchangeable term for any product, business, brand, idea, organization, institution or movement. Although the emphasis here will be on organizational relevance, many of the same principles and patterns in the pages ahead apply to individuals too.

PHASE 1: EMERGENCE

Every entity begins the same way - with a point of creation or conception. Perhaps it's a spark of inspiration, an idea scribbled on a napkin over coffee, a moment of brilliance that wakes you from a deep sleep, or a meeting of minds during a brainstorming session. The seeds of the idea take root and before you know it, a new business opens its doors, a new product hits the market, a new movement or association gets underway.

In this early stage, your relevance is typically quite low. After all, before you can be relevant to a target audience you must first determine who 'they' are and why they should pay attention to you in the first place.

Phase One of the Relevance Curve is a time of exploration, experimentation and creativity. Often a small team of like-minded individuals rally round the new vision with a shared commitment and sense of anticipation.

Budgets are low, stakes are high and the smallest victory is cause for celebration. This is the "fake it till you make it" stage of any fledgling endeavor – and typically it is an enormously exciting and simultaneously challenging time.

During this first phase, business models, target markets and an entire product's design can change from week to week or month to month. Internally, processes are fluid and there is a high degree of openness to outside influences and new ideas.

Momentum and market awareness build slowly in this first phase – often at what feels like a glacial pace. Eventually, you begin to get a clear sense of who your market is; they just don't know yet who *you* are.

As the months and years pass, you become more deliberate and strategic... and your relevance steadily grows to the point where you reach a thrilling milestone that dreams are made of and bestselling books have been written about: the Tipping Point. It is at this point that relevance begins to grow exponentially and momentum really kicks in. You have entered a new stage of your relevance – Phase Two.

PHASE 2: PROMINENCE

This new phase is an exciting time on the Relevance Curve. If you were to liken it to a season it would undoubtedly be summer. The entity goes from strength to strength, emerging into the limelight from relative obscurity.

You are getting an ever-clearer idea of the needs and nature of your target market. Even more exciting is the fact that they are also beginning to know who *you* are too. Over time you develop a band of raving fans who love what you do and influence the marketplace to do the same.

It is at about this time that the strategic focus shifts from creativity and innovation to an emphasis on growth and expansion. In order to support the burgeoning success, the entity's back-end administrative function also expands.

Staff numbers and office sizes increase. At the same time, internal systems and processes begin to form as 'best practices' are identified. Lines of authority are established and management structures solidify in the name of efficiency.

As you continue to ascend through the second phase, you become mainstream, popular, widely accepted and possibly even ubiquitous. Near the top of the curve in this second phase, you enter what Derek Zoolander would call the 'so hot right now' stage.

NEAR THE TOP OF THE CURVE IN THIS SECOND PHASE, YOU ENTER WHAT DEREK ZOOLANDER WOULD CALL THE 'SO HOT RIGHT NOW' STAGE.

This is a time where all manner of clichés could be used to describe your success. You are 'in the zone'; 'on message'; 'firing on all cylinders'; and in a 'sweet spot.' You can't seem to put a foot wrong and momentum feels effortless.

A SENSE OF INVINCIBILITY

By now, competitors have started to pay attention – emulating your success formula and viewing you as a benchmark for excellence. It is also at about this point that your reliance on market feedback begins to taper off. You are beginning to form a clear identity of who you are – but also who you are *not*. This is a time of streamlining and specialization.

While the 'so hot right now' stage can be enormously exciting, it is also the single most dangerous stage on the Relevance Curve for any entity. The reason for this is simple: with great success comes an enormous temptation to start resting on your laurels. It is easy to start believing your own press, become mildly complacent and even develop a sense of invincibility.

However, this stage is a time for vigilance and a re-doubling of effort. If you don't take active steps and keep doing the fundamentals that saw you succeed in the first place, slowly but surely you will begin to drift. It may take months, years or decades, but without deliberate effort you will eventually pass a second invisible trigger called the Turning Point – a point which marks the transition from Phase Two to Phase Three.

PHASE 3: IRRELEVANCE

While the transition from relevance to irrelevance is usually unheralded, it is not entirely imperceptible. In fact, I would suggest that organizations and leaders usually know the very moment they pass the Turning Point because there will be an undeniable, ever-growing, gnawing sense that something is missing.

It is as if the sense of freshness and vitality that once typified the entity seems to have evaporated. Staff members are doing the same things they've always been doing, but now it just feels like drudgery or "going through the motions". Even the entity's slogans, phrases and messaging which once held such meaning begin to feel like empty rhetoric.

The early stages of Phase Three can be very confusing because even though there is a sense that something is awry, typically there is no evidence of the fact. Sales graphs are often still pointing skywards; expansion plans may be on the boil; the balance sheet appears healthy. However, these lagging indicators mask weaknesses that have not yet become apparent.

As a result, leaders tend to ignore their gut sense that something has changed and continue with 'business as usual'. This is often under the justifiable but erroneous assumption that if they keep doing what they have always done, they will keep getting the results they have always enjoyed.

THE TRAP OF 'CHEAPER, QUICKER, MORE'

At an organizational level, the early stages of Phase Three tend to be when another set of dangerous dynamics come into play. The Phase Two focus on growth and expansion gives way to a drive for efficiency – the compulsion to do things marginally cheaper or faster than in the past.

At the same time, leaders unconsciously shift into management-mode with an emphasis on quality control and continuous incremental improvement. Internal processes and systems begin to ossify and harden at the cost of agility and responsiveness. The very successes of the past begin to hold you hostage making it difficult to introduce change. Openness to innovation gives way to a resistance of it; bureaucracy and red tape begin to slowly choke the entity from the inside out.

Somewhere around half to two-thirds of the way into Phase Three, typically the entity reaches a point of crisis. At first, it is a bad month. Then it is a bad quarter... and then a bad year. Perhaps you start experiencing attrition as members and clients drift away. Market share starts to fall as newer and more nimble start-ups begin beating you at your own game.

While at first these negative results are typically dismissed as an anomaly, a temporary downturn or just part of a cycle "we've seen before", eventually the writing on the wall becomes clear: you are not as 'hot' or relevant as you used to be.

Although this point of crisis may be confronting and even terrifying, it can also be a gift. After all, when times get tough, individuals and organizations suddenly become willing to try new things and make changes that they may otherwise have resisted when times were good.

Further still, crises have a unique way of stimulating creativity and innovation. Necessity is indeed the mother of invention.

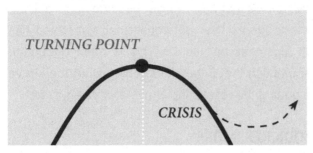

The good news is that if entities play their cards right at the point of crisis, they can turn things around and regain momentum, vitality and relevance.

Take the wrong steps or simply do nothing however, and you will inevitably continue on the downward slide toward a third trigger known as The Tanking Point.

PHASE 4: OBSOLESCENCE

As you pass The Tanking Point and enter the final phase of the Relevance Curve, momentum is now working against you. By this point, denial, scarcity and protectionism become dominant forces. Fear creeps in and becomes the key driver of behavior. The strategic focus shifts from efficiency to cost-reduction and damage control.

It is at this point that rash decisions are made and sweeping changes are introduced. However, akin to rearranging deck chairs on the Titanic, such activity is often too little, too late.

As the entity crumbles, staff members, customers and shareholders jump ship. By this point, everyone is asking the question 'what happened' or 'where did we go wrong?' Competitors begin to circle and hostile takeover bids are made. Eventually, the entity is acquired; re-badged; or slowly grinds to a halt having become completely and utterly obsolete.

While this cycle may appear fatalistic and even a little defeatist, in chapter 4 we will explore the important question of whether obsolescence and decline is indeed an unavoidable fate or merely the consequence of decisions made and actions taken.

In the next chapter however, we will look at how the Relevance Curve helps us make sense of the patterns we see in everything from the rise and fall of civilizations to the erosion of societal institutions and the passing parade of fads and fashions in popular culture. After all, what do the Portuguese Empire, the PTA and pay phones have in common? Read ahead and you'll find out.

CHAPTER 2:
REAL-LIFE RELEVANCE

While the cycle we discussed in the previous chapter may be a convenient theoretical model, the true value of the Relevance Curve becomes clear when it is applied to life.

German philosopher Friedrich Engels once argued that an ounce of reality is worth a ton of theory and I am inclined to agree. I believe that theories only prove useful if they help us make sense of the experiences and practical realities we are confronted with in everyday life.

To this end, in the coming pages we will look at a number of facets of society and culture where the Relevance Curve is clearly at work – whether we have realized it previously or not.

THE RELEVANCE CURVE IN HISTORY

A few years ago, my wife and I were on our first trip to Rome. Having spent almost a month travelling around Italy, we were a little cathedral-weary and yet we figured that as the saying goes, "When in Rome…" and so we booked in for a tour of the Vatican.

Halfway through our guided tour of the Sistine Chapel, our guide explained the origins of the Vatican City as a sovereign state and the importance of the Lateran Treaty of 1929. This agreement, we learned, was made between Italy's Prime Minister at the time, Mussolini, and Pope Pius XI, and established the Vatican City as a self-governing entity.

"The Lateran Treaty states that as long as the Vatican stands, it is to be given a guarantee of full and independent sovereignty from Italy," our guide explained.

As we set off again on our tour, a young boy in our group worked up the courage to ask a question. "But what if The Vatican falls one day?" he enquired. "Would the Vatican City become a part of Italy again?"

Our guide paused, turned around with a smile seeking out the boy and replied "That is a very interesting question. What's your name?"

"Isaac" said the boy stepping forward with a mixture of certainty and pride.

Crouching down, our guide explained, "Well Isaac, I guess if the Vatican fell the land would have to go back to Italy. But don't worry,' she continued 'The Vatican will never fall."

In the days that followed, Isaac's question stuck with me. Even though it may seem inconceivable that one of the worlds most powerful and wealthy institutions could one day fall, there is no reason why this could not and will not one day happen. After all, history features a long procession of empires that dominated culture and spanned the globe only to see their power and positions erode with time.

From the ancient Egyptians, Hittites and Chou Dynasty through to the Romans, the Vikings, the Portuguese and the Ottomans, every great empire or civilization has followed a pattern of rise and fall remarkably similar to the one described in the previous chapter.

In more recent centuries, we have seen the Dutch, the Spanish and the British empires lose their status as global powers. Currently, many analysts are pondering whether America is next.[1] Even U.S. President Obama acknowledged this question in his 2012 *State of the Union* Address rather aptly titled "An America Built to Last".[2]

The pre-eminent historian Norman Davies once said: "All states and nations, however great, bloom for a season and are replaced."[3]

To paraphrase Davies' observation, history shows us that even the

HISTORY SHOWS US THAT EVEN THE GREATEST NATIONS AND EMPIRES ARE NOT IMMUNE TO THE RELEVANCE CURVE CYCLE. greatest nations and empires are not immune to the Relevance Curve cycle.

THE RELEVANCE CURVE IN SOCIETAL INSTITUTIONS

The journey of community service organizations such as Apex, Rotary and Lions throughout the 20th Century has many ways epitomized the Relevance Curve.

The early 1900s saw a host of new service clubs and membership-based associations spring up throughout the western world. Many of these passed the Tipping Point in the late 1930s and by the early 1940s were well and truly into the 'so hot right now' stage of Phase 2. Indicative of this, community service organizations in the U.S. saw their membership *double* in size between 1940 and 1945.[4]

Somewhere during the 1960s, however, many of these organizations passed their respective Turning Points and entered Phase Three on the Relevance Curve with growth and momentum stagnating. By the mid-1980s, community service groups began a steady decline to the point where by 1997, membership of these organizations in the U.S. was half the size of the 1960's peak.[5]

The Parent Teacher Association (PTA) in America is another good example of the Relevance Curve in action. In the 1960s the organization boasted a larger membership base than any other secular organization in America, but by the mid-90s the PTA had lost over half a million members.[6]

Curiously, this attrition occurred over a period when the number of American families with children under the age of 18 grew by 2 million.[7] In other words, it wasn't that there were fewer parents in the 1990s than in the 1960s, but rather that PTA membership had become seen as less appealing to parents 30 years on.

In his book *Bowling Alone*, Professor of Public Policy at Harvard Robert D Putnam, observes: "Somehow in the last several decades of the twentieth century, community groups started to fade. It wasn't that older members dropped out, but that community organizations were no longer continuously revitalized by new members."[8]

Naturally, this begs the question: *why aren't these organizations attracting new members?*

The simple answer comes back to relevance. Organizations that are relevant to their time and to the needs of their respective communities will always attract new members naturally and effortlessly. However, the opposite is also true: organizations that lose touch with the times or the needs of their members find it near impossible to attract new members.

Looking to a very different societal institution, trade unions have faced similar relevance challenges in recent decades.

For many years, unions provided valuable security and empowerment for working class employees who may otherwise have fallen prey to unfair work conditions or exploitation. At it's peak in the 1950s, union membership in the U.S. stood at about 32.5% while in other countries like Australia union membership topped 57% of the working population during the mid-1970s.[9] Just a handful of decades later however, it is a very different story. Unionization in the US today has sunk to around 12% and around 18% in Australia.[10]

While there are a number of reasons for this decline, research indicates that the primary cause is that people are simply not as interested in, or feel they are in need of union representation as they were previously. In short, unions are seen as less relevant to the working class today than they once were.[11]

As an interesting contrast, at the same time as union membership has declined, affiliation with industry associations has grown. In the 1950s, less than 10% of American workers belonged to a professional association but by the mid-1990s this number had doubled.[12]

Returning to a theme we began with in the opening

AT THE SAME TIME AS UNION MEMBERSHIP HAS DECLINED, AFFILIATION WITH INDUSTRY ASSOCIATIONS HAS GROWN.

pages of this book, one area where the Relevance Curve is particularly apparent is in religious adherence and church attendance.

While people's spiritual beliefs might not have changed enormously over the last half century – with the vast majority of people still believing in the existence of God and in life after death[13] – levels of religious affiliation and engagement have fallen significantly over the same time period.

In the United States, the rate of formal religious adherence dropped roughly 10-12% between the 1960s and 1990s[14] while the percentage of Americans who described themselves as having no formal religion rose from 2% in 1967[15] to over 20% in 2012.[16]

More tellingly, almost 90% of respondents in a 2012 Pew Research Center study said they did not find organized religion attractive - describing religious institutions as too concerned about money, power, rules and politics.[17]

Similar trends are unfolding in the U.K. In the 2011 census for England and Wales, the percentage of the population calling itself Christian fell to 59.3% - down from almost 72% a decade earlier. Further still, the census revealed that the number of people professing no religious faith had increased from 14.8% to just over 25% in the space of 10 years.[18]

In Australia, a wide-scale study looking at religious adherence in the City of Melbourne found that a staggering 80% of the metropolitan population had little or no church affiliation and that religious institutions were losing members at a rate of 4,500 people per year. This, at a time when the city's population is growing by 90,000 people annually.[19]

The very practical implications of this trend cannot be underestimated – namely what to do with increasingly underutilized traditional church buildings. In the UK for instance, the Church of England closes about 20 churches a year and The Roman Catholic Church in Germany has shut about 515 churches in the past decade. [20]

In Montreal, a former Roman Catholic stronghold where Mark Twain once said you couldn't throw a brick without breaking a church window, questions about what to do with underutilized churches have lingered for years. The Canadian Catholic Church has sold off about 50 of Montreal's churches in the past 15 years and deconsecrated religious buildings in Quebec are so plentiful that the province established an advisory board to help tackle issues such as the disenchantment that often arises when the buildings are sold.[21]

But it is in the Netherlands where the trend appears to be most advanced. The country's Roman Catholic leaders estimate that two-thirds of their 1,600 churches will be out of commission by the mid-2020s, and 700 of Holland's Protestant churches are expected to close by 2018.[22]

This data can leave us with little doubt that at some point over the past few decades, many churches and religious institutions have started becoming less relevant to the needs and lives of their local communities – a theme we will pick up on in chapter 5.

THE RELEVANCE CURVE IN POPULAR CULTURE

Finally, popular culture offers us a long list of fads, fashions and products that have followed the cycle of emergence to prominence and then obsolescence. Consider:

- How 'talkies' came along in the late 1920s and rendered silent movies obsolete within a few short years;
- How cultural fixtures such as pinball parlors and drive-in movie theatres have all been relegated to the realm of nostalgia;
- How CDs and then MP3 players have replaced gramophones, long-playing records and cassette tapes. In each case, the rise to prominence of one technology has hammered the nail in the coffin of its predecessor;
- How public pay phones were once a familiar sight on every street corner until mobile phones triggered a decline in popularity and use;
- That children's toys like *Tickle Me Elmo* Dolls and Tamogotchis were children's playthings of choice for a season or two before becoming yesterday's news;
- Fads like Troll Dolls, Mood Rings and Baseball Cards which were commonplace in school playgrounds for a few years before disappearing.

I hope you are left with as little doubt as I am that the Relevance Curve is more than just a convenient theory. Whether in the form of social institutions, fads and fashions or the annals of history, the path from prominence to obsolescence is in fact a well-worn road.

The next chapter is dedicated to helping you determine where you are on the Relevance Curve at this very moment. Are you on the way up, riding high in the 'so hot right now' stage or are you on the downward slide?

WHERE YOU ARE RIGHT NOW ON THE RELEVANCE CURVE WILL DETERMINE THE STEPS YOU WILL NEED TO TAKE.

The reason this is so important is that where you are right now on the Relevance Curve will determine the steps you will need to take in order to win the battle for relevance in the years to come.

CHAPTER 3:

WHAT IS YOUR SILENT PULSE?

A few years ago I visited an acupuncturist following the recommendation of a good friend. Having seen scores of chiropractors and physiotherapists over the years, I was curious to see how acupuncture would differ.

The moment I walked into his clinic, it was clear that Warren was not your typical health practitioner. His waiting room was jam-packed with herbs and trinkets; a strong scent of incense permeated his rooms; and the music playing softly in the background was something I'd expect to hear at a Balinese massage house rather than a medical clinic.

In person, Warren had a disarming manner and sense of humor that immediately put me at ease. He began with all the usual questions about my personal and medical history and I expected him then to examine my posture and alignment, perhaps even ordering an X-ray like everyone else I've seen over the years. Instead, Warren asked to examine my tongue.

Looking intently into my mouth, he rattled off a series of observations about my diet, stress levels and sleep patterns – all of which were spot-on. Then, reaching for my right wrist, he said, "Now let's check the health of your liver."

I was intrigued. "How can you tell by looking at my wrist?" I asked.

"I'm checking your liver's pulse," he replied pointing to a different part of my wrist to where you'd normally check your heart rate.

"Just as I suspected, your liver pulse is weak," he said. Warren went on to prescribe a host of odd-sounding vitamins and supplements plus a diet rich in raw fruits and vegetables.

To this day, I am not sure how accurate Warren's diagnosis or methods were, though they certainly appeared to restore me to good health. My visit that day did however start me thinking – how many 'pulses' do our bodies have that we completely ignore? How many signals could we be missing and have no idea?

TAKING AN ORGANIZATION'S 'PULSE'

From an organizational and leadership perspective, I wonder the same thing. In measuring the health, vitality and relevance of a business or organization, I suspect that many leaders pay attention to only a narrow range of signals and therefore develop a warped view of how they are really tracking.

MANY LEADERS PAY ATTENTION TO ONLY A NARROW RANGE OF SIGNALS AND THEREFORE DEVELOP A WARPED VIEW OF HOW THEY ARE REALLY TRACKING.

In my role as a consultant, I always begin my work with clients by exploring how their organization measures success. The reason for this is simple – the way a business or organization measures their success drives everything else that they do: the decisions they make; the habits they discourage; and the behaviors they reward.

Regardless of the industry or country in which I find myself, it is fascinating to discover how similarly clients gauge their success - typically by measuring a range of quantifiable indicators which I refer to as an organization's *audible pulse*.

Below are some of the more common responses I have received over the years when asking clients to finish the sentence "We'll know we are successful when..."

- Profits increase
- Market share grows
- The balance sheet is healthy
- Our investment pipeline is strong
- Staff engagement is high
- Market ranking is good
- Member or customer numbers are growing
- We meet or exceed our Key Performance Indicators (KPIs)

While these traditional ways of measuring success can help to balance budgets, predict cash flows and monitor expenses, they can also be dangerously inadequate and notoriously unreliable indicators of an organization's true health.

History shows this to be the case. Consider the fact that of the 100 biggest and most financially successful companies in 1912, one in 10 was out of business a decade later.[23]

Similarly, when Tom Peters and Robert Waterman released *In Search of Excellence* in 1982, it was described at the time as the world's most comprehensive and accurate study of business success. Two years later, *Business Week* found that one-third of Peters' and Waterman's 43 'success stories' were in serious financial trouble or on the brink of collapse.[24]

One such company was consumer electronics giant Digital. Ironically, at the very time Digital was receiving accolades for business excellence, it was ignoring the arrival of desktop computers – an oversight which would put it out of business a few short years later.[25]

In their landmark 1994 book *Built to Last*, Jim Collins and Jerry Porras also compiled a list of 18 successful companies that they believed would stand the test of time due to their 'visionary' approaches. Paradoxically, at the 10-year anniversary of the book's release, seven of the original eighteen companies had stumbled from greatness.[26]

Looking at more recent failure stories like Blockbuster, Kodak and Borders, it was only a relatively few short years ago that these organizations were the outward picture of success. Sales were buoyant, profit margins healthy, market share enviable. The audible pulse of each organization was strong. As Forbes' Frederick Allen describes it, Kodak was still the darling of Wall Street many years after it had begun to lose the digital war.[27]

In the case of Borders, consider that just two years before the company's 2011 collapse, the bookseller boasted a staggering 1,249 retail outlets and $3 billion dollars in annual turnover. These outward indicators of business health gave little hint to the fact that the brand was in serious trouble following a series of staggering mistakes in previous years - namely a failure to enter the e-book market fast enough and an overinvestment in physical stores despite the consumer shift to online.[28]

Herein lies a principle that ought to give every reader pause for thought: businesses, organizations and institutions are often way down the track toward decline and obsolescence long before there is any external evidence of the fact. To put it more simply, it is possible to be on the brink of obsolescence and have absolutely no idea at all!

Naturally, I am not recommending that leaders ignore or dismiss the quantifiable measures of their organization's health such as sales figures and financial results. Rather, it is important that we see these things for what they are – lagging indicators.

While such 'audible pulses' offer an insight to the effectiveness of past decisions and investments, they give limited insight into an organizations *present* underlying health, much less an accurate forecast of the *future*. To gauge an entity's true health, leaders would be better served to pay attention to the measure of their relevance – something I refer to as a *silent pulse*.

AN ENTITY'S SILENT PULSE…IS THE CANARY IN THE COALMINE HERALDING THREATS THAT MAY NOT YET BE EVIDENT.

An entity's silent pulse is like an early detection alarm or a bellwether. It is the canary in the coalmine heralding threats that may not yet be evident.

Howard Schultz recognized the importance of a business's silent pulse upon his return to the helm of Starbucks in January 2008. Schultz recognized that even though Starbucks had been hitting home runs year on year in terms of growth, he sensed that nevertheless something was wrong.

As Schultz described it, Starbucks was failing to create the 'soulful, romantic experience' for customers for which it had once been renowned. "We'd lost sight of the experience around the coffee and we were too focused on ringing the register," Schultz admitted.[29] To put it differently, Schultz knew that while Starbucks' audible pulse was strong, the company's silent pulse was anything but. In chapter 10, we will explore the steps he took to turn things around.

When former Google executive Marissa Mayer took the reins at Yahoo, she also took immediate steps to focus the company on its silent pulse. One way Mayer did this was to simply remove Yahoo's live-feed share price indicator from the company's internal website.

"I want you thinking about *users*," Mayer stressed early in her leadership. In this, the incoming CEO was signaling to employees that it was more important for Yahoo to focus on their silent pulse by creating exciting web services than monitoring their audible pulse as expressed in company stock levels.[30] Former G.E. CEO Jack Welch agrees: "Shareholder value is a result, not a strategy. Your main constituencies must always be your employees, your customers and your products," he said.[31]

MEASURING AN ENTITY'S SILENT PULSE

When I share the concept of a silent pulse with clients, one of the common challenges that arises is that of objectivity and measurement. After all, it is easy to gauge audible pulse indicators like sales data and KPIs whereas implicit silent pulse indicators can be relegated to being little more than subjective 'gut feel' judgments.

In an effort to help clients objectify and measure their silent pulse, I have developed the simple diagnostic tool below which I urge you to take this opportunity to complete. A digital version of this diagnostic is also accessible online at www.mysilentpulse.com.

Reflecting on the questions below, indicate on a scale from one to 10 how true they are of your business, brand or organization at this moment:

In the past year, we have altered our operations due to market feedback

Not true   1 - 2 - 3 - 4 - 5 - 6 - 7 - 8 - 9 - 10   **Very true**

We have very few real competitors in the marketplace

Not true   1 - 2 - 3 - 4 - 5 - 6 - 7 - 8 - 9 - 10   **Very true**

Our internal operations today are vastly different from three years ago

Not true   1 - 2 - 3 - 4 - 5 - 6 - 7 - 8 - 9 - 10   **Very true**

There is a high sense of enthusiasm, energy & momentum internally

Not true   1 - 2 - 3 - 4 - 5 - 6 - 7 - 8 - 9 - 10   **Very true**

Our competitors tend to copy what we do and not the opposite

Not true   1 - 2 - 3 - 4 - 5 - 6 - 7 - 8 - 9 - 10   **Very true**

New ideas or process-innovations are rarely if ever met with resistance

Not true   1 - 2 - 3 - 4 - 5 - 6 - 7 - 8 - 9 - 10   **Very true**

There is a strong sense of internal unity and harmony

Not true   1 - 2 - 3 - 4 - 5 - 6 - 7 - 8 - 9 - 10   **Very true**

The last few years have been our best yet

Not true   1 - 2 - 3 - 4 - 5 - 6 - 7 - 8 - 9 - 10   **Very true**

I am more excited about our future plans than our past accomplishments

Not true   1 - 2 - 3 - 4 - 5 - 6 - 7 - 8 - 9 - 10   **Very true**

I spend more time in strategy than maintenance

Not true   1 - 2 - 3 - 4 - 5 - 6 - 7 - 8 - 9 - 10   **Very true**

Add up your circled ratings _____

Next, using the scale gradient on the curve below, put a mark where your ratings total would place you right now.

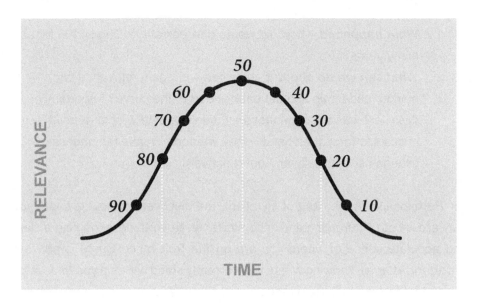

WHEN THE TRUTH IS HARD TO HEAR

Naturally, discovering just how relevant your business, brand or organization is can be confronting. I clearly remember working with one particular client for whom this was the case.

Spending the day consulting with this client company's sales and marketing team, I guided them through the above diagnostic and the results were unambiguous – their silent pulse was at about the 30 mark and they were perilously close to Tanking Point.

What was perhaps most confronting about this outcome was that the company had been at the top of their game for decades. Dominant, successful and highly profitable, they were envied by competitors and the benchmark of their industry. And yet, in just a handful of years, everything had changed.

As it happened, everyone in the company's senior management sensed that they'd passed the Turning Point a while back – some even described it as the organization's 'elephant in the room'. However, no-one was able to put their finger on exactly why things felt so out of sync.

Upon confronting the reality of their flagging silent pulse, discussion in the room revolved around two questions:

1. ***What happened*** – how did we go off-track after being so hot for so many years?

2. ***What can we do about it*** - how can we regain relevance and market leadership and get back ahead of the curve? Importantly, this client was adamant that they didn't want to wait for a point of crisis to force their hand – they wanted to make the necessary changes strategically and not reactively.

Perhaps like in the case of my client, the discovery of how relevant you truly are is both confronting and uncomfortable. Nevertheless, gaining a clear and accurate sense of where you are on the Relevance Curve is critically important. After all, knowing where you currently stand will help you to develop a map for the road that lies ahead.

EXERCISE: CONSIDER YOUR COMPETITORS

While it is valuable to discover your own position on the Relevance Curve, it is equally important to be clear on where your competitors stand.

List your top 5 competitors by assigning them a letter below. Next, place the letter for each competitor where you believe they are right now on the same Relevance Curve you used to determine your own position.

A. _____

B. _____

C. _____

D. _____

E. _____

Consider what the relative position of your competitors on the Relevance Curve may mean in for you the years to come.

CHAPTER 4:

IRRELEVANCE — FATE OR FAILURE?

A few years ago I had a revealing conversation with the president of one of the largest non-profit groups in the world. Following a presentation I made to the organization's leadership, the president and I walked backstage and in the course of our conversation I asked about his vision for the next few years. His response was surprising.

"I often wonder what the future holds," the leader said humbly. "After so much enduring success and influence I sometimes fear that the only way from here is downhill."

I reflected for days afterwards on his words. Is decline after success inevitable I wondered, in the way that winter follows autumn?

As I considered the possibility, I recalled a principle I'd learned in high school physics: the Law of Entropy. In layman's terms, this second law of thermodynamics states that everything in Nature is always moving from integration to disintegration. Nothing stands still nor lasts forever, and natural cycles of degeneration, decomposition and deterioration ensure that this is the case.

The great King Solomon reflected on this phenomenon when he famously wrote that there is a time and season for everything; for birth and death; for building up and tearing down.[32]

25

Modern thinkers echo the same sentiment. As one former Kodak chairman almost prophetically suggested, "No company has a God-given right to survive. Maybe there is a natural cycle to companies – they grow, are successful, then decline and end."[33]

This of course prompts questions about the future prospects of modern-day success stories such as IKEA, Google, and Apple. In the case of Apple for instance, the passing of Steve Jobs led many to wonder whether in fact he was the secret ingredient to the brand's success and that the company's best days are therefore behind them. Giving validity to this prediction, in 2012 Apple fell from 5th to 26th in Forbes' ranking of the world's most innovative companies.[34]

So while Apple are one of the world's most valuable companies and boasted revenues in 2012 which exceeded Microsoft, Google and Facebook combined,[35] analysts are already suggesting that the company's dream run cannot and will not continue forever.[36]

While the demise of a brand like Apple may seem implausible, history leaves us in no doubt that simply because a business or organization has been successful, dominant or powerful in the past does not automatically mean it will remain so in the future. In fact, the demise of businesses over time is so predictable that McKinsey & Co. consultant Patrick Viguerie invented a term for measuring it called *The Topple Rate*. This metric gauges the rate at which firms lose their leadership positions and one thing is for certain - it is speeding up. According to Prof. Richard Foster of Yale University, the average lifespan of a major listed company has shrunk from 67 years in the 1920s to just 15 years today.[37]

In a June 2015 address, outgoing Cisco CEO John Chambers went so far as to predict that 40% of businesses at the time would not exist in a meaningful way in 10 years. "If I'm not making you sweat, I should be," he said.[38]

Along these very lines, Jim Collins in his book *How the Mighty Fall*, argues: "There is no law of nature that the most powerful will remain at the top. Anyone can fall and most eventually do."[39]

To this extent, the president of the non-profit organization I spoke with backstage was correct to assume that what goes up, must come down. And yet, his assumption that day didn't sit

"THERE IS NO LAW OF NATURE THAT THE MOST POWERFUL WILL REMAIN AT THE TOP. ANYONE CAN FALL AND MOST EVENTUALLY DO."

well with me. It seemed too fatalistic. What about the human capacity for innovation, ingenuity and reinvention? What of the drive to survive, the ability to adapt, and the instinct to evolve?

A number of months following the conversation, I stumbled across a definition of the Law of Entropy which helped me reconcile all that we know about human capabilities while not discounting the natural cycles that are beyond human control. This definition described entropy as the process by which "anything left to itself will naturally tend towards decay".

What I like most about this definition are the four words "anything left to itself". After all, while it is true that nothing on earth lasts forever, it is also true that many great organizations, businesses, products and movements decline long before their time because of specific actions, or *inaction*.

In their 2008 business tome, *Billion-Dollar Lessons,* authors Carroll and Mui suggest that almost one in two business failures (of the 750 corporations they researched) could have been avoided if the companies had only taken action in the face of specific warnings.[40]

Naturally, no business or organization sets out to fail. However, while the battle for relevance may not be intentionally lost, that doesn't mean the decline is accidental. What are the warning signs that Carroll and Mui alluded to?

DESTINATIONS YOU MAY WISH TO AVOID

While the journey to irrelevance is often incremental and unconscious, it is also predictable and measurable.

In Section 2 we are going to look at five specific drivers of organizational entropy – or what I call the five roads to irrelevance. Each of these drivers in one way or another has contributed to the demise or obsolescence of almost every iconic business, brand or idea throughout human history.

If you have a sinking feeling that you may already be on the downward slide, take heart – the game is not over yet. Even if the momentum and vitality of the past seem like a distant memory, it is never too late to turn things around. In the next couple of chapters, you will discover that the challenges you face are neither new nor unique.

For those who are still ascending the Relevance Curve in phase one or two, the coming chapters are designed to serve as signposts to destinations you may prefer to avoid in the future.[41] As the adage says, *a wise person learns from their mistakes, a much wiser person learns from someone else's.*[42]

Certainly, I have always found it smarter to place a warning sign at the top of a cliff in preference to stationing an ambulance at the bottom! My hope is that section 2 offers just the warning signs you need to stay clear of danger.

SECTION 2:
The 5 Roads to Irrelevance

CHAPTER 5:

ROAD 1 - SHIFT HAPPENS

On the 23rd of February 1905, four young businessmen met at a downtown Chicago office boardroom for an informal lunch. Enjoying their time together, they agreed to meet the following week and before long, their lunch meetings became a regular occurrence.

Over the coming months, each member of the group invited colleagues and friends to join the weekly gatherings and within a year these meetings had become so popular that breakaway groups formed. And thus, an organization that would change the course of human history was born. Its name: Rotary.

From these humble beginnings, Rotary grew in popularity at a breathtaking pace. The organization's focus on drawing together business people in local communities for the purpose of networking and community service saw membership grow to 20,000 by 1925.

In the decades that followed, Rotary's size, stature and influence continued to grow to the point where in 1985 the organization set out a bold plan to eradicate polio from the face of the planet. While a feat of this magnitude had never been attempted by any one organization, the determination and commitment of Rotarians worldwide saw this ambitious goal all but reached by the late 2000s.

Today, Rotary is one of the world's preeminent non-government organizations with over 1.2 million members across 200 countries. However, while this headline membership figure may be impressive, what it doesn't show is that Rotary, like almost all service organizations, has seen its growth rates stagnate in recent decades.

Although Rotary continues to expand rapidly in countries like India and South Korea, 2010 saw the organization lose 35,000 members in the USA and 11,000 members in Australia. In addition to natural attrition (many Rotary clubs have an average age of well over 60), there is a huge churn rate in Rotary membership – people join, but simply don't stay.

So why is this? Well, it is certainly not that local businesspeople are disinterested in networking with their peers – the myriad professional networking groups and industry associations attests to this. Nor is it that people are unwilling to give back to society, or to volunteer their time. Certainly it is not because social needs requiring the attention of service organizations are any less today than they have been in the past.

Rather, I would suggest that the reason Rotary and other similar organizations are experiencing such rapid and concerning falls in membership across their 'mature markets' is that *a shift has happened:* the world has changed and service organizations like Rotary have failed to keep pace.

STEP BACK IN TIME

If you walk into a Rotary club meeting in any city around the world on any given day of the week, you are likely to be confronted by scene that could seem both foreign and strange.

At the front of the room, you'll see the Rotary club president sitting in a place of honor wearing a chain of ceremonial medals around his or her neck. The beginning of the meeting will be punctuated with the ring of a Rotary-branded brass bell fashioned specifically for the occasion. Looking around, you will likely see an array of faded banners and flags from different clubs around the world – each bequeathed to the local group over the years by visiting Rotarians from faraway lands.

As the meeting gets underway, grace may be recited, the national anthem sung, and a toast to the nation's head of state will usually be offered. In some of the more traditional clubs, there may even be song – a ritual whereby members sing from a songbook of old choruses featuring altered lyrics which reflect Rotary's values of service, fellowship and philanthropy.

In conversation at Rotary meetings you are likely to pick up on other cultural norms peculiar to the organization. One of these is a stated or implied expectation that members will either attend every weekly meeting or endeavor to do a 'make-up' meeting at another club or through an online registering system. A failure to comply with the 100% attendance rule in some clubs will result in a loss of membership.

Having worked extensively with Rotary around the world in recent years, I have seen first-hand this organization's work and the difference it makes. And I have found Rotarians to be among the most generous, selfless and dedicated people on the planet. However, when I was invited to be a keynote speaker at the 2011 Rotary International Convention, an event which draws over 20,000 delegates from across the globe, I felt it was imperative to respectfully impress upon those in attendance a harsh reality: *You must change or you will not survive.*

To its credit, Rotary's leadership have recognized that times have changed and are aware that the organization needs to "catch up." Whether they can change fast enough in order to do so is yet to be seen.

Every organization, business or leader would do well to learn from Rotary's experience. After all, the very shifts that have caused Rotary to lose relevance in recent decades pose a real threat to any industry or idea. The world is changing faster than most of us appreciate, and more swiftly than many of us like.

THE WORLD IS CHANGING FASTER THAN MOST OF US APPRECIATE, AND MORE SWIFTLY THAN MANY OF US LIKE.

When shift happens, it is almost as if someone moves the goal posts mid-play or changes the rules of the game altogether - and you are left holding the ball trying to figure out what to do next. Suddenly everything that once seemed predictable and linear is unpredictable and chaotic. Charles Darwin dubbed such chaos 'random mutation' and modern business authors describe it as a 'disruption.'

Over the coming pages, we take a look at five key disruptive shifts that have the ability to cause a brand or organization to become irrelevant in what can seem like the blink of an eye. These include:

a. Societal Shifts
b. Demographic Shifts
c. Market Shifts
d. Technological Shifts
e. Legislative Shifts

A. SOCIETAL SHIFTS

One of the oldest and most cherished social institutions in the U.K., the local pub, is rapidly falling prey to this first type of shift. In the U.K., these cultural icons are becoming endangered as, on average, 25 publicans a week shut their doors for good.

Although some analysts have explained this decline by pointing to lower-priced alcohol in supermarkets; unreasonably high excise taxes; new smoking laws; or, perhaps, general economic woes, in reality the shifts threatening British pubs are more fundamental and far-reaching.

While the traditional local pub was once the place where beer-loving blokes went to swig a few pints, watch a sports match, and get some time away from 'the missus', the simple fact is that this Anglo, blue-collar male archetype is no longer as commonplace in modern-day Britain. Not only are today's metrosexual men looking for different things in a pub – quality food, an extensive range of wine and spirits, clean facilities, and Wi-Fi – pubs are also under ever-increasing pressure to become family-friendly environments where women can also feel welcome and comfortable. In short, British society is changing and pubs that fail to recognize this and respond are finding that their days are numbered. [43]

In his book, *The Wisdom of Crowds*, James Surowiecki describes the extent to which similar social changes led to the decline of another social institution: America's bowling alleys.

In the late 1950s, the bowling alley was the common man's country club with more than 12,000 of them nationwide. Over the next few decades, however, bowling alleys went out of vogue as social needs and preferences changed. Today there are half as many bowling alleys across America as there were four decades ago despite the overall population of the U.S. increasing by 100 million people in the same time period.[44]

Naturally, things come and go with time. What is popular one season will likely be passé in the next. What is cutting edge this year may well be perceived as cliché in 2 years time. While tastes and preferences

> **THINGS COME AND GO WITH TIME. WHAT IS POPULAR ONE SEASON WILL LIKELY BE PASSÉ IN THE NEXT.**

can be as fickle as the emotions that drive them, more fundamental social shifts can cause institutions and businesses to quickly be left behind and therefore cannot be underestimated.

Consider for instance Britain's long lost love affair with the seaside. In the late 1870s, England's southern coast became *the* place to holiday and Britons began flocking to towns like Weymouth, Blackpool, Margate and Whitstable en masse. In their heyday, these towns boomed. New hotels, restaurants and leisure facilities were opening as fast as they could in an effort keep up with demand.

However, during the early 1970s, everything changed. As cheap package holidays to the Spanish coast and other exotic locations grew in popularity, suddenly the British seaside lost its attraction. Hotels closed down, restaurants began shutting and fairgrounds sat motionless rusting by the seashore. As CEO of British Destinations Peter Hampson describes it, this shift caused British resort towns to "fall off a cliff into a 30-year recession."[45] It has only been in recent years that these seaside destinations have finally started experiencing a resurgence – not as summer vacation spots but rather as year-round weekender destinations for cashed-up Londoners.

Changes in consumer tastes and preferences are also having a significant impact on the U.S. dairy industry. In an age of bottled water, vitamin beverages and energy drinks, the humble glass of milk seems to be becoming a thing of the past. Milk consumption across the U.S. has fallen almost 30% since 1975 and dairy industry spokesman Tom Gallagher suggests that milk providers need to recognize they are facing an imminent crisis. "We cannot simply assume that we will always have a market," Gallagher warned.[46]

SHIFTING SOCIAL STRUCTURES

Anytime the shape and power structure of society changes, those organizations and institutions that depend on the *status quo* tend to feel the effects sharply.

Consider the impact of the Bubonic Plague as it swept through Europe in the 14th century, killing roughly half of the continent's population. Because so many plague victims were from the working classes, wages rose sharply in the years that followed, forcing many business owners who had grown accustomed to exploiting cheap labor to either adapt or go out of business.[47]

Similarly, the shape of England's working population morphed dramatically in the first half of the 20th century due to the impact of WWI and WWII. In the early 20th century, hundreds of thousands of men and women were employed as butlers, housekeepers, maids, valets, footmen and chauffeurs. By the close of WWII however, many of Britain's grandest and oldest households had become unviable as domestic help became harder to procure. This societal shift marked the beginning of the end of feudal Britain and the growing unviability of an entire level of aristocracy, as portrayed in the award-winning television series, *Downton Abbey.*

WHEN THE SHAME SUBSIDED

Women's refuges have also been heavily impacted by societal shifts. In the 1950s and 60s before the development of effective contraception, these refuges were filled with women who had fallen pregnant 'out of wedlock'.

While the stated purpose of women's refuges was to provide healthcare and support for expectant single mothers, to many they were a convenient way of hiding the shame of a disgraceful pregnancy until the baby could be born and offered up for adoption. The whispers among older women that a 17-year old girl had been 'sent away for 6 months' were met with knowing nods.

By the 1970s, social attitudes began to change. Terminations were more accessible and Government-support parent benefit payments made it financially possible and viable for a single woman to keep her child. In addition, attitudes towards single mothers changed as more pregnant young women were encouraged to stay home under the protection of parents until the baby was born. One by one, women's refuges closed their doors as demand tapered off and their relevance declined.

Another social institution that has seen its relevance wane due to shifting social attitudes to gender is that of women's auxiliary groups. Typically made up of the wives of an association's or organization's members, various ladies' auxiliary groups have steadily declined as women's roles and time-commitments evolved from the 1960s onwards. Rather than fund-raising in support of their husbands' interests, women nowadays prefer to play a far more active and independent role.

POLITICAL PARTIES TAKE HEED

In the political arena too, shifts in society's attitudes and values mean that the battle lines of old are beginning to make less sense. As times and needs evolve, the old guard is struggling to define itself in a new context.

One of the changing social norms re-defining politics is in the sphere of industrial relations. In past decades, leftist parties typically defined themselves by giving the working class a voice in sectors ranging from manufacturing to primary industries, while their right-leaning adversaries asserted the basic premise of small government, free enterprise and commercial autonomy for employers. As Western economies and workforces have become more service-driven, entrepreneurial and white collar, the causes championed by the left-leaning political parties of old are less vital than they once were.

AS TIMES CONTINUE TO CHANGE AND NEEDS EVOLVE, THE POLITICAL LANDSCAPE WILL LOOK VERY DIFFERENT IN THE FUTURE. According to retired Australian Labor Party minister, Lindsay Tanner, the old narrative of 'material deprivation and broad economic injustice' that garnered left-leaning party voter support 50 years ago no longer resonates with the voting public to the same degree.[48]

As times continue to change and needs evolve, the political landscape will look very different in the future. We are already hearing the early rumblings of disquiet at the status quo.

In the United States, Google co-founder Sergey Brin describes the current state of American politics as "a bonfire of partisanship". According to Brin, the vast majority of elected officials are well-meaning, yet "90% of their effort seems to be focused on how to stick it to the other party".[49]

In his 2012 *State of the Union* address, President Obama expressed similar concerns regarding the current state of affairs in politics to the point of describing Washington as "broken". He said: "Some of what's broken is to do with the way Congress does its business these days. A simple majority is no longer enough to get anything – even routine business – passed through the Senate. The judicial branch also needs to change. Too often, it is inefficient, outdated and remote. We need to end the notion that the two parties must be locked in a perpetual campaign of mutual destruction; that politics is about clinging to rigid ideologies instead of building around common sense ideas."[50]

As voters become increasingly disillusioned, parties and leaders must respond if they are to stay relevant. Political parties who can read the times, and respond accordingly, will fare well in the years ahead while those who fail to do so will likely fade into obscurity.

B. DEMOGRAPHIC SHIFTS

This second type of shift is one on which I have focused much of my career. When I initially began tracking trends in 2004, my emphasis was on the changing shape of society, specifically the shifts in values and attitudes of younger generations.

Between 2004 and 2007, I travelled the globe speaking to, interviewing and researching over 80,000 young people in order to get an idea of what is driving and defining Generation Y (or the Millennials as they are sometimes known). My first book, *The 'New' Rules of Engagement* was essentially an exploration of the key findings of this research.

There are a number of reasons no leader or organization can afford to ignore this group born between the early 1980s and late 1990s. Chief among these is the fact that the Gen Y cohort is enormous in size and therefore holds massive economic and commercial clout.

In his book *The Great Depression Ahead*, leading global economist Harry S Dent argues that age-based demographic trends are the single most significant driver of our economy. Dent shows how it is possible

> **IT IS POSSIBLE TO ACCURATELY PREDICT ECONOMIC BOOMS AND BUSTS SIMPLY BY EXAMINING THE SPENDING PATTERNS OF DIFFERENT AGE GROUPS.**

to accurately predict economic booms and busts simply by examining the spending patterns of different age groups.[51]

According to Dent, an individual's peak spending years are between the ages of 46 and 50. So, if you consider that the vast bulk of the enormous Baby Boom generation passed through this window between the mid-1990s and mid-2000s, it is no surprise that our economy prospered during those years.[52]

To understand how Gen Y may have a similar kind of impact in the future, consider these facts:

- In North America, Gen Y are 60 million-strong which makes them only marginally smaller in number than the Baby Boomers. Sometimes Gen Y are even labeled the 'echo-boomers' owing to the fact that they are the offspring of the Baby Boom generation;
- In the Asia-Pacific region, Gen Y makes up over 30% of the population – in China alone there are 200 million people between the ages of 18 and 30. In India, roughly *half* of country's population is under the age of 25;

- In parts of the Middle East and North Africa, the influence of the youth demographic is even more pronounced with 65% of the region's population under the age of 30.

Our globe, and particularly the regions where growth is set to be strongest in the coming decades, is staring down the barrel of what sociologists call a 'Youth Bulge'. The good news for businesses and organizations is that if they can position themselves

OUR GLOBE IS STARING DOWN THE BARREL OF WHAT SOCIOLOGISTS CALL A 'YOUTH BULGE.'

appropriately, this Gen Y demographic offers enormous potential for growth and prosperity. And that opportunity is not only in the future – it is here *now*.

In the U.S., Gen Y already wields almost $200 billion in purchasing power. As a result, some economists suggest that Gen Y's impact on society, business and economics will be similar in magnitude to that of the Baby Boomer generation.[53] In Australia, academics showcase similar data. The Centre for Retail Studies at Monash University have estimated that Gen Y possesses half the nation's discretionary spending power.[54]

Despite the opportunities that Gen Y present, the challenge facing most organizations and brands is that they are ill equipped to engage this young group. In recent years, much of my work has been with clients whose business models, distribution channels, product offering and messaging are geared toward the Baby Boomers. Naturally, if these organizations don't quickly take steps to become relevant to Gen Y, they may soon find themselves on the endangered species list.

One industry coming to terms with generational change is that of golfing.

Between 2009 and 2013, golfing participation rates of people aged 18 to 34 fell roughly 13%, while participation rates for this demographic in other active sports like running rose 29%. Reflecting on why this may be the case Matt Powell of SportsOneSource points to the fact that "Golf is slow, takes a long time to play and is expensive. As a sport it doesn't reflect the kind of values millennials like such as diversity and inclusion."

This dropoff is beginning to take a toll. In July 2014, 46-year old Florida chain Edwin Watts Golf Shops filed for bankruptcy blaming a decline in the sport's popularity. Just days later, Dick's Sporting Goods laid off more than 400 golf professionals as it reduced store space for golf in favor of women's and youth apparel. The bigbox retailer is also rethinking its specialty retailer Golf Galaxy, which was acquired in 2007 for $226 million.[55]

Looking to a very different industry, social media behemoth Twitter is fighting generational battle of it's own. Just a few short years ago, Twitter was the undisputed second place to Facebook in the social media world. More recently, however, a host of younger and hotter social apps have taken the spotlight. At the time of writing, apps such as Instagram, Snapchat, Dubsmash, WhatsApp and Pinterest all rank ahead of Twitter in download rankings for iPhone and Android devices. Further still, Instagram's monthly active user count of 300 million is roughly equal to that of Twitter and industry insider Tero Kuittinen suggests that it won't be long before Snapchat is nipping at Twitter's heels too.

According to Kuittinen, one of the main things Twitter is missing is the "fun, adventurous, funky, experimental" feeling users get on younger social apps such as Snapchat and Dubsmash. Twitter has been slow to make the platform more visual; however, its acquisition of the live-video app Periscope in early 2015 could help.[56]

For Twitter, the stakes are high. They cannot simply rely on historical strength or brand recognition. They must reach out to and engage the next generation of users lest they become, as one technology commentator friend of mine recently described it, the Blackberry of social media.

LEARNING FROM OTHERS' MISTAKES

Organizations and brands wishing to stay relevant would do well to learn from the mistakes of those who missed the last demographic wave represented by the Baby Boomers.

Of all the organizations who struggled to find relevance with this group when they were adolescents and young adults, it is perhaps religious institutions and churches that stand out the most.[57]

Many mainstream Christian churches failed to engage the Baby Boomer generation as they entered adulthood. Studies of religious observance in the 1960s and 70s show that Baby Boomers (in their 20s at the time) were significantly more disaffected from religious institutions than previous generations at the same age. American sociologist Wade Clark Roof estimates that two-thirds of all Boomers raised in religious families 'dropped out' somewhere along the way with less than half returning to the church later in life.[58]

Today many churches face the challenge of engaging the Baby Boomers' offspring. This was highlighted in a recent Australian study which found that the proportion of people attending church aged over 70 was 10 times the number of those aged in their 20s.[59]

In the commercial realm, the same demographic imperatives apply.

In recent decades, car manufacturers have relied on connecting with Baby Boomers' sense of nostalgia in order to drive sales. They have succeeded in doing this by re-releasing iconic cars from the Boomers' youth like the VW beetle, Chevrolet Camaro and Dodge Challenger – essentially targeting a generation who want to re-capture their youth literally and figuratively.[60] More recently however, Ford has embarked on a shift away from this retro trend and is now focusing on a younger demographic. The company realized that cars like the retro-shaped Ford Mustang which appeal to Baby Boomers, were unlikely to resonate with Gen Y consumers who have no nostalgic connection with the original models. The company also recognized that Gen Y is entering their peak car-buying years as their parents exit at the other end. In response, Ford's newest Mustang looks more like an Aston Martin - a significant departure from the shape and image of old.[61]

Consider too the choice facing Volvo at the dawn of the 21st century when it discovered that Gen Y was responsible for a quarter of new car purchases, and would be buying half of all new cars sold by 2020.[62] Realizing how un-attractive the Volvo brand was to younger consumers, the company embarked on an ambitious and enormously successful re-positioning exercise which we will explore in the final chapter of this book.

McDonald's has also had to face the harsh reality that younger generations want different things from their elders. Recognizing that emerging consumers had become more health-conscious owing to influences such as the *Super Size Me* documentary, McDonald's was forced in the mid-2000s to gravitate away from their fast food roots.[63] In chapter 15 we will look at the steps McDonald's took during those years to turn business back in their favor.

Rather than waiting till their hand is forced as in the case of McDonald's, smart leaders always keep one eye on the demographic horizon ahead. After all, one of the great things about demographic shifts is that, while they can be difficult to predict, they do have long lead times.[64]

| **ONE OF THE GREAT THINGS ABOUT DEMOGRAPHIC SHIFTS IS THAT THEY DO HAVE LONG LEAD TIMES.**

DEMOGRAPHIC SHIFTS ARE MORE THAN GENERATIONAL

While much of the focus in previous pages has been on generational trends, demographic shifts take a much broader form than simply the age-breakdown of society. They can include everything from immigration rates to changes in a population's ethnic makeup and socio economic status.

It was the changing demographic landscape due to immigration, for instance, that caused the financial giant Rothschilds to fall from greatness in the late 19th century. As massive swathes of the population migrated from Europe to the Americas, Australia and New Zealand, the financial and economic impact was enormous. Up until this shift in the 1860s, Rothschilds had been the world's dominant financial power. However, as demographic shift happened they failed to recognize the significance of trans-Atlantic migration and started to lose relevance and power in the early 1870s. Their position was taken over by JP Morgan who recognized the opportunity of this migratory shift and exploited it by creating a worldwide bank headquartered in New York rather than Europe.[65]

Looking at a more recent example, a key driver in the demise of Kmart in America during the latter part of the 20th century was the migration of the retail giant's customers not across oceans but from cities to suburbs. In her book *Kmart's 10 Deadly Sins*, Marcia Turner argues that the retailer willfully ignored this trend in the demographic nature and composition of their market to their detriment.[66]

Whether in the form of new generations, evolving socio-economic conditions or population changes, organizations and brands that ignore demographic shifts do so at their peril. [67]

C. MARKET SHIFTS

When I was at university, I worked at a local specialist bookstore that had an enviable reputation for service after 30 years of operation. Customers were loyal, the atmosphere welcoming and almost family-like, and the business's bottom-line healthy. However, gradually things began to change. A larger chain store in a city nearby started advertising in local newspapers and on radio. It aggressively positioned itself as having a greater range and cheaper prices – a claim our store couldn't refute. Our competitor also had many times the floor space and in most instances their retail prices were lower than we could order stock at wholesale cost from suppliers.

To their credit, many of our customers still chose to shop locally. However, as the price differential increased and our inability to compete on range grew, even devoted customers became infrequent. When they'd visit after a long absence, they'd make any number of excuses for where they had been.

The writing on the wall was clear: we were fighting a losing battle against the competition. A few years later, the owner sold up.

This story, of course, is anything but unique. The last few decades have seen countless family-owned businesses go to the wall as a result of market shifts. Regardless of whether they were selling fresh produce, ladies' fashion or hardware, many small businesses have been unable to compete with the 'big guys' and their economies of scale.

In many ways, this consolidation of competition is a natural process in business and is nothing new. In 1921, for example, there were almost 200 automobile companies in the U.S., but this number shrunk to 20 by the 1930s and was down to four by 1960.[68] Almost a century earlier, a similar pattern unfolded in the railway business: in 1830 there were over 100 railroad companies in England; 50 years later, only a half dozen companies remained.[69]

REAL-TIME EVOLUTION

Evolutionary theorists argue that all development in the realm of biology is a function of changes which prove advantageous to some species and devastating to others. In the same way, market economists point

> **MARKET ECONOMISTS POINT TO A CONSTANT PROCESS OF NATURAL SELECTION WHERE ONLY THE "FITTEST" SURVIVE.**

to a constant process of natural selection where only the "fittest" survive.

The fast-moving IT world allows us to see such an evolution in real time. Look at the way Google usurped the once-dominant search engine AltaVista in the space of a few years during the late 1990s and early 2000s.

Consider too how marketplace dynamics impacted on IT giant, IBM. Founded in 1911, the company didn't rise to dominance until the introduction of its 360 main-frame computer in the mid-1960s. For some time thereafter everything seemed to be going IBM's way. The company was powerful, successful and wealthy. In the early 1980s, however, things started to change. A market newcomer named Intel started to develop microprocessors that were more powerful than IBM's. Furthermore, Intel was designing processors for lower priced machines like mini computers and PCs. The proliferation of these smaller and cheaper products significantly eroded IBM's competitive advantage.

Although IBM responded by investing heavily in PCs – even managing to dominate that market within a few years – their chief focus remained on main-frame computers. In essence, IBM saw PCs as bait that would lure customers into purchasing more expensive main-frame solutions. Over time, IBM's PC customers grew frustrated and turned to newer and more nimble competitors like Compaq, Dell and HP. All of this culminated in IBM posting cumulative losses of $16 billion between 1991 and 1993.[70]

In recent years, marketplace shifts in the form of web-based software and cloud computing have posed a significant threat to software giant Microsoft.

Google Apps is continuing to win over corporate users that traditionally relied on Microsoft's Office suite – a trend which Microsoft admits poses "a very serious threat to our company".[71]

Interestingly, only a few short years ago, Microsoft was the underdog challenging an incumbent market leader. When web search engine Netscape first launched in 1995 it was a phenomenon because it allowed a whole new generation to surf the Internet quickly and easily. Netscape gained millions of users almost overnight. In an effort to get a piece of the action, Microsoft opted to embed its own web browser, Internet Explorer, into their market-leading Windows operating system and by 2002, the company had all but crushed Netscape by capturing 95% market share.[72]

Recent assaults by browsing solutions such as Mozilla Firefox and Google's Chrome have in turn significantly eroded Internet Explorer's domination – and further relegated Netscape to the annals of history.

THE WORLD OF CONSUMER ELECTRONICS

Similar market forces to those at work in the IT sector have also caused a number of consumer electronic giants to falter. Phone manufacturers such as Nokia, Ericsson and Motorola struggled to retain their market share as consumers opted for smartphones over traditional mobile devices and then, with breath-taking swiftness and fickleness, demonstrate a changing appetite for different kinds of smartphone.

Consider the fate of Blackberry and Taiwanese smartphone maker, HTC, who have both struggled in recent years to stay relevant in a market dominated by Apple's iPhone and Google-powered Android devices.[73]

Once the pioneer of smartphone technology, BlackBerry enjoyed a staggering 51 per cent of the North American smartphone market in late 2009.[74] Just 5 years later, this had slumped to 1.9% and is projected to be a mere 0.3% by 2018.[75] From a financial perspective, recent years have not been kind to Blackberry either. The company's share price dropped from a 2007 peak of $236 per share to an embarrassing $10 per share six years later[76] (Blackberry shares lost almost 75% of their value in 2011 alone).[77]

It is a similar story at HTC where the company's 2013 second-quarter profits fell by 83%.[78] This is a far cry from HTC's peak in 2010 when it was the world's biggest provider of smartphones using Google's Android operating system.[79] Tellingly, the company's stock prices lost 80% of its value between 2011 and 2013.[80]

Interestingly it is not only *external* market forces that can cause a consumer product or brand to become irrelevant as competitive dynamics change. Consider how Apple essentially put its own iPod out of business. The popularity of the iPod, once the 'must have' technology device for music lovers everywhere, was largely eroded by the iPhone's release in 2007. Once a consumer could listen to his or her music on their phone, there was no need for a separate device. This, however, had been a deliberate cannibalization on the part of Apple. In 2005, Steve Jobs warned Apple's board that the ubiquity of mobile phones would render the iPod obsolete almost

> **"IF YOU'RE NOT WILLING THE CANNIBALIZE YOUR OWN BUSINESS, SOMEONE ELSE WILL DO IT FOR YOU."**

overnight. Apple's solution, rather than waiting for a competitor to beat them to it, was to invent the "iPod killer" themselves. As Steve Jobs famously observed at the time, "If you're not willing the cannibalize your own business, someone else will do it for you."

Looking outside the technology sector, the manufacturing and retail industries have had their fair share of competitive wrangling's in recent decades. The demise of the iconic textile manufacturer Pillowtex is a case in point.

Starting out in 1954, Pillowtex grew to dominate the pillow manufacturing and retail business between the 1960s and the 1980s. By the mid-1990s, the company had reached almost half a billion dollars in annual sales – a milestone of success that was only to be short lived. In 1994, the U.S. government had begun a decade-long phase out of import quotas in keeping with international trade agreements. In essence this meant that manufacturing companies like Pillowtex would be increasingly subject to competition from international companies whose costs of manufacture were substantially lower. Realizing this, many of Pillowtex's competitors rushed to move their production facilities offshore to developing countries where labor costs were lower. In contrast, Pillowtex chose to continue production domestically in the U.S.

Within a few short years, Pillowtex found themselves hopelessly undercut on price by cheaper imports. Unable to compete, the company quickly lost ground and after filing for bankruptcy in late 2000, finally went into liquidation in 2003.[81]

TROUBLE IN TOYLAND

Once the darling of the toy industry, Mattel's Barbie doll has had something of a rough ride in recent years with young girls gravitating to other dolls from the Monster High franchise and those based on the hit Disney movie "Frozen."

Though still by far the largest doll brand globally with annual sales of $1 billion, Barbie no longer generates the attention she used to. Barbie sales in North America experienced declines for nine straight quarters throughout 2013 and 2014 in the face of growing competition.

"The Barbie brand is not as strong as it used to be and a generic fashion doll will suffice," BMO Capital's Donald Johnson said.

The decline of Barbie is further bad news for Mattel, which lost the title of the world's top toy maker to Lego in late 2014.[82]

While the influence of market forces and the dog-eat-dog world of competition can seem unfair at times (particularly for those whose livelihoods it effects), it is inevitable in a free market economy. The marketplace by its very nature is constantly changing and

THE FUTURE WILL ALWAYS BELONG TO THOSE WHO CAN READ THE MARKET AND RESPOND.

evolving. As such, the future will always belong to those who can read the market and respond. While we may bemoan, demean or even resent the competition there is one thing we can never do – ignore them. As former Intel CEO Andy Grove so aptly observed: 'Only the paranoid survive'.[83]

D. TECHNOLOGICAL SHIFTS

This fourth type of shift typically gets the most press coverage. Almost weekly there are reports of another business, product or industry that has been made obsolete because of the onward march of technology.

Consider some of the more notable examples of technology-induced obsolescence in recent years:

Blockbuster Video. In its Nineties heyday, Blockbuster was opening a store somewhere in the U.S. every 24 hours[84] and by 2005 had over 5,700 stores across America.[85] A few short years later in 2011, the company was bankrupt and its final stores closed in early 2014.[86] Why this turn of events? New streaming services like Netflix and Apple TV meant consumers no longer needed to rent DVDs, Blockbuster's bread-and-butter.

Encyclopedia Britannica. In early 2012, Britannica shocked the world with the announcement that it would cease production, after almost 250 years, of their printed volumes. The reason was pretty obvious: consumers no longer needed to spend $1500 on a set of books that would quickly date while the same information is available online for free via a Google search. At its peak in 1990, Britannica sold 120,000 sets per year, but by 2006 this number had dropped to 40,000 and by 2010 only 12,000 units were sold.[87]

Postal Services. Around the world, traditional postal services are shrinking at an astonishing rate. Mail volume in the U.S. has declined by 20% in recent years[88] and in Australia to levels below what they were in 1990.[89] The U.S. postal service as a consequence is in the process of closing one in 10 of its outlets and ceasing Saturday deliveries. In New Zealand, proposals have been made to reduce delivery days from six to three per week.[90] Again, the reason for this decline is fairly clear. Since the introduction of fax machines and then email, Skype and social media, we are simply sending fewer letters. The speed and magnitude of this trend was highlighted at a conference recently where I was a guest speaker. At the end of my presentation, one young delegate came up to me and asked if 'snail mail' which I had referred to was a smartphone app!

The Better Business Bureau. This iconic 100-year old American institution has found itself fighting for survival and relevance in a digital age. Having specialized in investigating complaints against companies and providing approved businesses with a coveted seal of approval, online consumer review and social networking sites have eroded the bureau's value proposition. As evidence of this, the BBB drew just 4.1 million website visitors in February 2012, compared with the 30.6 million online review giant *Yelp* attracted in the same time period.[91]

SkyMall Magazine. After 25 years selling quirky products like a Darth Vader toaster or a paper towel holder with USB ports, the company behind the in-flight catalog *SkyMall* filed for bankruptcy protection in January 2015. One of the key factors in the company's loss of relevance is that airline passengers can increasingly keep their smartphones and tablets powered up and connected to Wi-Fi during flights.[92]

While the pace at which technological shifts are driving obsolescence is greater than ever before, in many ways it is nothing new. There is a long list of products, brands and businesses throughout history that have lost the battle for relevance due to technological advancements. Consider the timeline below:

- **1830s:** The introduction of telegrams sounds the death knell for the Pony Express
- **1860s:** The discovery of kerosene effectively kills off the whale-oil industry in America's northeast. Within the space of a few short years, the thriving communities of Nantucket and New Bedford had become economic wastelands.
- **1910s:** Automobiles grow in popularity putting farriers out of work
- **1950s:** Transistor technology kills vacuum tube radios[93]
- **1960s:** New Boeing jets lead to the demise of the non-luxury ocean liner industry
- **1960s:** Television ends the dominance of radio as the primary form of home entertainment[94]
- **1990s:** Emails make fax machines redundant
- **1990s:** Mobile phones render pagers obsolete[95]
- **2000s:** Google Maps impacts sales of GPS navigation systems and printed directories

- **2008:** Voice-over IP (VOIP) technology begins to replace traditional landline telephones
- **2009:** Gaming apps like *Angry Birds* eat into the market share of traditional software-based video games[96]
- **2010:** Online photo sharing and digital photo books significantly erode the revenues of image printing businesses[97]
- **2010:** Free apps like *eBuddy* and *Pinger* threaten mobile phone companies that rely on text messaging revenue
- **2011:** Cookbooks lose relevance as wannabe Masterchefs use tablet devices in the kitchen.

The business landscape is changing continually and right now we are experiencing a range of fundamental technological disruptions that will have widespread ramifications in the years to come.

Consider the impact that driverless car technologies will have in the coming years.

Although many believe the reality of autonomous vehicles is still a long way off, nothing could be further from the truth. Researchers at Boston Consulting Group predict that self-driving cars will be a reality by the mid-2020s and a common sight on our roads by the mid-2030s.[98]

Indicative of how far self-driving technology has come in recent years, an Audi A7 drove itself 550 miles from San Francisco to Las Vegas to attend the Consumers Electronics Show in January 2015.[99]

Recent research indicates that a surprisingly high number of consumers would be eager to use autonomous cars if they were available. A full 60% of U.S. adults surveyed stated that they would ride in an autonomous car, and nearly 32% said they would not continue to drive once an autonomous car was available. So while the notion of traveling in a car with no driver elicits a sense of anxiety in some and fascination in rest of us, the true significance of this new technology will be seen in the disruptive impact it will have on a wide range of businesses and industries.[100]

First cab off the rank to face possible annihilation will be the cab industry itself. A January 2013 Columbia University study suggested that with a fleet of just 9,000 autonomous cars, Uber could replace every taxi cab in New York City, and that passengers would wait an average of 36 seconds for a ride that costs about $0.50 per mile. It came as no surprise when Uber CEO Travis Kalanick recently hinted that the ride-sharing giant will eventually replace all of its drivers with self-driving cars.[101]

Looking further afield, industries such as the $198 billion automotive insurance market, $98 billion automotive finance market and the $100 billion parking industry could take a huge hit as demand for their services weakens. Further still, we may well see the obsolescence of rental car companies, panel beaters, public transportation systems, and, best of all, speeding tickets. [102]

Naturally all of these projections are based on the assumption that we as consumers will actually own cars in the future (driverless or not). One business analyst recently predicted that owning a car in 30 years time will be like owning a horse today – something you do if it is a personal interest or hobby but not as your primary means of transportation. If indeed our future communities are serviced by a range of convenient driverless ride-sharing services, owning a car would certainly look increasingly unnecessary – much less financially attractive. According to recent research, cars today are driven just 4% of the year, which is an astonishing waste considering that the average cost of car ownership is nearly $9,000 per year.[103] Once we have a viable alternative to personal car ownership, many of us may well take advantage of it – a possibility that ought to send chills up the spine of automakers worldwide.

While it is easy to talk about the disruption of business models and large-scale industries, the more sobering reality is that the very people working in the industries above will pay the greatest price of all in the form of lost jobs and livelihoods. According to the U.S. Bureau of Labor Statistics, 915,000 people are employed in motor vehicle manufacturing alone while truck, bus, delivery, and taxi drivers account for nearly 6 million more jobs. Virtually all of these roles could be eliminated within a few decades, and this list is by no means exhaustive.[104]

Despite the potential for business upheaval and large-scale job losses, the shift towards driverless cars does bring with it a number of significant positives. First and foremost, driverless cars will likely make our roads far less dangerous with autonomous vehicles predicted to be safer than manually controlled cars by a factor of ten.[105] Morgan Stanley estimates that autonomous vehicles will result in a 90% reduction in crashes which would save nearly 30,000 lives and prevent 2.12 million injuries in the U.S. alone each year. On top of this, driverless technologies will save millions of hours of lost productivity and could lead to a dramatic reduction in city traffic congestion as driverless cars do not need to park. Currently 30% of city traffic is made up of drivers on the hunt for a parking spot.[106]

While this is just one of many technological disruptions that will shape industries and economies in the future, here are three broad technology trends that few businesses can ignore:

A. THE DEATH OF THE GATEKEEPER

I recently heard it said that ever since the dawn of the Internet, any profession with the word 'agent' or 'broker' in the title became an endangered species. It's a compelling thought really and one that has a lot of truth to it. Modern technologies and the Internet in particular have brought about a profound change in the nature of distribution. Consumers can now connect directly with suppliers and have access to ample information with which they can make intelligent buying decisions.

One sector in which this shift is having an enormous impact is that of travel and tourism. In a 2010 survey of 12,000 consumers across 12 countries, two-thirds of respondents admitted that the Internet was their first port of call when looking to book a holiday.[107] Furthermore, almost half of the respondents indicated that when researching a trip online, they purchase travel services such as accommodation, flights or tours directly from the supplier rather than through a travel agent.[108]

This removal of the middleman – known as 'disintermediation' – is a trend that poses an enormous threat to industries ranging from retailing and real estate to professional and financial services. Each of these sectors, and many others like them, must make a choice: find new ways to become indispensible or run the risk of becoming irrelevant.

In *How Companies Win*, authors Kash and Kalhoun suggest that the 20th century model for business success centered on protecting, controlling and defending distribution channels. They point to companies like AT&T, Ford and IBM who succeeded by doing just this.[109] In the 21st

> **THE 20TH CENTURY MODEL FOR BUSINESS SUCCESS CENTERED ON PROTECTING, CONTROLLING AND DEFENDING DISTRIBUTION CHANNELS.**

century, however, this protectionist approach simply won't work. The age of empowered consumers means product and service providers can no longer simply be gatekeepers standing between suppliers and end users. On the contrary, middlemen must be adding real value (and not merely adding 'clip the ticket' costs) in the distribution process if consumers are to continue using them.

THE CHANGING FACE OF RETAIL

Perhaps nowhere more acutely do we see the impact of disintermediation than in the traditional retail sector where online retailing is wreaking havoc. Whereas in the past consumers had little option but to purchase goods from a local retailer, the age of the Internet means that consumers can now go directly to wholesalers or suppliers – and in any country around the world.

> **PERHAPS THE MOST INSIDIOUS AND CONFRONTING ELEMENT OF THE ONLINE RETAIL TREND IS THE GROWING INCIDENCE OF 'SHOWROOMING.'**

Perhaps the most insidious and confronting element of the online retail trend is the growing incidence of 'showrooming.' This recently coined term describes the tendency of shoppers to visit a physical store to see and touch a product only to then go online and make their purchase – often via a smartphone before they've even left the store![110]

While comparison-shopping is nothing new, web-enabled smartphones have made it easier and more prevalent than ever.[111] According to market research firm *ClickIQ*, about half of all online purchasers have engaged in 'showrooming' prior to making their digital transaction.[112] Another recent poll of 1,000 people found that 61% had tried an item on in a store only to buy it later online – with almost half this number admitting to doing so more than five times.[113]

While many bricks-and-mortar stores have bemoaned the showrooming trend over the past few years, retail giant Best Buy recently decided to see showrooming as an opportunity rather than a threat in the belief that once customers are in store, the company has every chance it needs to win them.

"We love showrooming," Best Buy's Chief Executive Hubert Joly declared in late 2012. "We want to turn the tables and embrace it." Best Buy has offered to match online prices in its stores, removing another reason— perhaps the biggest reason—why customers might head online to competitors such as Amazon.[114] In the lead up to the 2013 holiday season, Best Buy even ran television ads that touted its stores as "the ultimate holiday showroom." Analysts estimate that less than 10% of shoppers take advantage of Best Buy's pricematch offer, but executives have said the pledge alone is enough to keep the company from losing customers to online rivals.[115]

Validating the wisdom of Best Buy's change in attitude towards showrooming, a 2015 Deloitte study found that customers' use of digital devices in-store to do product comparisons actually *increased* sales volumes by an average of 21 per cent.[116]

THE DAY THE MUSIC DIED

While traditional retailers are only now coming to terms with the impact of disintermediation, the music industry was forced to confront challenges of an even greater magnitude in the early 2000s. For music companies, it wasn't just that consumers were able to access their products more *cheaply* over the Internet – it was that they could suddenly do so *for free*!

As early as 1997, things began shifting in the music world with digital downloads rising 45% in the space of one year - and music industry revenues plummeting 15% as a result.[117] While at first these digital downloads were largely done through illegal sites like Napster, within a few years legitimate online music retailers like iTunes grew to prominence. Suddenly consumers were empowered like never before. Rather than being forced to buy a whole album to get access to the 2 or 3 songs they wanted, music lovers could simply purchase the tracks individually and never have to step foot inside a store to do so.

As a result of this shift, by 2012 the global recorded music industry had shrunk to roughly half the size it was at the turn of the 21st century.[118] According to one peak industry group, physical recorded music sales fell by 20% between 2007 and 2011 while digital sales had doubled during the same time period.[119] In 2012 alone, a staggering 4.3 billion songs and albums were downloaded worldwide.[120]

In recent years, everyone involved in the previously lucrative music supply chain - from artists to record labels and retail stores – has suddenly found themselves fighting for viability and survival.

The collapse of iconic British music retailer HMV in January 2013 was clear evidence of an industry in turmoil. By late 2012, HMVs market value was just £4.7 million – down from £1 billion 7 years earlier. [121] The 92-year old chain that started life selling gramophones and sheet music seems to be yet another casualty of the digital age.

Indicative of how significantly the music business has shifted in recent years, David Bowie released his long-awaited new single in early 2013 straight to iTunes – skipping the CD format altogether. One industry analyst reflecting on Bowie's move suggested it was the way of the future and predicted that "physical music products will all but disappear by the year 2020".[122]

Recognizing these trends, traditional record labels have been forced into the realization that they increasingly exist to provide content for digital music suppliers like iTunes. Interestingly, however, the very structural shifts that propelled iTunes to a position of market domination now threaten it. The emergence of streaming services like Spotify, Pandora, Google Play Music and Apple's own streaming solution may well mean that purchasing music becomes a thing of the past once again. Further still, the growing popularity of YouTube as a music platform represents a significant threat - a recent Nielsen study found that nearly two-thirds of teenagers use YouTube as their primary medium for listening to music – and are paying nothing for the pleasure.[123]

While the internet and web-enabled devices have disrupted many business models and industries over recent years, the most significant and profound form of disintermediation set to have an impact in the coming years is that of 3D printing.

Unlike previous forms of disintermediation which has forced middlemen such as retailers, wholesalers, distributors and brokers to clarify the value they add, the significance of 3D printing is that it disintermediates those at the very beginning of the supply chain: the manufacturer.

We first saw an indication of how fundamentally 3D printing would impact the world of manufacturing and when Nokia released the design files for their smartphones a number of years ago encouraging consumers to print their own case at home – removing the need for an entire supply chain. More recently, a company named Mink has developed a 3D printer for eye shadow which allows consumers to literally 'print' the required amount of a cosmetic matched to any color in the spectrum. At a much larger scale, property developers in China have printed entire houses and apartment blocks at blistering speeds in recent years – a development which could have a massive impact on the construction industry.

While 3D printers remain a fringe product for the moment, it will not be long before they become commonplace in households – a trend that many businesses would be wise to pay close attention to.

B. THE DEATH OF PAPER

In August 2012, it was announced that the legendary British comic series, *Dandy*, would cease printed production by the end of the year. First released in the mid-1930s, *Dandy* was the U.K.'s longest-running comic series and a childhood favorite of several generations. At its peak in the 1950s, *Dandy* sold two million copies per week but by 2011 this number had shrunk to just 8,000. Curator of London's Cartoon Museum, Anita O'Brien, suggested *Dandy,* quite simply, was yet another victim of the Digital Age.

While the comic book industry worldwide is at a point of crisis, it is part of a much broader shift away from paper-based media, news and entertainment.

In the mainstream publishing world, seismic shifts are afoot. According to Pew Research, nearly one-third of Americans now own an e-reading device and sales continue to climb.[124] In late 2011, Amazon announced that sales of e-books had, for the first time, exceeded sales of hardcover and paperbacks combined.[125] The shift to digital books is forcing publishers to re-think their business model. As evidence of this, in November 2012 giant publishing house HarperCollins announced it would close its last two warehouses in an effort to streamline operations.[126]

THE NEW WORLD OF NEWS

Much has been said in recent years about the future of newspapers. Rupert Murdoch may believe in a future for print, but few share his optimism. Australian Broadcasting Corporation's Mark Scott suggested in September 2012 that "media empires share the fate of all empires: so strong for so long, not wanting to see that the world is changing and that what worked in the past won't work in the future. Often by the time these empires respond, it's too late."[127]

While only time will tell whether newspapers are enduring or endangered, historical data offers a trajectory that favors the second view. Consider that in 1948, daily circulation in the U.S. was 1.3 newspapers per household but by 1998 newspaper readership had fallen by 57%.[128] Ten years later in 2008, a tipping point of sorts was passed where for the first time the number of people obtaining news online for free surpassed the number of readers paying for newspapers or news magazines.[129]

The challenge facing news providers today is how to charge for content without killing off their digital readership. Although some newspapers have had success in charging for premium content, the question still remains: how many people are prepared to pay for something for which they have become accustomed to paying nothing?

The commercial and ethical dilemmas regarding the monetizing of news are by no means new. In the 1922 tome, *Public Opinion*, social commentator Walter Lippman wrote, "The citizen will pay for his telephone, his railroad rides, his motor car, his entertainment. But he does not pay openly for his news."[130]

It is not only the *business model* of news media that is being challenged by technological shifts but also the entire journalistic process. Speaking in Sydney in 2010, U.K.s *Guardian* newspaper editor Alan Rusbridger suggested that there were significant parallels between the printing revolution of the 15th century and the social media revolution of the early 21st century.

"We are living at the end of a great arc of history which

> **WE ARE LIVING AT THE END OF A GREAT ARC OF HISTORY WHICH BEGAN WITH THE INVENTION OF MOVABLE TYPE.**

began with the invention of movable type. Today we see the mass ability to communicate with each other without having to go through a traditional intermediary," he said.

"Digital forces are threatening to weaken or even destroy the traditional basis, role and funding of the press. What's more, it has meant that the general public can publish more and speak louder than any journalist can. As with the early 16th Century, it is our privilege as a generation not only to imagine the future of information, but to take the first steps in re-crafting the ways in which it is created and spread."[131]

While the death of paper has been predicted since as far back as the mid-1960s, the physical printed word has perhaps never been more under threat than it is now. Although books, for instance, will always have some place, there is little doubt that in the years to come they'll play a less dominant role in education, communication and entertainment than they have in the past.[132]

C. THE DEATH OF THE PC

One final product that looks as if it will fall prey to technological advancements is the desktop PC.

While the early 1990s saw PC manufacturers like Compaq, Dell and HP usurp IBM's market dominance, in recent years it has been these very three companies who have borne the brunt of disadvantageous shifts. According to HP, the growth of tablets and smartphones is significantly eroding worldwide demand for PCs. Testament to this is the 2011/2012 fall in HP and Dell's PC revenue by 10% and 19% respectively.[133]

In the corporate environment long-dominated by Windows-based PCs, Forrester Research reports that spending on iPads is skyrocketing and unlikely to plateau any time soon. Reflecting on this trend, global research firm IDC suggest that PC manufacturers have reached a "make or break moment."[134] *The Wall Street Journal* goes further, describing the rise in tablet sales as the beginning of "the post-PC era."[135] Indicating that this prediction may well be true, IDC reports that PC shipments plunged 10% in 2013.[136]

Further eroding the dominance of desktop PCs is the rising number of consumers using mobile devices to browse the Internet. A 2011 survey of 15,000 consumers across 12 countries found that one in four U.S. and U.K. respondents "infrequently" or "never use" desktop computers for browsing the Internet – preferring instead to use mobile devices. In India, a staggering 59% of consumers reported using mobile devices as their primary web access.

IN INDIA, 59% OF CONSUMERS REPORTED USING MOBILE DEVICES AS THEIR PRIMARY WEB ACCESS.

Of all the shifts discussed in this chapter so far, no single one has more potential to decisively and swiftly cause obsolescence than shifts in technology. According to global accounting firm Deloitte, we have only just seen the beginning with one third of our economy facing 'imminent and substantial' upheaval and turmoil due to digital technologies.[137]

The message is clear. The onward march of technology will mean that the future will look very different from the past. The question is, are you ready?

E. LEGISLATIVE SHIFTS

Perhaps more than any other of the four previous shifts, changing legislation can be the hardest to predict. After all, governments

DECISIONS MADE BY THOSE IN PUBLIC OFFICE HAVE A SIGNIFICANT INFLUENCE ON EVERY ASPECT OF COMMERCE AND THEREFORE CANNOT BE IGNORED.

don't necessarily respond to market forces. Rather, they are typically driven by political pressure and tend to be swift and ruthless rather than evolutionary, leaving those affected with little warning or time to prepare. Nevertheless, decisions made by those in public office have a significant influence on every aspect of commerce and therefore cannot be ignored.

Consider the impact that the legalization of ride-sharing services like Uber and Lyft has had on the taxi industry. The potential impact of autonomous vehicles notwithstanding, the price of an individual New York yellow-taxi medallion fell about 19% in 2014 according to the New York City Taxi and Limousine Commission. Other cities have seen an even steeper drop.[138]

In order to prevent similar impacts in their own sector, The Hotel Association of New York City has lobbied city officials heavily in recent years to enforce bans on room-sharing apps like Airbnb, FlipKey and HomeAway. Hotel owners say that many Airbnb hosts who rent out their homes are violating a 2010 New York state law that prohibits people from renting their apartments for fewer than 30 days if the occupants aren't also present.[139] The extent to which laws such as these can be enforced, or will even remain in force over the years to come, could have significant implications for the hotel industry at large.

WINE CORKING UNDER PRESSURE

A few years ago my wife and I visited a beautiful vineyard in a region of Tuscany famous worldwide for its high quality Chiantis. During a tour of the winery, I remarked to our guide that is was a long time since I had seen a traditional cork in a bottle as synthetic corks or metal screw caps had become so commonplace.

Our guide, also a co-owner of the vineyard, explained that he would dearly love to use metal screw caps on his bottles. He explained that cork is notoriously unreliable for sealing wine bottles and that he loses a sizable percentage of stock each year due to spoilage – a cost that would disappear almost immediately with the use of steel caps. I was stunned to learn that Italy's powerful cork lobby (yes, they have one) has pressured the government into legally compelling winemakers to use cork to seal their wine bottles. Even though such a ruling doesn't make economic sense, political influences prevail.

LEGISLATION: THREAT OR OPPORTUNITY?

There are countless examples of businesses and industries that suddenly found themselves on the path to irrelevance due to legislative shifts.

Recently I was on a speaking tour in the southern U.S. states of Alabama and Tennessee. As I travelled between engagements, I learned from my driver that long before it was known for country music, the area surrounding Nashville, Williamson County in particular, was famous across America for horse racing. Following the civil war in the late 1800s, however, the State of Tennessee made the decision to outlaw gambling. Almost overnight, an entire industry and social institution collapsed. Horse breeders and racers were forced to relocate west to Kentucky where the horse-racing establishment remains strong to this day.

While many companies see legislative shifts as a threat, they can also be an opportunity to innovate. This has certainly been the case with automaker Ford in the U.S. In response to tough fuel-economy targets imposed by the government, Ford recently set about overhauling the design of its cars. A key element of Ford's strategy has been to replace steel parts with aluminum in their new trucks – a move that has resulted in a 15% weight reduction and a 25% improvement in fuel economy.

Rival carmaker, GM, is taking a different approach, installing hybrid motors as standard in their vehicles. Audi meanwhile has focused on designing engines that shut off at traffic lights to minimize fuel consumption.[140]

GOVERNING FOR THE GREATER GOOD

While legislative shifts often contradict the principles of a free market economy, there are times when they are necessary for the greater good. Worldwide legislation to limit the scope and influence of cigarette manufacturers, for example, has had a dramatic effect on the viability and relevance of tobacco companies. While these companies aren't happy, few would argue with the rationale behind such policies. Similarly, when governments empower consumers to switch banks without fear of exit fees, this may not please the banks but the rest of us are thrilled.

In the U.S., the government's decision to deregulate the airline industry in the late 1970s was also nothing but good news for consumers. Up until the industry's deregulation, airline giants like Delta, United and American dominated the market due to their control over hub airports and lucrative routes. The introduction of competition from newcomer airlines, however, quickly saw the price of airline tickets fall – and with them some of the incumbents who didn't adapt fast enough.[141]

Thanks to legislation too, the man in the street wins when pharmaceutical patents for drugs expire, allowing for more affordable generic brands to be introduced. While such laws are a wonderful thing for competition and affordability, they can dramatically undermine the entire revenue model of established companies in the blink of an eye.

Even though legislative shifts can be the bane of many organizations existence, they are often necessary for the greater good. However, even in cases where policy changes represent little more than political point scoring or vote grabbing, it is absolutely critical that businesses and industries respond to legislative shifts. A failure to do so, as in the case of each of the five shifts discussed in this chapter, will quickly set an organization or industry on a collision course with irrelevance.

WAVES AND TIDES

While it is important to be aware of these five shifts and the way they can threaten the relevance and longevity of any business or organization, it is equally important to distinguish between underlying trends and the fickle procession of fads.

Typically, short-term fluctuations are given far more attention than they deserve, especially in the media's short-term, 24/7 news cycle. People obsess about the rise and fall of short-term fads which I liken to waves – they come and they go, they don't last long and their mark is far from permanent.

Broad-based trends and shifts that every leader must pay attention to, on the other hand, I liken to tides. They may be slow-moving and less dramatic than the waves, but in the longer term such shifts are all-pervasive. Leaders and organizations ignore the shifting tides at their peril.

LEADERS AND ORGANIZATIONS IGNORE THE SHIFTING TIDES AT THEIR PERIL.

Shift is indeed happening and the ability to predict, prepare for and pre-empt change is vital. As media mogul Rupert Murdoch once said; "The essential ingredient to business success is the ability to consistently see round the corner."[142]

FOR REFLECTION:

Which of the 5 shifts pose a threat to your brand or organization? In what way?

- Societal Shifts
- Demographic Shifts
- Market Shifts
- Technological Shifts
- Legislative Shifts

CHAPTER 6:

ROAD 2 — THE INTOXICATION OF SUCCESS

A few decades ago, if I had asked you which industry you most closely associated with Switzerland, there would have been no hesitation: watchmaking. Switzerland and watchmaking were synonymous with one another and had been for centuries. Until the early 1970s, the Swiss dominated the timepiece market worldwide, producing half the watches sold each year around the globe.[143] 15 short years later, however, everything had changed.

When Japanese company, Seiko, released its *Astron* Quartz-movement watch in time for Christmas sales in 1969, the Swiss incumbents met the news with resistance and suspicion.[144] This new electronic watch represented a dramatic departure from traditional mechanical design and was largely dismissed as a fad.

The reason for such a dismissal was clear. Over the years, Swiss watchmakers had understandably developed a series of set beliefs about how watches were meant to be produced and what customers wanted in a timepiece. They confidently assumed they were the masters at creating quality watches and no-one was going to come in and tell them how to do what they did best.

By the mid-1980s, however, the Swiss watchmakers were in crisis. In the preceding decade and a half, the industry had shed almost 70% of its workforce and two-thirds of Swiss watchmakers went out of business.[145]

The moral to this story is clear: something dangerous happens when everyone starts looking at things from the same perspective or with the same set of assumptions about the way things are or should be. Group-think develops and collective blind spots begin to form, resulting in an inability to

SOMETHING DANGEROUS HAPPENS WHEN EVERYONE STARTS LOOKING AT THINGS FROM THE SAME PERSPECTIVE OR WITH THE SAME SET OF ASSUMPTIONS ABOUT THE WAY THINGS ARE OR SHOULD BE.

detect threats or to identify new opportunities outside the current frame of view.

Switzerland's watchmakers offer a compelling example of an industry that blindly wandered down the second road to irrelevance – something I call 'The Intoxication of Success'. Put simply, the Intoxication of Success is a belief that says "Look how successful we have been... we must be on the right track." At best, this mentality results in decision-makers becoming closed-off to different perspectives and points of view, while at worst it can lead to a deadly blend of arrogance and complacency. Naturally, the greater an organization's success or longevity, the greater the likelihood of it becoming blinded by its own triumphs and achievements.

In contrast with the Swiss watchmakers, Nike CEO Mark Parker is patently aware of the ever-present danger of complacency. "One of my fears is being this big, slow, constipated bureaucratic company that's happy with its success' he said. 'Companies fall apart when their model is so successful that it stifles any thinking that challenges it."[146] If only more business leaders had such foresight and wisdom.

EXPOSING THE NEGATIVES AT KODAK

Looking at the more recent demise of photographic giant Kodak, it would appear that an intoxication borne of success also played a key role. Notwithstanding external factors such as technological shifts as we discussed in the previous chapter, it was also a combination of *internal* forces that contributed to the spectacular downfall of this corporate giant.

During its 131-year history, Kodak was renowned for its innovation, flexibility and responsiveness. In the early years, founder George Eastman pioneered a cellulose film technology to replace the bulky glass plates previously used by photographers and this innovation put Eastman Kodak on the map.[147]

At the turn of the 20th century, Kodak demonstrated further agility when it released high quality color film in response to new products introduced by German competitors, thus solidifying its leadership.[148] Kodak subsequently grew in strength. By the 1960s, it was the 'Apple' or 'Google' of its day and investing in Kodak stock was "a sure bet".

Former Kodak employee Robert Shanebrook recalls Kodak's heyday in the 1960s. "At lunch, employees would crowd into the auditorium to watch a daily movie at an on-site theatre. Other employees would play basketball on the company courts. We had this self-imposed opinion of ourselves that we could do anything, that we were undefeatable."[149]

In almost every arena of life, Kodak enjoyed prominence and influence. Any occasion worth capturing on film, including Queen Elizabeth II's coronation in 1953 and the moon landing in 1969, became known as "a Kodak moment." The company's most famous product, Kodachrome, was used to shoot over 80 Oscar-winning Films while Hollywood's Kodak Theatre hosted the Academy awards each year.[150]

Somewhere between the mid-1960s and late 1980s, however, Kodak went from being an industry pioneer to a prisoner of its success. The very prosperity and profitability of Kodak's film

| KODAK WENT FROM BEING AN INDUSTRY PIONEER TO A PRISONER OF ITS SUCCESS.

business left the company ill-prepared to face what would become the biggest threat to its survival – the advent of the post-film era. According to former Kodak executive and author of *Surviving Transformation*, Vince Barabba, Kodak's leadership first became aware of the threat that digital technology posed to its business in the early 1980s.[151] After extensive analysis, however, the company's management concluded that digital photography lacked the quality, compatibility, affordability and appeal necessary to supersede traditional film.[152]

In *Management Today,* analyst Leon Gettler argues that this conclusion was not unreasonable. "You wouldn't have expected Kodak to invest in an unproven new technology at a time when it enjoyed 90% of film and 85% of camera market share."[153]

Justifiable or not, Kodak believed it was bullet-proof and used the analysis of digital technology to justify its inaction. When Kodak did finally explore the possibilities of a digital product range, it did so without a great deal of enthusiasm. Engineer Steven Sasson presented Kodak with its first digital camera in the mid-1970s and his superiors dismissed it as "cute" – all the while instructing Sasson and his fellow engineers not to tell anyone about it.[154]

This response was indicative of an insular and protectionist culture that had begun to form within the company. Former Kodak CEO, George Fisher, described that the company regarded digital photography as 'the enemy, an evil juggernaut that would kill the chemical-based film and paper business that had fueled Kodak's sales and profits for decades.'[155] Kodak's leadership team even formally vetoed plans for digital camera production proposed by the company's then vice-president Don Strickland saying it would represent the 'cannibalization of film."[156] One wonders how different things could have been if Kodak's leadership viewed cannibalization as a necessary opportunity the way Steve Jobs did four decades later.

Put simply, Kodak's management proved unwilling to consider any alternative to the exceptionally high manufacturing margin the company enjoyed on its cash cow film and equipment businesses. Anyone who championed low margin digital photography was consequently shunned or marginalized.[157]

The reality is that if Kodak had been a *startup* company at the onset of the digital age, it would have jumped at the opportunities and possibilities that digital photography offered. However, when contrasted with its traditional revenue channels, digital was never going to measure up. It would never deliver the fat margins and recurring long-tail revenues that film, paper and chemicals had.[158]

Kodak's resistance to digital photography saw the company make the very mistake its founder, George Eastman, had avoided seven decades prior when he embraced the emergence of color film.[159] As authors Carroll and Mui describe it, Kodak "kept its plane on autopilot until it flew into the side of the mountain."[160] By the turn of the 21st century, Kodak's profits plummeted 95% from $1.41 billion to $76 million in the space of a single year,[161] forcing the company to close dozens of its factories and processing labs.[162] By 2005, Kodak had shed two-thirds of its workforce and the company eventually filed for bankruptcy in January 2012.

While the factors that lead to success intoxication are many and varied, there are four remarkably common *symptoms* of this second road to irrelevance which every leader and organization must remain vigilant to:

1. Complacency
2. Conceit
3. Closed-mindedness
4. Conformity

1. COMPLACENCY

In the late 1980s senior vice president of the Bank of America, K. Shelly Porges, observed: "The greatest challenge we have as we become successful is not to rest on our laurels, never feel like we've done it. The minute you feel like you've done it, that's the beginning of the end."[163]

The pages of history suggest that Porges is on the money. Success can be a dangerous thing. It tends to erode a healthy appetite for invention and innovation. When you are riding high and in that 'so hot right now'

THE GREATEST CHALLENGE WE HAVE AS WE BECOME SUCCESSFUL IS NOT TO REST ON OUR LAURELS, NEVER FEEL LIKE WE'VE DONE IT.

stage, the lure of contentment and temptation to bask in the glory of triumph is enormous. It's easy for an organization or leader to 'let themselves go' - becoming fat, lazy and happy. This sense of complacency is one of the key factors that can cause an entity to slowly but surely pass the Turning Point on the Relevance Curve. Success creates a sense of satisfaction with the status quo and dulls a leader's motivation to grow and to keep learning.

In his 2011 best-selling book, *Adapt*, author Tim Harford speaks to this point suggesting that the great challenge for dominant and successful organizations is not that they lack the *capacity* to innovate, but rather that they lack the *will* to do so.[164]

In a similar vein, Robert Kriegel in his landmark book, *If it ain't broke, break it,* suggests that when companies become successful, they typically stop attending to the basics; forget the things that made them successful; and start taking success for granted.[165] He cites the case of IBM who got comfortable and shifted into cruise mode at the peak of their success in the early 1980s. IBMs complacency gave Digital Equipment Corporation (DEC) just the opportunity they'd been waiting for. DEC came to the fore with an innovative strategy and captured a significant slice of IBMs midrange computer pie. Between 1984-1988, DECs sales doubled and their earnings quadrupled as they ruthlessly pounded IBM.

Ironically, by 1987 the roles began to reverse – DEC was now the giant and was enjoying the spoils and accolades of success. In the midst of their celebrations, they failed to notice that customers were shifting to low-cost desktop networks which lowered their need for midrange computers. The result was a complete reversal of the previous year's success. In one year alone, DEC saw a 17% drop in profits.[166]

Simultaneous to the IBM/DEC wrangling's, a similar riches-to-rags story was being played out in the world of kitchen appliances. In the early 1970s, Carl Sontheimer revolutionized home cooking with his *Cuisinart* product. Celebrity chefs of the day including Julia Childs endorsed his range and the *Cuisinart* brand quickly rose to prominence. However, forgetting his formula for success which had centered on innovation,

Sontheimer failed to evolve the product as times and needs changed. Fifteen years after its launch, the *Cuisinart* had scarcely changed and competitors began to offer products that were cheaper, more efficient and fresher in design. *Cuisinart* eventually filed for bankruptcy having been, as Forbes magazines described it at the time, "chopped up by far hungrier, less complacent companies".[167]

American retail giant Sears is another business that fell into the trap of complacency. While it pioneered the mail-order catalogue business and then dominated it, new competitors like Victoria's Secret and Patagonia entered the mail order business and introduced slick new magazine formats, toll-free telephone numbers, 24-hour service and next-day delivery. Despite this, Sears' mail order operations remained unchanged and within a few years, their once highly profitable cash-cow catalogue business simply stopped producing milk.[168]

Sears really should have known better than to fall into the very trap that had led to the demise of the great retailer Atlantic & Pacific Tea Company (A&P) just a few decades prior. From the 1920s to the 1950s, A&P had risen to become the largest retailing organization in the world. However, over time the company's leadership grew comfortable with the success formula that had served them so well and failed to evolve as big low-cost operators like Wal-Mart expanded in the grocery business and players like Whole Foods pitched to the higher-end shopper.[169] The latter part of the 20th century saw A&P follow a steady downward trajectory with the company eventually filing for bankruptcy in December 2010 and then again in July 2015.[170]

Just as comfort is the enemy of progress, becoming complacent in success is one of the most dangerous traps an organization can fall into. After all, the moment you think you've made it, you've

| EMBRACING THE STATUS QUO IS A DEATH SENTENCE FOR ANY BUSINESS TODAY.

passed it. As Starbucks CEO Howard Schultz remarks "Embracing the status quo is a death sentence for any business today."

2. CONCEIT

Defined in the Oxford dictionary as *an excessive pride in oneself*, conceit is an exceptionally common indicator of success intoxication.

The Greek historian, Herodotus, was the first to make explicit links between arrogance (what he called *hubris)* and the process of decline in empires. Drawing on patterns in history, he described a simple dynamic whereby a successful leader or nation oversteps the boundaries of prudence and decency to commit an act that brings about their ultimate fall. This helps account for the arrogant display of power which sparked the Peloponnesian war and ultimately brought Athens to its knees.

The pattern in human history is clear: conceit is directly related to demise. The moment those in power begin to see themselves as indestructible or invincible, they start making the very mistakes that lead to their destruction. As King Solomon noted many centuries ago, "Pride goes before destruction and haughtiness before a fall."[171]

While no organization or individual ever sets out to become conceited on purpose, conceit is all too often a by-product of enduring success. Examples of this in the modern business world abound.

Consider the ill-fated approach that Sony took as the post-CD age dawned. Rather than embrace the MP3 format, Sony arrogantly assumed that their market dominance meant they could 'own' the entire music ecosystem and therefore attempted to force consumers to use their proprietary ATRAC format. While Sony was attempting to force the market's hand, audio file sharing services like Napster were quickly making the MP3 format ubiquitous. By the time Sony realized it could not take consumers for granted, Apple had dealt it a final blow with the release of the iPod – a product that all but killed off Sony's Minidisc range.

Mobile phone manufacturer Motorola fell into a similar trap with the release of its StarTAC phone in 1996. The world's number one cell phone maker at the time, Motorola assumed it could demand retailers and carriers play by its rules. Motorola dictated, for instance, that in order to be able to stock the StarTAC phone, as much as 75% of retailers' inventory had to be

Motorola. The company went further, stipulating that retailers showcase StarTAC devices in stand-alone displays in-store.

Naturally, retailers and phone carriers reacted badly to Motorola's strong-arm tactics and the pushback gave competing phone manufacturers the opening they had been waiting for. The subsequent fall for Motorola was as spectacular as it was embarrassing. The company went from industry leader with 50% share of the mobile phone market in the mid-1990s to a mere 17% in 1999.[172]

WHEN DOMINANCE BECOMES DANGEROUS

In his book, *Innovation and Entrepreneurship,* Peter Drucker suggests that conceit tends to arise in any industry where a small number of key players have dominated and remained unchallenged for a long time. Drucker describes a process by which arrogance inevitably creeps in amongst these established

> **CONCEIT TENDS TO ARISE IN ANY INDUSTRY WHERE A SMALL NUMBER OF KEY PLAYERS HAVE DOMINATED AND REMAINED UNCHALLENGED FOR A LONG TIME.**

operators. Clinging to historical and increasingly dysfunctional practices, incumbents tend to ignore or even scoff at new market entrants until the more agile and responsive start-ups begin eroding the dominance of established players. Typically, at this point, the incumbents take action but often find that it is too late.[173]

THE IVORY TOWER SYNDROME

While conceit typically results from enduring success, at other times it can simply be a by-product of an organization becoming out of touch with those it is seeking to influence – something known as the 'ivory tower syndrome'.

At Microsoft, many of the company's challenges during the 2000s arose from the fact that the young hot shots who had built the company in the 1980s were now middle-aged managers. "Microsoft bosses just didn't understand the burgeoning class of computer users who hadn't been born when Microsoft first opened its doors," was how one market analyst put it.[174]

More dangerous than the fact that managers didn't understand the next generation of computer users was the fact that those in power dismissed input from this younger cohort too. A culture developed in Microsoft during the early 2000s where young company engineers were met with disinterest or resistance when they tried to communicate to their superiors the emerging trends among their peers. "Most senior people were out of touch with the way home users were starting to use computers, especially the younger generation" one young Microsoft developer said. As a result, when AOL moved ahead creating it's instant messenger program, AIM, Microsoft trailed a full 2 years behind with the release of MSN Messenger.

In the years that followed, Microsoft continued to trail the market. In 2003, for instance, a young Microsoft employee noticed that his college buddies were making extensive use of AIMs 'status' feature to share personal information like 'gone shopping' or 'studying for finals.' When the employee suggested to his middle-aged boss that MSN follow suit by developing a short-messaging status feature of its own, his suggestion was dismissed as silly. As far as the employee's supervisor was concerned, no young person would want to upload a few words on his or her profile page to tell friends what they were doing.[175]

In reality, what this young developer had picked up on were the embryonic stages of the social networking revolution – something Microsoft could have pioneered and dominated had they been more in tune with and open to what their customers were thinking and doing.

Losing touch with consumers was also a key driver in the Japanese electronics industry losing its market leadership position during the late 1990s and early 2000s. As Panasonic President Kazuhiro Tsuga admitted in June 2012 "Japanese firms became too confident about our technology and manufacturing prowess. We lost sight of the products from the consumer's point of view."

One analyst went further arguing that Japan's greatest strength became its greatest weakness. "Japanese firms strived to create products that were the world's thinnest and smallest while losing sight of factors that really mattered to people such as design and ease of use." It was this oversight that allowed players like Apple, Google and Samsung to gain a foothold in a market traditionally dominated by Japanese giants like Sony, Sharp and Panasonic.[176]

While conceit as a result of the 'Ivory Tower syndrome' is not necessarily malicious or intentional, it is no less damaging to the long-term relevance of an organization, business or brand.

3. CLOSED-MINDEDNESS

Success tends to solidify people's points of view and in many ways, this is natural. After all, if a set of assumptions and beliefs has led to triumph in the past, information or ideas outside this frame of reference will almost automatically be viewed with suspicion.

Leading Australian demographer and social researcher Hugh MacKay describes closed-mindedness this way. "If you've adopted a rigid worldview, you tend to see everything through the filter of your convictions and, not surprisingly, you see what you're looking for. The more you use a particular theory for making sense of things, the more things seem to fit the theory".[177]

THE MORE YOU USE A PARTICULAR THEORY FOR MAKING SENSE OF THINGS, THE MORE THINGS SEEM TO FIT THE THEORY

Recent centuries offer many examples of predictions and assumptions that were as flawed as the paradigms that shaped them:

- Napoleon Bonaparte's dismissal of Robert Fulham's steamboat invention. "How, sir, would you make a ship sail against the wind and the currents by lighting a bonfire under her deck? Excuse me; I have not the time to listen to such nonsense" Napoleon famously said.
- The Michigan Savings Bank chief executive who, in 1903, advised investors not to sink their money in the Ford Motor company, believing "the horse is here to stay, but the automobile is a fad."

- A Boeing engineer who boasted "there will never be a bigger plane built" when Boeing's 10-seater 247 model was launched in 1933.
- Sir William Preece, inventor and former head of the British Post Office, who suggested in the early 1900s that "the Americans have need of the telephone, but we British do not. We have plenty of messenger boys."
- Finally, consider New York governor Martin von Buren's anti-railroad appeal to then U.S. president, Andrew Jackson, in the early 1830s: "Dear Mr. President: The canal system of this country is being threatened by a new form of transportation known as 'railroads'... As you may well know, Mr. President, 'railroad' carriages are pulled at the enormous speed of 15 miles per hour by 'engines' which, in addition to endangering life and limb of passengers, roar and snort their way through the countryside, setting fire to crops, scaring the livestock and frightening women and children. The Almighty certainly never intended that people should travel at such breakneck speed."

The reason closed-mindedness is so dangerous to the relevance and longevity of an organization is that as the world around us changes, so too must our frames for understanding it.

PLAYING BY OUTDATED RULES

When American football legalized the forward pass in 1906, suddenly it was possible to gain 40 yards with the flick of a wrist. Curiously, however, most teams chose not to take advantage of the rule change, opting instead to stick with what they knew.

A coach at St Louis University was one of the first to break from the pack, instructing his players to use the forward pass extensively. His open-minded embrace of a new approach produced outstanding results: St Louis outscored their opponents that season 402-11.[178]

In the world of armed combat too, it is those who embrace innovative tactics that typically prevail. As a tragic example of this, historians and analysts estimate that as many as four million soldiers lost their lives in WWI simply because wartime leaders stuck to traditional military tactics rather than taking advantage of modern weaponry and approaches.[179]

In WWII, it was a similar story in the clash between German and French forces. The French adopted an entrenched defense, best exemplified in the 150-mile long fortification called the Maginot Line. The Germans, in contrast, opted for a new mobile artillery tactic. When these two ideologies clashed, the German offensive using tanks and aircraft meant the French did not stand a chance.[180]

The very same dynamic exists in a business context.

As we saw in the case of the Swiss watchmakers, to dogmatically stick with a set of assumptions that were appropriate in the past may not serve us in the future. Rejecting outright any new ideas that fail to fit into the existing assumptions we hold can cause us to miss the very innovations that may be the key to our future success. Focused attention can become tunnel vision and niches can turn into ruts – a phenomenon known as 'inattentional blindness'

REJECTING OUTRIGHT ANY NEW IDEAS THAT FAIL TO FIT INTO THE EXISTING ASSUMPTIONS WE HOLD CAN CAUSE US TO MISS THE VERY INNOVATIONS THAT MAY BE THE KEY TO OUR FUTURE SUCCESS.

Consider how a belief system that had served Kmart well for decades gradually led the company off course as times changed. Kmart's origins as a five-and-dime store resulted in the company seeing itself as a place where customers received low prices but essentially paid for these with long checkout lines, poorly lit stores and out-of-stock items.[181] This mentality led to Kmart to become stuck. Market researcher George Rosenbaum argues that Kmart never got past the belief that "if you give the customer something, you have to take something away such as comfort, service or convenience."

Kmart's competitors, meanwhile, offered low prices but not at the expense of user-friendly, clean and well-stocked stores. Before long, customers came to understand that they did not have to suffer in order to save – an approach that was way outside Kmart's frame of reference.[182] The results were devastating. By 2003, Kmart in the USA was experiencing nationwide store closures, had cut almost 70,000 jobs, and was posting multi-billion dollar losses.[183]

WHEN INDIVIDUALS BECOME INTOXICATED

While organizations can grow intoxicated by success to the point of being closed to new approaches, individual leaders are highly susceptible to this too. In his book, *Why Good Companies Go Bad,* Donald Sull explores a phenomenon he calls "the cover curse". Sull pointed to case after case of leaders such as Compaq's CEO Eckhard Pfeiffer who, having won critical acclaim and being featured on the covers of business publications, fell from greatness soon after.

In exploring why this may be the case, Sull suggests that the 'cover curse' doesn't indicate lack of editorial insight on the part of business publications but rather is a function of the fact that praise from the business press reinforces managers' attachment to their success formula. Further still, by the time a company's success formula has won critical acclaim, it's leaders should be rethinking it rather than "gold-plating it into dogma" and arrogantly assuming it is the only or best way to do things.[184]

It takes great humility and self-awareness for organizations and individual leaders to remain open to new ideas. Nevertheless, doing so is critical in order to remain relevant and ahead of the curve. After all, before we can change anything else, we must be willing to change our mind.

> **BEFORE WE CAN CHANGE ANYTHING ELSE, WE MUST BE WILLING TO CHANGE OUR MIND.**

4. CONFORMITY

"You become like those you associate with."

"Birds of a feather flock together."

"Like attracts like."

We all know these timeless truths: parents become acutely aware of their significance when their children begin forming friendships at school.

The simple reality is that over time, human beings in proximity to one another begin to resemble each other. You see this expressed at an interpersonal level in long-time married couples who begin to mimic one another unconsciously and finish each other's sentences.

The same process occurs in successful organizations and businesses.

As organizations grow over time, a culture built on shared values and attitudes becomes self-perpetuating – the more success an organization achieves, the more clearly defined its culture becomes. In *Built to Last,* authors Jim Collins and Jerry Porras argue that developing a strong and even 'cult-like' culture is in fact a critical ingredient in organizational success.

While a strong culture does create an important sense of cohesion and belonging, it can also leave an organization vulnerable to blinkered thinking or collective blind spots. This is due to the fact that those who do not subscribe to

> **WHILE A STRONG CULTURE DOES CREATE AN IMPORTANT SENSE OF COHESION AND BELONGING, IT CAN ALSO LEAVE AN ORGANIZATION VULNERABLE TO BLINKERED THINKING**

or fit with the organizations mind-set either fail to join in the first place, or are swiftly ejected in the same way white blood cells attack and neutralize a foreign pathogen in our bodies. The result is that views, opinions or ideas that are divergent or dissenting go unheralded and unrewarded – even when these views may be necessary and important to hear. In the same way that in-breeding results in weaker genetic strains, cultures lacking diversity can weaken an organization with time. As Hala Moddelmog, former president of Arby's Restaurant Group, says, "You really don't need another you."[185]

Conformity threatens in many different ways, and can lead to disaster. Psychologist Irving Janis argues that the lack of diversity in a group insulates it from outside opinion and convinces members over time that the group's judgment on important issues must be right. These kinds of groups, Janis suggests, share "an illusion of invulnerability, a willingness to rationalize away possible counter-arguments to the group's position, and a conviction that dissent is not useful."[186]

While conformist cultures in organizations can be inherently unhealthy, they become particularly dangerous when, like the village in the award-winning movie *Chocolat*, those on the 'outside' are viewed with fear, suspicion or a sense of superiority.

CONFORMITY AT THE TOP

In *Why Good Companies Go Bad,* Donald Sull argues that conformity in leadership played a key role in the woes of companies such as Firestone Tires, Compaq and failed automaker Daewoo. Prior to these companies' fall from greatness, he suggests that the respective leadership teams had become 'like clones', each executive tending to reinforce a collegial point of view. In the case of Daewoo in particular, six in 10 of the company's senior management graduated from the same university, and almost a third graduated from the same high school.[187]

Sull suggests that organizations, particularly those with longevity and success behind them, do a 'clone test' in an effort to combat such in-breeding. He exhorts management teams to do a quick survey of those in leadership and ponder questions like:[188]

- What is the executive team's gender breakdown?
- What is its average age?
- How many leaders rose from within the organization?
- How many dress in similar ways?
- How many look physically similar?
- How many come from a similar background?
- How many share a common alma mater?
- How many socialize outside work hours?

Underscoring the importance of diversity, a recent McKinsey & Co study of 366 public companies worldwide found a statistically significant relationship between companies with women and minorities in their upper ranks and better financial performance. Businesses with the most gender-diverse leadership were 15% more likely to report financial returns above their industry average and an even more striking link was found between business success and ethnic diversity.[189]

In order to combat homogeneity in organizations, it is critical to focus on competence rather than commonality when hiring or identifying future leadership talent. Simply because past or current leaders fit a certain mold (in skills, appearance or temperament), beware of making the assumption that they were successful *because* of these largely superficial characteristics. This erroneous and misleading assumption is sometimes referred to in business circles as the Halo Effect.

While success ought to be the aim of any organization or leader, it is also important to recognize that with success come inherent dangers.

Regardless of whether it is expressed in the form of complacency, conceit, closed-mindedness or conformity, becoming intoxicated by success will always leave organizations and leaders with a nasty hangover

BECOMING INTOXICATED BY SUCCESS WILL ALWAYS LEAVE ORGANIZATIONS AND LEADERS WITH A NASTY HANGOVER

when they finally do wake up... hopefully before its too late.

FOR REFLECTION:

Looking at the four symptoms of success intoxication below, truthfully consider which of them may apply in your context:

1. **Complacency**
2. **Conceit**
3. **Closed-mindedness**
4. **Conformity**

While this may be a confronting realization, what steps can you take to combat the intoxicating effects of success in the future?

CHAPTER 7:

ROAD 3 - PRESERVATION OBSESSION

We live in an age where the pace of change is such that in order to stay in the same place we must run faster and faster.[190] As best-selling business author Robert Kriegel says: "Today's innovations are tomorrow's antiquities…

TODAY'S INNOVATIONS ARE TOMORROW'S ANTIQUITIES…

Thinking that you can stay ahead by repeating the past is folly. If you or your products don't grow, improve and evolve, as in nature – they (and you) will face extinction."[191]

The dizzying pace of change in recent years has left many business leaders feeling disoriented and out of control. However, while the current rate of change may be greater than in the past, the challenge of recognizing and responding to change is far from new. Many decades ago, Wal-Mart founder Sam Walton observed: "You can't just keep doing what works one time, because everything around you is always changing. To succeed, you have to stay out in front of that change."[192]

While the need to keep pace with change may seem like common sense, it is far from common practice.[193] On the contrary, we are creatures of habit that tend to crave the predictable. Most organizations and many leaders have a natural reflex to resist and even *fear* change. The stronger this reflex, the more at risk a company, brand or organization will be of losing relevance.

Fear is a funny thing. While it can be healthy and necessary for self-preservation, fear can also be highly counter-productive when it becomes an irrational, all-consuming and debilitating phobia. Although people can have many different types of phobia, the one that I am especially interested in is the irrational and debilitating fear of new things and/or change – known as *neophobia.*

I suspect that deep down we are all neophobes to varying degrees. My wife could certainly attest to the fact that I am. For instance, if I find a particular brand of business shirt or jeans that fits just right, or is cut and designed to my taste, I will buy two of every color in my size. When I find what I like, I am very resistant to change.

While such a desire for the familiar is natural, the type of neophobia we are going to explore in this chapter is so dangerous that it is in fact the third road to irrelevance. Such a fear of the new is perhaps best characterized in the rarely stated yet often held belief within organizations that *everything old is automatically good* and *everything new is automatically bad.* This belief leads to a relentless and irrational drive to preserve the past at all costs.

Drawing on both my observations of working with clients and also my research over recent years, I would suggest that there are 3 common symptoms of Preservation Obsession within organizations.

PRESERVATION OBSESSION SYMPTOM 1:
A GLORIFICATION OF THE PAST

A colleague of mine named Graham told me about a memorable boardroom meeting he chaired after his appointment as CEO of a non-profit organization. At the meeting Graham made a recommendation for a relatively minor change to the organization's day-to-day operation. A brief discussion ensued and none of the attendees expressed any opposition. When it was time to vote however, one board member vetoed the proposal, and Graham sought out the naysayer at the close of the meeting to find out why.

"I was voting on behalf of my father," the board member said.

"Oh I haven't met your father – he wasn't able to make it today?" Graham responded.

"No of course not," the board member replied. "My father died 12 years ago!"

Not knowing how to respond, Graham changed the topic, but he remained aghast. Here was a colleague so obsessed with preserving the past to the point of voting on behalf of someone who represented agendas, needs and challenges which existed 12 years ago. Far from being focused on the future, this board member wasn't even willing to embrace the present!

While remembering the past, reflecting on milestones and valuing heritage are important for any organization, there is a danger when these things are over-valued or placed on a pedestal. It doesn't take long before the organization becomes stale, dated and falling behind.

It's a dangerous place to be when key leaders or influencers in an organization are perpetually wearing rose-colored glasses, living off past successes or longing to return to the 'good old days'. Like a driver who is so focused on the rear-view mirror they stop looking out the windscreen, glorifying the past will always put an organization on a collision course with irrelevance. After all, while enduring organizations value where they have been, they are always more loyal to their future than their past.

ENDURING ORGANIZATIONS ARE ALWAYS MORE LOYAL TO THEIR FUTURE THAN THEIR PAST.

PRESERVATION OBSESSION SYMPTOM 2: AN OVER-EMPHASIS ON PROCESS

Associate Professor of Strategy and Entrepreneurship at the London Business School, Frank Vermeulen, describes an experiment at San Diego Zoo that highlighted the behavioral tendency to over-emphasize process.

As part of the experiment, scientists placed five monkeys in a room with a staircase in the center and a bunch of bananas hanging at the top of the staircase. Whenever one of the monkeys would try to climb the steps to reach a banana, the scientists would use a hose to spray the other four monkeys with ice-cold water – much to their irritation.

Very quickly, a dynamic developed where any time a monkey attempted to climb the staircase the other four would hold it back in order to avoid a further drenching. The monkeys learned that climbing the ladder to retrieve the bananas was 'against the rules' and the scientists put away the hose.

After a while, the scientists removed one of the original monkeys and replaced him with a new one. Naturally, this new entrant spotted the bananas immediately and made a beeline for the steps. The remaining four monkeys set upon the new entrant, beat him up, and gave him the clear message that the staircase and bananas were out of bounds – even though the new entrant had no idea why.

Over the next half hour, the scientists replaced the remaining original monkeys one by one until none of the initial group remained in the room. Interestingly, as each new monkey entered the room, it would quickly learn through threat of force that climbing the stairs was not to be attempted. Each of the monkeys would beat the others if they even attempted to scale the stairs in pursuit of the bananas - even though none of them had any experience or knowledge of the cold-water treatment. The staircase became off-limits even though none of the monkeys knew why. It was simply "the way we do things around here".

ARE WE THAT DIFFERENT FROM MONKEYS?

Vermeulen points to the fact that the behavior of the monkeys is not unlike what happens with human beings. Naturally, all businesses and organizations develop processes, routines, habits and practices. Over the course of years, however, the reasons for these may well be forgotten and all that remains is an expectation of compliance even though no reason for doing so is given or apparent.

As times change, the 'rules' for doing business are changing with them. Almost daily, new success formulas are being created, new paths are being trodden, new approaches being explored by others in the marketplace.

However, despite the opportunities and competitive advantages that these new ways of operating may offer, many organizations resist embracing them - opting rather to stick with processes, rhythms, routines that are tried and true.

"Once managers find a process that works well enough, they usually stop experimentation and commit to what works," explains Donald Sull in his book *Why Good Companies Go Bad*.

"Over time, any company develops a 'success formula' of processes that allow for economies of scale. As the success formula continues to facilitate success, this positive feedback reinforces management's belief that they should fortify and reinforce the formula. With time and repetition, processes become second nature; people stop considering alternatives to

OVER TIME, PROCESSES SETTLE INTO ROUTINES, RELATIONSHIPS BECOME SHACKLES, AND VALUES OSSIFY INTO DOGMAS.

their formula and grow less flexible. Strategic frames become blinders, processes settle into routines, relationships become shackles, and values ossify into dogmas."[194]

As time goes on, these outdated and uncompetitive processes get embedded in the organization's culture and become *sacred cows*. Defined as "an outmoded practice, policy, system, or strategy," sacred cows have a unique ability to inhibit change and prevent responsiveness to new opportunities.[195] A dead giveaway that someone in an organization is engaging in cattle worship is when he or she utters that insufferable phrase: *"But that's the way we've always done it."*

Any suggestion of change offends a sacred cow worshipper. They will point defensively to historical data, drag out codes of conduct documentation and even make accusations that someone is "reinventing the wheel". Naturally, I am not endorsing change for change's sake (something we will discuss in the next chapter), but by the same token while the wheel may not need reinventing, sometimes it does need a change of tire.

Courageous leaders recognize that it is more important to be purpose-driven than popular and are therefore willing to forego processes that are inefficient and outdated - no matter how much others may cling to the familiarity of rote and ritual. This is something we will explore further in chapter 14.

MAKE UNCERTAINTY YOUR FRIEND

In addition to eroding efficiency, an over-emphasis on process can prevent risk-taking and creativity. Although it is predictable and comfortable to do things in a tried-and-trusted fashion, staying

ONLY THOSE COMMITTED TO THE RISK AND PROMISE OF UNCHARTED WATERS WILL THRIVE.

relevant typically involves carving new paths. Or as former Motorola CEO Robert Galvin put it: "Only those committed to the risk and promise of uncharted waters will thrive."[196]

Steel production processes in the U.S. are a case in point. Up until the early 1960s, large integrated steel mills were profitable and successful – that is, until a new type of steel mill labeled the 'mini-mill' came onto the scene. Mini-mills operated quite differently from their traditional counterparts and worked on vastly different economies of scale. They were cheaper to build ($6 billion each as opposed to $100 billion) and less labor-intensive to run (0.6 as opposed to 2.3 labor hours per ton of steel produced).[197]

Increased efficiency notwithstanding, governments, labor unions and integrated steel companies opposed the mini-mills every step of the way.[198] Those in charge of the integrated steel giants saw this new approach as a risky departure from the safe and proven methods of old. When vetoing a proposal to incorporate mini-mill technology in his plant, one steel executive said: "The integrated steelmaking process is the only right one... Everything else is cheating – a fad, unhealthy, and unlikely to endure." Ironically, 10 years on from this statement being made, the only prosperous providers in the American steel industry were those using the mini-mill technology.[199]

Although leaders fear changing the things that garnered them success, an unwillingness to take necessary and intelligent risks is likely to make a business stale at best, or a failure at worst.

I have personally found this to be true as a speaker on the conference circuit. I can easily get comfortable with material that works; jokes that get a predictable response; and stories that make the required impact. However, I have found it critical to keep pushing myself to take risks with new material, and to discard content that is safe because I recognize that an unwillingness to do so will result in me becoming stale, outdated and irrelevant. Many of my professional speaker colleagues have fallen into this trap by delivering the same canned content year after year, decade after decade.

CONSISTENCY AT THE COST OF CREATIVITY

Process-focused organizations tend to train people to perform tasks *consistently*, but not creatively. Consider, for example, how fast food employees are expected to follow scripts when serving customers at the front counter. Such scripts are designed with efficiency and consistency in mind... and work well as long as the customer also follows the script. If a request

> **PROCESS-FOCUSED ORGANIZATIONS TEND TO TRAIN PEOPLE TO PERFORM TASKS *CONSISTENTLY*, BUT NOT CREATIVELY.**

is made that falls outside the scope of the normal ordering process however, the register operator typically get flustered, thrown and confused.

Why does this happen? Because the employee has been trained to *do* but not to *think*. Therefore when something goes wrong or there is a disruption to the normal process, they are unable to respond in the moment, understand the problem, or think outside the box (and the script) for a solution.

The reality is that creativity at all levels of an organization is critical in responding to change. Processes that remove the need for and even discourage creative thought leave an organization increasingly vulnerable to disruptions that could render it uncompetitive and irrelevant. What's more, a process-driven approach tends to condition individuals in an organization to comply with the status quo rather than look for creative alternatives and innovations.

PROCESS IS NOT THE ENEMY

In saying that over-emphasizing processes can cause an organization to lose relevance, it is important to be clear that processes in and of themselves are not the enemy. You don't need to look far to see how quickly things can go off track when due process is ignored or non-existent.

Consider the case of one state law enforcement organization within which it had become accepted practice for police officers to ignore the required process of verbally swearing affidavits when an offender was arrested. The failure to comply with this simple procedure resulted in many years of evidence in a high profile criminal investigation being deemed inadmissible and the case being dropped.[200]

Process is a necessary means to an end. The problem arises when process becomes the end in itself - with both risk-taking and creativity being stifled as a result.

PRESERVATION OBSESSION SYMPTOM 3: A STUBBORN COMMITMENT TO TRADITIONS AND RITUALS

A few years ago when touring tropical northern Australia, I came across an ecological phenomenon unique to the area known as the Curtain Fig Tree. This unusual tree is, in fact, not a tree at all but a series of vines in the shape of a tree.

What is unusual about the Curtain Fig is the way in which it comes to exist. At the outset, a fig germinates high up in an existing tree and starts sending out roots that crawl down the tree's trunk towards the ground. Once the initial roots take hold in the ground below, many other roots repeat the same pattern until the fig begins to take over - strangling the original host tree to death and growing independently of it. Eventually, the original tree rots away and all that is left is a skeleton of figs resembling the shape of a tree that no longer exists.

In many ways, traditions within organizations can do a similar thing. While they start small and inconspicuous, traditions can grow in size and influence to the point where they take over and even strangle

TRADITIONS CAN TAKE OVER AND EVEN STRANGLE AN ORGANIZATION TO DEATH.

an organization to death. Eventually, all that remains are a series of habits, routines and activities that resemble the shape of the organization they once served but have effectively killed.

In fairness, traditions have their role and place in organizational life. After all, they can be a key part of building a strong culture, a sense of belonging and a connection with heritage. However, every organization and leader must make a choice: will you view traditions as a rudder that can positively shape your future course, or will you allow them to be an anchor that ties you to the past and holds you back?

CORPORATE SING-ALONGS

Probably the best example of how a stubborn commitment to tradition can undermine the relevance of a company would be the case of party plan giant, Tupperware.

For many years, up until the 1970s, Tupperware parties typically commenced with the singing of songs featuring company-themed lyrics. One of the more popular and commonly sung tunes went like this:

> *I've got the Tupper feeling up in my head,*
> *up in my head, up in my head*
> *I've got the Tupper feeling up in my head,*
> *up in my head today.*
> *I've got the Tupper feeling deep in my heart,*
> *deep in my heart, deep in my heart,*
> *I've got the Tupper feeling deep in my heart,*
> *deep in my heart to stay.*[201]

By the late 1970s, Tupperware's executive team realized that these songs and the corresponding 'actions' that accompanied them were becoming outdated and needed to go. However, there was uproar in the ranks. Some claimed it would be the end of Tupperware – even that the company would "lose its soul". Undeterred, the company's leadership pushed ahead and Tupperware party sing-alongs were relegated to the history books. Would

Tupperware have become the $2 billion company it is today, I wonder, if it had held on for dear life to its traditions and rituals? I suspect not.

It was a strangely similar story at computer giant IBM who from the 1930s to 1950s published a collection of company songs in an official songbook named *Songs of the IBM*.

While companies like Tupperware and IBM had the foresight to kill off some of their sacred cows, many other organizations remain heavily bogged down in outdated traditions and rituals.

THE INSIDIOUS CREEP OF TRADITION

Throughout history it is clear – as humans we crave tradition. We love to build monuments, establish memorials and settle into routines and rhythms that help us feel connected to our past and comfortable in the present.

> **WE LOVE TO SETTLE INTO ROUTINES AND RHYTHMS THAT HELP US FEEL CONNECTED TO OUR PAST AND COMFORTABLE IN THE PRESENT.**

Consider, for instance, the Protestant reformation in the 16th Century. One of the issues Protestants had with the Catholic Church was its array of traditions and rituals. The breakaway Protestants felt these traditions compromised the intentions of God and therefore established austere houses of worship in stark contrast to the relic-rich Catholic Church. Within a couple of hundred years, however, the Protestant churches had developed their own intricate framework of rites, processes and traditions. Today it is difficult to spot the difference between a high Anglican or Episcopal Church service and a traditional Catholic mass!

Even in modern evangelical and Pentecostal churches, known for their ruthless commitment to being contemporary and free of the stifling rituals of their older-denomination counterparts, traditions still take root. Whether it is the number and type of songs at the beginning of a service, the length and style of the minister's sermon or the way in which communion is served, traditions seem to grow as effortlessly as weeds in a garden.

California's iconic Crystal Cathedral is a case in point.

When Pastor Robert Schuller looked to establish a church in southern California in early 1955, there was little doubt that he was a pioneer with tremendous vision and a willingness to forge new paths. With limited funds, boundless creativity and a belief that churches were about people more than buildings, Schuller's Garden Grove Community Church spent its first 6 years operating out of a drive-in movie theatre and bore the motto *'Come as you are in the family car'*.[202] This unorthodox move raised eyebrows amongst the establishment but it worked. Schuller's message to the community was clear – his vision was to build a church that was fresh, new and different. Six years later, Garden Grove Community Church was attracting thousands each Sunday and a decision was made to build the world's first ever walk-in/drive-in church – an impressive structure of functionality and aesthetic.

As the church continued to grow, Schuller embarked on a series of ground-breaking initiatives including the construction of the 14-storey 'Tower of Hope' in 1968, America's first 24-hour suicide and crisis intervention telephone service, and the cutting-edge 'Hour of Power' television broadcast which first aired in 1970.[203]

At the Garden Grove Community Church's 20th anniversary celebration in November 1975, Schuller announced his most ambitious plan yet: to construct a 3000-seat sanctuary using thousands of panes of glass. This 'Crystal Cathedral', as it became known, took four years to complete and cost almost $17 million.[204] In the years that followed, the Crystal Cathedral became more than a southern Californian landmark – it became a source of inspiration to millions the world over. The gleaming church facilities themselves became a headquarters for community outreach and service.

During the 1990s, the influence of Robert Schuller and the Crystal Cathedral grew exponentially. The *Hour of Power* broadcasts expanded around the globe even airing in the former Soviet Union to an estimated audience of over 200 million people. Closer to home, the Crystal Cathedral's membership and facilities continued to expand with the church's world famous Christmas and Easter productions attracting 200,000 people from around the world each year.[205]

Somewhere during the early 2000's, however, the Crystal Cathedral's sparkle began to fade. As new generations of churchgoers sought contemporary services and music, Schuller doggedly insisted that clergy wear formal church gowns and that pipe organ music feature prominently during services. Even when his own children suggested the church was becoming out of touch, Robert Schuller stuck with what was tried and true. By the end of the 2000s, it was clear that the Crystal Cathedral was in serious trouble. Church attendance and revenue plummeted, and the Hour of Power ratings nosedived.[206] Amid mounting debts, the Crystal Cathedral filed for bankruptcy in October 2010 and sold its iconic facility to the Roman Catholic Diocese of Orange County in February 2012.

Speaking in July 2011 at a conference nearby the Crystal Cathedral, I stopped in to see the iconic church for myself and attended a Sunday service. The congregation that evening would have numbered no more than 70 - in an auditorium designed to seat over 3000. I was impressed by the minister who led the service. Amidst all the turmoil she was likely facing, her message was upbeat, sincere and well meaning. Despite this, there was simply no denying the fact that she was at the helm of a sinking ship.

The Crystal Cathedral that evening was one of the starkest pictures I have ever seen of faded glory. Here was an institution that had once been at the cutting edge, that had blazed new trails and accomplished great things but had become dated, tradition-bound and stuck in the past. This trap is one that the Crystal Cathedral is far from alone in falling into.

As we draw this chapter to a close, I wanted to do so by sharing one of my favorite examples of preservation obsession which comes from an institution known for valuing its past – the military.

For many years, U.S. military requirements stated that firing a cannon required 3 men. According to a detailed operations manual, one soldier holds cannon, one loads ammunition, and third one literally stands there. The reason for this third person requirement was simple: originally the third man's job was to hold the horse so that it wouldn't be spooked by the sound of the cannon's explosion. Naturally, this role was necessary when the operations manual was written as cannons were always hauled into battle by a horse. Despite the fact that horses had been superseded by new technology many decades ago, the old three-person rule stuck even though that it no longer served any purpose or made any sense. It was not until relatively recently that this outdated procedure was called into question and the operations manual updated – about 150 years after it should have been![207]

While we may naturally be creatures of habit, those who are committed to staying current and relevant must resist every urge to get stuck in patterns and routines from the past. After all, what has served us well yesterday may prove to be a shackle tomorrow. As Will Rogers once said, "Even if you are on the right track, you'll get run over if you don't keep moving."

EVEN IF YOU ARE ON THE RIGHT TRACK, YOU'LL GET RUN OVER IF YOU DON'T KEEP MOVING.

FOR REFLECTION

Looking at the three symptoms of Preservation Obsession below, which of these could apply in your context?

1. **Glorifying the past**
2. **Over-emphasizing process (at the cost of risk taking and creativity)**
3. **A stubborn commitment to traditions and rituals**

While valuing heritage is important, are there things you need to let go of in order to move forward? If so, what could they be?

CHAPTER 8:

ROAD 4 - PROGRESS ADDICTION

Britain's first female Member of Parliament, Lady Astor, once observed: "The main dangers in this life are the people who want to change nothing – or everything."

How true that is. As we saw in the previous chapter, those who hold onto the past and are unwilling to change will always prove hazardous to an entity's ongoing relevance. However, as Lady Astor observed, the very opposite fixation is just as dangerous – an addiction to progress.

This may come as a surprise when the remedy prescribed for every business challenge in recent times has been typically one thing: *innovate*. Consider the degree to which 'innovation' has become the buzzword of late:[208]

- In the first three months of 2012, more than 255 books were published with the word 'innovation' in their title;
- According to Cap Gemini Consulting, four in 10 companies now boast a *Chief Innovation Officer*;
- The frequency of the word 'innovation' in company documents filed with the Securities and Exchange Commission increased by 64% between 2006 and 2011.

THE DARK SIDE OF INNOVATION

While innovation is important, HP co-founder David Packard recognized its dark side with the following insight: "A great company is more likely to die of indigestion *from too much opportunity* than starvation from too little."[209]

> A GREAT COMPANY IS MORE LIKELY TO DIE OF INDIGESTION *FROM TOO MUCH OPPORTUNITY* THAN STARVATION FROM TOO LITTLE.

Steve Jobs also knew what it was like to want to do too many new things at once. "People think 'focus' means saying yes to the thing you've got to focus on," he once said. "But that's not what it means at all. It means saying no to the hundred other good ideas that there are. You have to pick carefully. I'm actually as proud of the things we haven't done as the things we have done,' Jobs continued. 'Innovation is saying 'no' to 1,000 things."[210]

In researching business success, author Jim Collins says the downside of innovation took him by surprise. "We anticipated that most companies fall from greatness because they become complacent. It's a plausible theory, with a problem; it doesn't square with the data,' he said. 'Certainly any enterprise that becomes complacent and refuses to change or innovate will eventually fall. But, and this is the surprising point, of the eleven companies we studied that had declined from a place of prominence or success, *only one* showed strong evidence of complacency. In every other case, there was tremendous energy and substantial innovation. Certainly, the evidence does not support the hypothesis that a decline in innovation precedes the fall of a great company. *Over-reaching* much better explains how the once-invincible self-destruct."[211]

What Collins describes as 'over-reaching', I call Progress Addiction: a compulsion to over-innovate driven by the false and dangerous assumption that *everything old is bad and everything new is good.*

In any organization or brand, there are 5 telltale indicators of Progress Addiction that every leader must be wary of:

A. THE UNBRIDLED PURSUIT OF GROWTH

This first symptom of Progress Addiction is characterized by leaders who drive a brand or business to grow too quickly.

An unbridled pursuit of growth was one of the key reasons Kmart in the U.S. went into decline during the 1990s. "It was the effort to expand its market, broaden its product lines and increase its influence that ultimately led to Kmart's loss of focus," notes Al Ries of research firm, Ries & Ries. "For Kmart, growth became its reason for being, rather than a means to an end."[212] The rate of Kmart's expansion was startling to say the least. During the 1960s and 1970s, the company's strategy was to open 100 new stores every year.[213]

It was a similar story for the once-great Ames Department store. Although Ames had pioneered the concept of discount retailing - even growing to the point of becoming the third or fourth largest discount retailer in America - the pursuit of growth and a series of bad acquisitions led them down the path of decline. As Ames heedlessly expanded beyond its stronghold markets in America's northeast, things went downhill quickly with the company entering bankruptcy in 1990 and finally being liquidated in 2002.[214]

Similarly, U.K. supermarket chain Tesco has struggled to maintain service levels at home while expanding into overseas markets over recent years. According to the Wall Street Journal, "the money Tesco spent chasing foreign growth left the domestic operation starved for investment. Stores in Britain weren't properly staffed, the fresh fruit and vegetable aisles started looking picked over, and the chain didn't invest in refreshing their private-label products to entice shoppers."[215]

When in 2002 McDonald's posted its first quarterly loss in almost 50 years,[216] analysts suggested that an unbridled pursuit of growth was, again, partly to blame. Despite opening an average of 2,000 new stores a year in the previous decade, all this expansion had not translated into new income growth. Further still, the pace of expansion had resulted in store cleanliness and customer service, for which the company was renowned, begin to slip across the board.[217]

Many organizations and brands make the mistake of growing too rapidly but not all recover from the consequences as well as McDonald's did in the late 2000s. Consider manufacturing giant Rubbermaid, once described by *Fortune* magazine as more innovative than 3M, Apple or Intel.

Rubbermaid prided itself on its pace of invention and innovation. Introducing new products almost daily and entering a new product category every 12 to 18 months, fatigue started to beset the company in the early 1990s. By late 1995, Rubbermaid posted its first quarterly loss in decades and within three years, the company was sold off.[218]

More recently, industry experts have suggested that one of Sony's biggest mistakes has been to enter too many new markets simply for the sake of being in them. In comparison, Apple has been far more selective in its approach and has only entered markets it had the potential to dominate or define.[219]

A dangerous dynamic develops whenever a leader slips into 'empire building' mode and forces a company, brand or organization to grow in a non-strategic and unsustainable way. While a desire to stay ahead of the curve may motivate leaders to pursue new horizons and expand, the result

THE CHALLENGE FOR LEADERS IS TO RESIST THE TEMPTATION FOR SHORT-TERM GROWTH AT THE EXPENSE OF LONG-TERM SUSTAINABILITY.

can be disastrous. The challenge for leaders is to resist the temptation for short-term growth at the expense of long-term sustainability.[220]

As the great empire-builder Caesar Augustus himself warned, *Hasten Slowly*.

B. CHANGING TOO MUCH, TOO QUICKLY

A dramatic example of this second symptom of Progress Addiction occurred at Hewlett Packard only a few short years ago. After HP CEO, Mark Hurd, resigned in 2010 amid a sex scandal, his replacement, Leo Apotheker, immediately implemented an agenda for widespread change.

Although he was in the role for just 11 months, in that short time Apotheker spun off HP's $64 billion PC business, launched and then abandoned the company's TouchPad product, and controversially acquired software vendor, Autonomy, for $10 billion. The result of such rapid, chaotic and widespread change was that HP's share price lost nearly half its value and the possibility of takeover became a genuine threat. "HP managed to lose its way in just 357 days," was how one analyst described the company's torrid time.[221]

A few years before the unraveling of HP, a similar story had played out within the telecommunication giant, Nortel. Appointed CEO in October 2005, Mike Zafirovski set out to turn around the struggling company by changing it from the inside out. Drawing inspiration from his 25 years at GE, Zafirovski laid off scores of employees, sold off assets and wasted no time in implementing Six Sigma projects designed to increase process efficiency. However, as one former company insider reported to me, Nortel's workforce responded badly to the raft of changes, believing them to be rushed, irrational and counterproductive. With each new initiative, employee morale declined along with the company's efficiency and profitability. In 2008, Nortel shares plummeted to $0.25 a share – down from $15 the previous year!

Although there were fundamental problems at Nortel long before Zafirovski took over as CEO, there is little doubt that the fast-paced sweeping changes he implemented exacerbated the company's problems and sped up its decline. In June 2009, the once $250 billion company filed for bankruptcy protection.[222]

Individual products and brands can also lose relevance when they change too much too quickly. Consider Coca-Cola's infamous decision in 1985 to change its iconic Coke drink formula, or Schlitz Beer, once hugely popular in the U.S., which altered its brewing process and thus the beer's taste causing it to rapidly lose appeal and eventually disappear.

Similarly, when auto manufacturer Datsun repositioned its U.S. operations under the Nissan brand in 1981, consumers and dealers were left confused. Prior to this point, Datsun had been the second-biggest selling foreign car brand in the country, but the re-branding confusion contributed significantly to the company's decline in the years that followed. The *Wall Street Journal* went as far as to describe the Datsun/Nissan rebrand as "one of the worst marketing decisions in automotive history."[223]

C. KNEE-JERK RESPONSES TO COMPETITOR'S MOVES

This third symptom of Progress Addiction tends to be most evident when insecure leaders consistently make decisions in a reactionary rather than a strategic way. Instead of running their own race, these leaders constantly change course in response to what competitors are doing without considering the implications for their own organization.

While imitation does have value, mindlessly copying how competitors do things is a dangerous trap to fall into. Like human beings, no two organizations or brands have the same DNA. Therefore, superficially imitating a competitor's strategies and methods is risky. Implementing

MINDLESSLY COPYING HOW COMPETITORS DO THINGS IS A DANGEROUS TRAP TO FALL INTO.

practices that don't fit your DNA will likely steer an organization off-course. This is something we will explore further in chapter 10.

D. MOVING AWAY FROM CORE STRENGTHS

In his book, *Humilitas,* John Dickson describes a tendency in leaders and organizations he calls 'competency extrapolation'. This is when individuals or entities conclude that because they do one thing well, they will be able to do other non-related things equally well. Such an assumption is often driven by a sense of invincibility that comes from success as described in chapter 6.

In a commercial context, research indicates that competency extrapolation in the form of entering adjacent markets where a company lacks skill or expertise is a key factor in as many as 75% of business failures.[224]

Consider, for instance, how moving away from core strengths played a role in the fall of Kodak. In January 1988, Kodak took the disastrous step of acquiring Sterling Drugs for $5.1 billion. Failing to recognize that producing chemically treated photo paper is vastly different from the manufacture of hormonal agents or cardiovascular drugs, Kodak took six years to acknowledge that the venture was not a good fit - a mistake which cost them handsomely.[225]

One of the world's largest cement makers, Blue Circle, also strayed beyond its capabilities and paid a heavy price. In the late 1980s, Blue Circle made a series of failed attempts to enter new markets ranging from property management and brick production to industrial minerals, gas cookers, bathroom furnishings and even lawn mowers. During its diversification push, Blue Circle lost significant ground against competitors in its core business and Lafarge SA bought it in 2001.[226]

Of all the examples we could point to, Colgate's dabbling in the microwave meal market is by far one of the strangest and most ill-conceived. In 1982, the toothpaste manufacturer embarked on what author Matt Haig called "one of the most bizarre brand extensions ever." With packets featuring colourful images of vegetable-laden stir-fries, Colgate's microwave meal range was designed to compete with established brands such as Healthy Choice and Lean Cuisine. As you could imagine, the new range didn't fly off the shelves. "For most people the name Colgate does not exactly get their tastebuds tingling," Haig wrote. [227]

In *How the Mighty Fall,* author Jim Collins suggests that moving away from core strengths is nothing short of a recipe for disaster in organizations and brands.

"Launching headlong into activities that do not fit with your economic or resource engine is undisciplined," he notes. "To neglect your core business while you leap after exciting new adventures" is equally foolish.[228]

E. BLATANTLY DISREGARDING THE PAST

This fifth and final telltale sign of Progress Addiction is one that younger managers and leaders must be particularly careful of. In an effort to modernize an organization or brand and define it as distinct from

DOING SOMETHING A DIFFERENT WAY FOR THE SAKE OF DOING SO IS SHORTSIGHTED, PRESUMPTUOUS AND EVEN ARROGANT.

its past, many leaders dispense with traditions and rituals and in doing so throw out the baby with the bathwater.

While it is necessary to confront unhealthy traditions and sacred cows in an organization, simply doing something a different way to how it has been done in the past for the sake of doing so is shortsighted, presumptuous and even arrogant.

As discussed in the previous chapter, traditions and rituals do have a place and often serve an important purpose. In the same way that a smart tradesman always checks to see if a wall is load-bearing before removing it, gung-ho leaders would do well to ensure that a tradition is not central to the culture and DNA of an organization or brand before simply removing it in the name of "progress".

The natural tension between Preservation Obsession and Progress Addiction is one that can be difficult to get right in an organization. One tends to counter the other and each keeps the other in check. To strike a balance between preserving the past and embracing the future my suggestion is that leaders 'value what is timeless, and time what is valueless'.

To put this more simply, leaders and organizations that are committed to remaining relevant must place great value on timeless principles - while simultaneously putting an expiry date on the traditions, habits and processes that have little value in and of themselves.

This distinction may at times be difficult to make but it is critical for long-term success and relevance.

FOR REFLECTION

Innovation does have a dark side. Looking at the 5 telltale signs of an addiction to progress, are there any that stand out as applicable for you or your organization? If so, in what ways?

    a. The Unbridled Pursuit of Growth

    b. Changing too Much, too Quickly

    c. Knee-jerk Responses to Competitor's Moves

    d. Moving Away from Core Strengths

    e. Blatantly Disregarding the Past

CHAPTER 9:

ROAD 5 — THE HUMAN FACTOR

Although we have spent the last four chapters examining a number of the most common roads to irrelevance, there is no escaping the fact that *human nature* has a key role to play in causing organizations and brands to fall from greatness.

For all our virtues and capabilities, there are also three universal human traits that spark decline and obsolescence with remarkable consistency:

1. POOR JUDGMENT

We all like to imagine ourselves to be rational beings and yet the empirical evidence suggests otherwise. Far from logical, we as humans have a unique capacity to make illogical, biased and emotionally driven decisions

> WE ALL LIKE TO IMAGINE OURSELVES TO BE RATIONAL BEINGS AND YET THE EMPIRICAL EVIDENCE SUGGESTS OTHERWISE.

based on selective information – all the while justifying them as "rational". If in doubt, look at the annual Darwin Awards that recognize individuals who have contributed to human evolution by self-selecting out of the gene pool through their own stupidity.

Perhaps if there were a business equivalent to the Darwin Awards, first prize would go to now defunct book retailing giant, Borders. Back in 2001, Borders' leadership took the ill-fated step of handing over the company's online business to a fledgling electronic retailer named Amazon. Believing that online book sales were unlikely to take off, Borders made a decision described by some as tantamount to "corporate suicide".[229]

Mobile phone giant Motorola made an equally flawed error of judgment with the failed development of its Iridium Satellite Phone system. Although reliable data early on had questioned the new technology's viability, key members of Motorola's leadership ignored this advice and pressed on with a project that never had any hope of working. The results spoke for themselves – eventually Motorola ended up writing off $2.5 billion due to the failed technology.[230]

Motorola rival Blackberry also fell into the trap of making ill-fated decisions when it came to company strategy. While Blackberries were once the company-issue handset of choice,[231] as white-collar employees began bringing their own devices to work en masse, Blackberry executives raised the alarm. Despite this, company CEO Jim Balsillie dismissed their concerns as not worth worrying about - an error in judgment that has cost the company very dearly.[232]

Of course it is always easy to judge decisions as good or bad with the benefit of hindsight. But the point still stands; human error and bad decisions are a key cause of decline.

2. DENIAL

A group of neuroscientists have recently discovered that denial is more than a propensity toward naivety and foolishness – it is actually the result of a physiological phenomenon unique to humans. According to research, a section of the brain's frontal cortex causes an 'optimism bias' that prevents us from believing that even the most likely and reasonable negative things could happen in the future.[233]

Long before this discovery, psychologists recognized the capacity humans have for denial - otherwise known as cognitive dissonance.[234] This term describes the human ability to hold two apparently contradictory thoughts at the same time – to understand the scope and nature of a threat and then choose to ignore the facts, and "look the other way".

A fascinating study published in 2004 that looked at how denial manifested within organizations, found that in the face of a competitive threat, roughly one in six respondents reported that they would *deliberately* ignore a genuine threat assuming it would disappear.[235]

In the 1980s, denial had become endemic in the once-great corporate icon IBM. When things were at their most dire, the company surveyed 1200 of its top managers and found that four in 10 did not accept the need for change – despite the fact that the company was sliding perilously close to the Tanking Point.[236] It would appear that this culture of denial within IBM went right to the top. At one point in the late 1980s, a young analyst submitted a report to senior management highlighting the new technologies eroding IBM's traditional mainframe business. Rather than heeding the report's warning, one senior executive member famously dismissed the analyst with the words: "There must be something wrong with your data."[237]

Denial was also running rampant at Sony in the mid-2000s. Although it was plainly obvious that the Japanese electronics giant was losing its competitive edge, Sony's leadership chose to live in the past repeatedly pointing to old sales figures and presuming that its current products would automatically reach the same levels its previous successful lines had.[238]

Denial not only pervades an organization's broader culture, it plays out at an interpersonal level too. Take the case of the former CEO of U.K. banking giant HBOS, Sir James Crosby, who sacked whistle-blower Paul Moore in 2004 rather than

LIKE IGNORANCE, DENIAL MAY BE BLISS — BUT CAN ALSO PROVE DEADLY.

accept Moore's valid critique of the bank and its practices. Joseph Stalin did much the same thing, famously ordering Peter Pachinsky's execution as punishment for daring to criticize Soviet engineering projects. [239]

Like ignorance, denial may be bliss – but can also prove deadly.

3. SHORT-SIGHTEDNESS

I was recently reading about a humanitarian organization called Outreach to Africa that works with impoverished people in the developing world by helping them plant gardens to improve nutrition and self-sufficiency. The programs founder, Evelyn Komuntale, described how she and her team recognized early on that they could not simply give seeds to the people they were working with, as the recipients' natural instinct was to eat them. Instead, Komuntale's team had to explain the value of sowing the seeds so that more food could be reaped in the future.[240]

Although a modern business context may be vastly different from the one Evelyn Komuntale describes, the principles are remarkably similar. In our modern 'seize the day' age where the

> **WE MUST BE WARY OF BECOMING "HOSTAGES TO THE PRESENT.**

pressing concerns of the current quarter, financial year or funding cycle can dominate our thoughts, it is critically important that leaders avoid short-term thinking. As James Kouzes and Barry Posner argue in their book *A Leader's Legacy*, we must be wary of becoming "hostages to the present."[241]

While self-interest and short-term thinking come naturally to human beings, such qualities impact the long-term sustainability and relevance of a brand, business or organization.

Reflecting on the challenges facing the Benrus Watch company when he took on the role of president and chairman in 1967, Victor Kiam noticed an ingrained culture of short-term reactionary thinking rather a long-term strategic approach. "We were constantly saying 'If we do this now, what's it going to do to our earnings in this quarter?'"[242] Unsurprisingly, the company went bankrupt a few short years later.

Microsoft also experienced the repercussions of a culture of short-term thinking when they began conducting six-monthly performance reviews in the early 2000s. Understandably, these reviews focused staff on short-term performance rather than longer-term efforts to build and grow steadily. "They forced a lot of bad decision making," said one Microsoft software designer. "People planned their days and years around the review rather than on doing what was right for the company."[243] The result of this short-term focus was, as one analyst described it, a lost decade of opportunity for Microsoft.[244]

FOR REFLECTION

Of the three human-nature traits described in this chapter, which have contributed to decline and irrelevance most clearly in your own experience?

1. **Poor Judgment**
2. **Denial**
3. **Short-sightedness**

CORRELATION VS CAUSALITY

Before we end Section 2, it is important to acknowledge the inherent dangers in drawing fixed conclusions about the causes of decline and obsolescence.

Firstly, we must resist the temptation to reach for overly simplistic explanations for what we see in the world around us, or to look for evidence that merely supports what we already believe **THE SIMPLE REALITY IS THAT REALITY IS RARELY SIMPLE.** to be true. The simple reality is that reality is rarely simple. In studying the demise of iconic institutions and movements, there are always a multitude of complex and interdependent factors at play. The study of decline is far from an exact science.

A second danger in studying decline and obsolescence is to confuse correlation with causality. To conclude that because two things occurred *at the same time* or in a sequential order that one therefore led to the other.

A few years ago, I was at a Colorado radio station for a live interview. Following the broadcast, I came across a printed notice on one of the station's staff bulletin boards that listed 10 things people could do in order to live longer. The list included a number of the usual suspects – exercise for 20-30 minutes 3 times per week, eat five serves of vegetables each day, and so on. Point number 8 however intrigued me. *'Floss daily,'* it exhorted. *'Flossing will add 10 years to your life'.* As someone who flosses only on the morning of my annual visit to the dentist so I can say with integrity that I have indeed flossed since my last visit, this claim stopped me in my tracks.

Having tried unsuccessfully to verify the fact that flossing adds years to life, it appears that this is a good example of when correlation and causality get confused. While I doubt that the act of flossing extends a person's life expectancy, it does make sense that people who floss each day are probably more *likely* to also eat well, exercise and generally take good care of themselves. So while flossing is *correlated* with longer life expectancy, the relationship is not *causal*.

Look around and you see the confusion of correlation and causality everywhere:

- A few years ago, a major national insurer ran an advertising campaign stating that 90% of car accidents happen within a three-mile radius of a driver's home. The erroneous conclusion one could draw is that driving in your local neighborhood is inherently dangerous. On the contrary, it is simply indicative of the fact that people do the majority of their driving within a few miles of their house. Hence, it is more likely that accidents will happen closer to home.
- In early 2012, Barclays Capital released a study that showed that there is a link between the construction of skyscrapers and financial crashes. The report suggested China was economically vulnerable because it was building roughly 54% of all skyscrapers in the

world at the time.[245] However, tall buildings in and of themselves, do not lead to stock market crashes. Rather it is that countries that build skyscrapers on a grand scale are more vulnerable to economic risks due to their rapid growth. Thus, the relationship between skyscrapers and economic crashes is correlated, but not necessarily causal.

- In the Middle Ages, doctors and medical experts believed that polluted or foul-smelling air – otherwise known as miasma – caused and spread the bubonic plague. In an effort to stem the disease's spread, doctors advised people to relocate to areas of fresh air. Such relocations did in fact help, but not for the reasons thought. By relocating people away from poor sanitation and pollution, the populace was escaping the rats that harbored the fleas that carried the infection.[246] It was not until years later that scientists discovered that pollution correlated with plague, but was not the cause of it.

Looking at some even more humourous and bizarre examples of the correlation/causality mismatch, consider the fact that statisticians have established a direct correlation between:

- The per capita consumption of cheese and the number people who die each year by becoming tangled in their bedsheets,
- The age of Miss America and murders by steam, hot vapors or hot objects
- Marriage rate in Kentucky and people who drowned after falling out of fishing boats!

Bringing all this back to the purposes of our discussion, while it is difficult to make definitive judgments about the causes of decline and obsolescence, there are certainly signs and symptoms which emerge time after time. My goal in the last 5 chapters has been to draw these threads and patterns together in order to provide something of a map through the minefield of irrelevance.

In the coming pages, we will turn our attention from understanding and identifying threats to learning from those who have managed to win the battle for relevance – even when the odds were against them.

FOR REFLECTION:

Considering each of the 5 roads to irrelevance we have discussed, rate from one to five the degree to which each is a threat to you and your organization in the years ahead (1 = low threat, 5 = high threat):

    1. Shift Happens   **1 – 2 – 3 – 4 – 5**

    2. The Intoxication of Success   **1 – 2 – 3 – 4 – 5**

    3. Preservation Obsession   **1 – 2 – 3 – 4 – 5**

    4. Progress Addiction   **1 – 2 – 3 – 4 – 5**

    5. The Human Factor   **1 – 2 – 3 – 4 – 5**

SECTION 3:
Winning the Battle
for Relevance

In the previous section, we looked at the key factors that have caused even the greatest to become obsolete in an effort to answer the question *why do the mighty fall?* However, while this question is an important one, I believe a far better question we need to explore is *why do the enduring prevail?* Why do some brands and organizations emerge from change and upheaval stronger than ever, while their counterparts get knocked out of the game?

Compare, for example, the fortunes of Kodak with Fuji, Meccano with Lego, SAAB with Volvo, Pan Am with Delta Airlines and Atari with Nintendo.

The evidence is clear - decline need not be inevitable. For every organization or brand that has fallen by the wayside, you will find another offering similar products or services to similar markets, which is flourishing.

WHAT SEPARATES THE ENDURING FROM THE ENDANGERED?

There are numerous brands and businesses that have successfully remained relevant year after year, decade after decade. What can we learn from these success stories? What insights can we extract from their experiences? What separates the enduring from the endangered? These questions will be the focus of section 3.

We are going to explore six strategies for achieving enduring viability and vitality. By the end of this section, my hope is that you will have a clear game plan for winning the battle for relevance in the years ahead.

As we launch into this section however, I am aware that readers will typically fit into one of two groups or categories.

GROUP #1

The first group are those whose brand, business or organization is still in the first or second phase of the Relevance Curve we discussed in chapter 1. Your entity is still on an upward trajectory or could quite possibly already be in a position of market dominance or social prominence.

For this first group, the challenge ahead is to *retain* relevance – to harness momentum, stay on message, stick to what you do best, and stay one step ahead of marketplace shifts. The steps you will need to take in order to retain relevance may require humility, courage and foresight.

Only a visionary leader will take the steps necessary to win the battle for relevance long before it is clear that you are even engaged in a battle at all. The temptations of success intoxication, inertia and complacency are likely significant but resist them you must.

After all, while smart leaders re-invent themselves when the going gets tough, but much smarter leaders re-invent themselves BEFORE they are forced to.

GROUP # 2

The second group is in a different position. By now you are probably aware of the fact that you have passed the Turning Point and you are not as hot as you once were. You may be in the early stages of phase three of the Relevance Curve or even be past the Tanking Point and well into the final relevance phase. Either way, the possibility of obsolescence is a looming reality.

The challenge for you is to *regain* relevance and get back ahead of the curve. As we discussed in chapter 4, the good news is that it is not too late to turn things around. Data shows that companies that come back from the brink of downfall end up being stronger as a result of the experience.[247]

> **COMPANIES THAT COME BACK FROM THE BRINK OF DOWNFALL END UP BEING STRONGER AS A RESULT OF THE EXPERIENCE.**

Perhaps your current predicament is in fact a blessing in disguise.

In the chapters ahead, we will explore story after story of companies and institutions of every kind who have successfully turned around what seemed like irreversible decline. This is, in fact, one of the core premises of this book: that any brand or organization can regain relevance regardless of how weak their silent pulse is or how far behind the curve they have fallen. However, simply because something can be done doesn't mean it *should* or *must* be.

The choice that every reader in this second group must face is whether or not to throw in the towel. You have to honestly assess whether your brand, business or organization is worth salvaging. This may seem harsh, but it is a question that must be confronted. As singer Kenny Rogers put it: *You got to know when to hold 'em, and when to fold 'em/Know when to walk away and when to run.*

The reality is that some things become obsolete for a good reason. If an idea or enterprise has had its day, reviving it at any cost is likely to be frustrating and fruitless. It may also be inappropriate. Some commentators have suggested that charities and social cause organizations, for instance, *should* have an in-built expiration date. "Charities exist to cure something, address an issue, or elevate the status of a group of people. Once that purpose is achieved, the charity should close up shop," an editorial in *Fast Company* noted. "Organizations shouldn't exist to exist. Once a charity has achieved what it set out to do, it should wear termination as a badge of honor."[248]

This argument has the ring of common sense. Was it not natural that various women's suffrage associations faded from prominence once women achieved the right to vote? In the same way, it should have been no surprise when The Pearl Harbor Survivors Association announced its December 2011 meeting would mark the association's end. As one association leader described it, "You can't have an organization that by its very nature cannot replenish itself with new members."[249] Likewise, is it possible that your brand or organization has reached its use-by date and that it would be smarter to relinquish rather than rescue it? As confronting as this question may be, it is a prospect that must be considered.

Bearing all this in mind, if you can state with conviction that your company, movement, idea or product is worth fighting for, in the coming chapters you will learn how to take the steps necessary to regain your former glory. The path ahead will not always be convenient, easy or popular, but it is a path that arrives at a worthwhile destination, with a spectacular view. Many before you have gone down this road, and so can you.

CHAPTER 10:
RELEVANCE STRATEGY 1 — RE-CALIBRATE

Back when I was in Scouts as a teen, I vividly remember weekends away in the bush where my buddies and I would be dropped off at some isolated location in the middle of nowhere. The scout master would specify the co-ordinates of a destination point and give us three days to get there. Long before Google Maps or GPS, we had to engage in old-fashioned 'orienteering' and find our way through the wilderness guided by nothing more than a compass and the contours of our map.

One of orienteering's most important lessons was drummed into us on day one. In order to counteract the variation between magnetic and true north, we learned to place our compass on the map with its heading arrow aligned with true north and rotate the compass housing until it lined up with the magnetic north line. Once our map and compass were calibrated, we were ready to embark on our journey. In training we had heard stories of groups who got hopelessly lost because they failed to do this. Presuming the difference between the two norths was insignificantly small, some Scouts figured they could just work it out as they went along. However, the diversion of a few degrees, compounded over many hours or days of walking, typically led them many miles off-course.

The notion of calibration is common in many arenas: pianists, IT technicians and car mechanics each calibrate their respective apparatus to enable optimum performance. In the commercial arena too,

RE-CALIBRATION IS CRITICAL IF A BUSINESS, BRAND OR ORGANIZATION IS TO STAY RELEVANT AND ON TRACK.

continual calibration or re-calibration is critical if a business, brand or organization is to stay relevant and on track.

FORD AND THE 3 PS

One of the most enduringly successful brands in the world would have to be Ford. However, in the early 1980s, the great automaker was in serious trouble. In the space of just three years, Ford had lost over $3.3 billion, or almost half of the company's net worth.[250] In the face of crisis, Ford's executive leadership team was courageous. Instead of knee-jerk responses, the executive team chose to ask some fundamental questions: *Who are we as a company? What do we stand for? What made us great in the first place? Is it possible we have lost sight of these things along the way?*

After a period of reflection, Ford's leadership identified what became known as the company's 3 Ps – *people*, *products* and *profits* – in that order. More than some formulaic mission statement or an exercise in navel gazing, this process of reflection Re-Calibrated Ford with the very ideology the company's founder had championed in the business's early days. Furthermore, it gave Ford's leadership a simple blueprint for future decision-making which contributed to the company's sustained turnaround in the years that followed.

Put simply, Re-Calibration is about ensuring there is alignment between a brand or organization and its key values. It

RE-CALIBRATION IS ABOUT ENSURING THERE IS ALIGNMENT BETWEEN A BRAND OR ORGANIZATION AND ITS KEY VALUES.

is about making sure that *what* you are doing and *how* you are doing it lines up with *who* you are and *why* you exist in the first place. It may not be sexy or spectacular, but it is critically important and being 'off' even by a few degrees can make all the difference when compounded over time.

KODAK'S WALK INTO THE WILDERNESS

It was Kodak's very failure to Re-Calibrate when the digital age hit that led to its demise. Quite simply, Kodak fell into the common trap of getting *who it was* confused with *what it did*. The company began to define itself by the products it sold and the markets in which it competed, losing sight along the way of why it was in business in the first place.

In the early days, Kodak had been in the business of helping people *preserve memories*. However, owing to the generous profit margins and lucrative residual income that resulted from selling film, Kodak began to see itself primarily as a company that sold film. In a sense, the company became a hostage to its own success. While a film-focused paradigm served Kodak well as long as everyone bought film and depended on it to take photos, the onset of the digital age posed a challenge. When the digital threat became clear, Kodak made the mistake of asking the question 'how can we ensure people keep buying film?' Instead, they should have asked, 'how can we help our customers *preserve their memories* in a digital era?'

Kodak could have dominated the digital camera industry. After all, they had invented the worlds first digital camera as far back as the mid-1970s. Kodak could have been the first company to introduce online photo sharing, and it could have pioneered cloud-based file backup systems. But instead they remained focused on film, and by the time Kodak realized just how far off track they were, it was too late.

Of course Kodak aren't the first to have made this mistake. Theodore Levitt observed the very same pattern of getting confused between what a company does and why it exists in his seminal 1960 piece for the *Harvard Business Review* titled *Marketing Myopia*. Levitt observed how railroad owners in the early 1900s mistakenly assumed that they were in the railroad business rather than the transportation business. As a result, when technology and customer needs evolved, these railroad companies missed the chance to embrace the opportunities these changes represented. Rather than providing new types of transportation solutions, they instead got stuck in the rail-oriented business model they knew best – a decision that saw them slowly but surely lose relevance.[251] Similarly, Greyhound Bus Company made the mistake of confusing what it did with why it existed.

"(Greyhound's) single biggest mistake was in thinking that it was in the bus business. So narrow was its vision that the company could not respond quickly to the trend away from bus travel to cars, planes, and light rail," Robert Kriegel notes in his book *Sacred Cows Make the Best Hamburgers.* "If Greyhound had realized they were really in the transportation or people-moving business, they could have jumped into other vehicles."[252]

WHAT BUSINESS ARE YOU REALLY IN?

Speaking at a bar licensee's conference recently, I asked attendees the question, "What business are you really in?" Unsurprisingly, the majority of responses centered on products and services – "We are in the food and beverage business". Although I understood why audience members responded the way they did, I challenged their assumptions and suggested that they were, rather, in the 'atmosphere and experience' business.

Seeing the puzzled expressions, I explained that when a customer enters a bar or restaurant and orders a glass of wine, they are aware that they are paying for one glass what they would otherwise pay for an entire bottle of the same wine at the liquor store down the road. "So why are they paying more?" I asked. "Why not just buy the bottle and drink it at home?" Answering my own question, I explained that it was the atmosphere and experience that enticed customers to pay up, and return again and again.

"See, you are in the experience and the atmosphere business – that's who you are and why you exist. Food and beverages are just one way that you create the experience and atmosphere your customers are looking for."

Most businesses and organizations set out with a clear idea of who they are and why they exist. However, as the 'what' and 'how' get

THE LONGER WE DO SOMETHING A CERTAIN WAY WITHOUT THINKING, THE HARDER IT BECOMES TO STAND BACK, AND MAKE SURE WE ARE STILL GOING IN THE RIGHT DIRECTION.

repeated, entities begin to focus on processes and lose sight of their purpose or outcome. Naturally, the longer we do something a certain way without thinking, the harder it becomes to stand back, get our bearings and make sure we are still going in the right direction.[253] When this happens, a groove becomes a rut and the harder we work, the further off track we go.

In order to win the battle for relevance, the first key for an organization is to Re-Calibrate itself with what the French call a *raison d'etre* - or the fundamental reason or purpose for existence. In corporate speak, this is often referred to as an organization's DNA.

In the pages ahead, I want to go well beyond business rhetoric, clichés and hyperbole. We are going to run through a practical process to help you identify your entity's DNA, and highlight strategies for Re-Calibrating with it in order to stay on track. Those of you familiar with the book *Built to Last* by Jim Collins and Jerry Porras will notice consistent messages in the pages ahead. Both Collins and Porras have had a significant influence on me over the years and their research in the field of helping organizations distill their DNA is unparalleled.

For the purposes of our discussion, I am going to define organizational DNA as being made up of two things that we will explore separately:

1. Defining Values
2. Driving Purpose

DNA = Defining Values + Driving Purpose

DEFINING VALUES

For decades, business leaders have had the 'corporate values' message drummed into them. Consultants have grown wealthy as boardrooms filled with well-meaning executives have spent countless hours hammering out and wordsmithing all that an organization holds near and dear.

Sadly, these exercises are often, at best, tokenistic and, at worst, a costly waste of time. They look good in the annual report, and sound impressive when espoused at the annual national conference, but more is required than a list of impressive sounding virtues. Values should be a guidepost for strategy and a touchstone for decision-making. They are

VALUES SHOULD BE A GUIDEPOST FOR STRATEGY AND A TOUCHSTONE FOR DECISION-MAKING.

a living thing – something central to the daily life of an organization or brand.

In the interests of clarification, below is a list of four things that organizational values are *not*:

1. AN ORGANIZATION'S VALUES ARE NOT *FORMULAIC*

Many organizations get wrapped up in the *form* by which their values are communicated. However, it is the function or impact of having clearly articulated defining values that matters most.

Consider the various forms that an organization's values messaging can take:

- Google's values are codified in a list of 10 guiding principles which include precepts such as: *You can make money without doing evil; You can be serious without a suit; Focus on the user and everything else will follow.* [254]
- Sony has been guided by a statement of ideology that has changed little since the company's founder, Masaru Ibuka, penned it in 1936.[255]
- The values of many other large corporations like 3M, American Express and Marriott take the form of a series of key words.[256]

The most powerful statements of values are not those with the greatest poetic symmetry, but rather those with piercing simplicity and clarity. It matters little what *form* the articulation of an organization's values take – there is no one right formula or best-practice approach. Further still, it is not the *content* of a values statement that counts, but how effectively the content captures the core essence of an organization's personality.[257]

2. VALUES ARE NOT *IMPOSED*

There is a common myth that the people who are best placed to describe and distill an organization's values are those at the top. As a result, values conversations are often restricted to those in senior management. Only once 'those who know best' have determined the values are they then passed down through the organization in the form of well-polished statements and platitudes. These imposed values tend to be announced and then quickly forgotten.

If the actions and decisions of individuals within an organization are to be truly values-driven, those individuals must have some input and involvement in the articulation of values in the first place.

3. VALUES ARE NOT *INTENTIONAL*

One of the common mistakes I see many of my clients make when attempting to identify their values is that they start by asking the wrong question. Rather than asking "What *are* our values?" they ask the question, "What *should* our values be?"

The values of an organization are not something that you have to work out – they are already being outworked every day. Rather than being intentional, an organization's values are implicit. The task then is not to ask what your values *should* be, but to discover what they already *are*.[258] To espouse core values that are not authentic will lead to cynicism in an organization – it's like hearing a morbidly obese person who takes no steps to get into shape say he or she values health and wellbeing. Actions do indeed speak louder than words!

Naturally, if it emerges that the core values of an organization or brand are destructive, restrictive or unsustainable, it is important to address this and take steps to change the organization's DNA over time. However, it is vital in the first instance to be upfront about what an organization's values are currently, even if they are not what you want them to be in the long-term.

4. VALUES ARE NEITHER *INNATELY RIGHT NOR WRONG*

While there are many words and themes that crop up repeatedly in values statements, there are no automatically right and wrong values for an organization or brand to have. Across the entire spectrum of

> **THERE ARE NO AUTOMATICALLY RIGHT AND WRONG VALUES FOR AN ORGANIZATION OR BRAND TO HAVE.**

enduringly successful companies and brands, there is not one single value that is common to all.[259]

It is not what an organization's core values are that determines their enduring success – but rather the fact that the organization *has* core values, *knows* what those values are and *allows* their decisions and strategy to be guided by them.[260]

EXERCISE: DISCOVER YOUR CORE VALUES

When working with clients, I use the following 3-question exercise to help them distill their core values. I would strongly encourage you to take the opportunity to do the same.

1. For what are you currently known? If you stopped a person in the street and asked them which four words come to mind when they hear your organization or brand's name, what words would they say?

-
-
-
-

2. What are the non-negotiables in your organization? In other words, what values would you stick to even if they became unpopular and unprofitable in the future?

In their book *Built to Last,* Jim Collins and Jerry Porras shared the story of a multi-billion dollar corporation who attributed their sustained growth to not compromising on their values: "We're willing to forego business opportunities that would force us to abandon our principles. We're still here after 100 years, doubling in size every six or seven years, when most of our competitors from 50 years ago don't even exist anymore. Why? Because of the discipline to not compromise our standards for the sake of expediency. In everything we do, we take the long-term view. *Always.*" [261]

_____

_____

_____

_____

_____

3. What basic philosophies and principles will stand the test of time? Which values will still be important in a hundred years' time and are more than simply the latest management or leadership fad?

_____

_____

_____

_____

_____

As you reflect on the questions above, I would encourage you to make a list of the words which encapsulate your entity's fundamental values. The aim is not to have an exhaustive list of everything that is important to your organization or brand, but to make a list no longer than six words. Research indicates that the more successful and enduring an entity is, the shorter the list of values it describes as 'core.'[262]

To help you compile a strong short-list, you may want to draw inspiration from the words below which list the values often suggested by my clients doing this exercise:

Common core values

Unity	Fairness
Quality	Generosity
Fun/Enjoyment	Balance
Teamwork	Passion
Empowerment	Innovation
Integrity	Authenticity
Compassion	Inclusiveness
Family	Creativity
Persistence	Work ethic
Originality	Equality
Education	Humility
Customer service	Patience/delayed gratification
Flexibility	Respect
Honesty	Courage
Ownership	Profitability
Accountability	Social responsibility

Our defining values are:

1. _____

2. _____

3. _____

4. _____

5. _____

6. _____

DRIVING PURPOSE

This second component of an organization's DNA is equally important. While defining values requires you to answer the question of *why do we do things* **the way** *we do*, the question of driving purpose is one that goes to the very heart of relevance: *why do we do what we do* **at all**?

Although many organizations have attempted to answer this question by crafting vision statements or mission statements, these are all-too-often a concoction of policies, practices, strategic aims and goals. True driving purpose, however, is more fundamental long-term and even philosophical than these things.[263]

Consider the purpose statements below which drive some of the world's most enduringly successful and relevant brands:[264]

1. **3M:** To solve unsolved problems innovatively
2. **Nike:** To experience the emotion of competition, winning, and crushing competitors
3. **Dyson:** To solve problems other seem to ignore
4. **Wal-Mart:** To give ordinary folk the chance to buy the same things as rich people
5. **Disney:** To make people happy
6. In reflecting on the driving purpose of your own brand or organization, there are several key issues to consider, including:

1. PURPOSE IS ABOUT *WHO* YOU ARE AND NOT *WHAT* YOU DO

As we saw in the case of Kodak, it is very dangerous for a business or organization to lose sight of why it exists and to start defining itself by what it does or the products it sells.

| **PURPOSE IS ABOUT WHO YOU ARE AND NOT WHAT YOU DO**

Consider the fact that 3M does not define itself in terms of its popular and iconic product lines.[265] Right from its inception in 1902 as the Minnesota Mining and Manufacturing Company, 3M would never have branched out from mining into sandpaper, Scotch Tape or Post-It Notes if it hadn't been for their driving purpose.

Confusing the 'who' with the 'what' was one reason IBM lost its way in the late 1980s. Although the company had clearly articulated its DNA in the form of three core values (respect for the individual; customer service; and excellence), somewhere along the way it started to define itself by specific corporate policies (such as dress codes for staff) and product lines (such as mainframe computers).[266] It wasn't until IBM Re-Calibrated in the mid-1990s under new CEO Lou Gerstner that things started to turn around.[267]

2. PURPOSE IS ABOUT *WHY* YOU DO THINGS, NOT *HOW* YOU DO THEM

One of the keys to enduring success in corporations is the ability for leaders to distinguish between purpose and practices. As we saw in chapter 7, one of the single biggest mistakes a brand or organization can make is to link its identity to its processes and traditions.

As such, a key element of Re-Calibrating is questioning the sacred cows in an organization by asking if these are connected to the entity's guiding purpose or whether they are simply entrenched practices. To clarify the distinction between guiding purpose and guarded practice, Collins and Porras point to the examples below:[268]

- Wal-Mart's commitment to *exceeding customer expectations* is its guiding purpose; stationing customer greeters at the front door is simply one way this is achieved;
- Nordstrom's desire to *serve the customer above all else* is its guiding purpose; hiring piano players for its store lobbies is just a means to this end.

Naturally, as times change, specific practices must change too. Guiding purposes are enduring, practices rarely are.

3. PURPOSE MUST BE *COMPELLING* BUT NOT *CONSTRICTIVE*

The most effective purpose statements inspire and guide an organization for years and even decades. To do so, they must be flexible, allowing for and even anticipating changes in the competitive environment.

THE MOST EFFECTIVE PURPOSE STATEMENTS INSPIRE AND GUIDE AN ORGANIZATION FOR YEARS AND EVEN DECADES.

For instance, Boeing's purpose of 'Being on the leading edge of aviation' allowed for and even prompted the company's daring shift in the 1950s from military bombers to the commercial passenger jet business. Had Boeing's purpose centered on being the 'leading manufacturer of military aircraft', this more narrow definition of purpose would have prevented the company from making the changes necessary to stay relevant as times evolved. Looking to the future, there may well come a day when Boeing exits the commercial jet liner business too. Regardless, its articulation of core purpose allows for the evolution and transformation of its business as necessary.[269]

Consider too that if the Disney Corporation's purpose statement had been to entertain kids by producing cartoons, the company would have stopped growing decades ago. However, Walt Disney's purpose to 'make people happy' allowed for and inspired the company to create feature-length hit movies, the Mickey Mouse Club, Euro Disney, and even online virtual world for kids called *Club Penguin*.[270]

We talked in chapter 5 about women's refuges that closed as social attitudes changed in the 1970s. If you remember, we discussed how up until the end of the 60s, the unstated purpose of these facilities was to provide a convenient solution for families shamed by a pregnancy out of wedlock. When this social stigma disappeared, so did the refuges' reason for its existence. Had the purpose of these refuges been to provide support for pregnant women regardless of marital status or age, the centers could have adapted the services they provided and stayed relevant to this day.

4. PURPOSE IS ABOUT MORE THAN PROFIT

In looking at what distinguishes enduringly successful companies from those that don't last the distance, the priority placed on profitability plays

THE KEY TO LONGEVITY AND RELEVANCE IS A COMMITMENT TO BE IN IT FOR MORE THAN SIMPLY THE MONEY.

a key role. Research shows that profit maximization is rarely, if ever, a driving purpose for enduring companies and organizations.[271]

Naturally profitability is necessary to the survival of any going concern, but the key to longevity and relevance is a commitment to more meaningful ideals, to be in it for more than simply the money. Paradoxically, companies and organizations with a non-monetary focus actually earn more than their profit-driven counterparts over time.[272]

As a case in point, consider pharmaceutical giant, Merck. In 1935, the company's founder George Merck II articulated a purpose that has guided the company ever since: "We are workers in industry who are genuinely inspired by the ideals of advancement of medical science and of service to humanity."[273] What is interesting is this purpose statement makes no mention of profitability or even pharmaceuticals. Exemplifying what we have discussed in previous pages, Merck's purpose statement is compelling without being constrictive and focuses on the 'why' rather than the 'how', and 'who' instead of 'what'. It should come as no surprise that many decades after this purpose statement was first articulated, Merck continues to flourish.

In contrast, consider American hotel and restaurant chain, Howard Johnsons. Throughout the 1960s and 70s, Howard Johnsons was the largest restaurant chain in the US with more than 1,000 outlets nationwide. When the company's founder passed away in 1972 however, his son took the reins and prioritized sales growth and return on investment over the company's former twin values of customer service and employee morale. Within a few short years the new CEO had all but destroyed the company and ended up selling the chain in 1979.[274]

Speaking in August 2012 at the Edinburgh International Television Festival, Rupert Murdoch's daughter, Elizabeth, openly criticized her father's company News Corporation for operating with an absence of values. Elizabeth Murdoch observed that "profit without purpose is a recipe for disaster" and that companies and their leaders need to "reject the idea that money is the

COMPANIES AND THEIR LEADERS NEED TO "REJECT THE IDEA THAT MONEY IS THE ONLY EFFECTIVE MEASURE OF ALL THINGS

only effective measure of all things". To this, she added that an absence of purpose could be one of the most dangerous things in a capitalistic world.

The last 100 years of corporate history give credence to Elizabeth Murdoch's insight. As HP co-founder David Packard once said: "Profit is not the proper end and aim of management – it is what makes all of the proper ends and aims possible.'[275]

EXERCISE: DETERMINING YOUR DRIVING PURPOSE

Below are a series of questions to help you articulate your entity's driving purpose. Like the values-clarification exercise, I encourage you to take this opportunity now.

1. Why do you exist?

As we have already discussed, the answer to this question needs to be expansive, inspiring, and more than simply profit-focused.

A few years ago I ran a program with the executive team for cosmetic giant Mary Kay and learned that the company's purpose was one that its founder Mary Kay Ash first espoused many years previously: "We are in the people development business." Mary Kay Ash stated, "Cosmetics are just the vehicle". This inspiring and stunningly altruistic purpose has guided the Mary Kay Corporation since 1963.

So what is *your* answer to the question 'Why do we exist?'

_____

_____

_____

2. How would you describe your business on the back of a T-shirt?

How could you capture the essence of your business, brand or organization in a couple of words, in an image or with a short slogan?

_____

_____

_____

3. If you were to cease to exist tomorrow, what would be lost?

Collins and Porras pose this question in a different way: "Why not shut the organization down, cash out, and sell off the assets?"[276]

_____

_____

_____

4. What would make you volunteer?

If you didn't need the money or there was no financial compensation available, what would motivate you to still give your time and energy to the organization?

_____

_____

_____

Come up with a statement

Drawing on the responses above, try and condense your purpose down finishing the sentence below:

We exist to _____

_____

My hope is that you now have a clearer idea of what the defining values and driving purpose of your organization or brand are. The reason we have spent so much time on this point is that your DNA will be central to the application of a number of other strategies we will discuss in the coming chapters. That said, it is not enough to simply _know_ what your DNA is. What matters more is that your values and purpose are _known_ and _owned_ throughout the organization. The larger and more complex a business grows, the more difficult this can become.

This was the challenge that confronted Starbucks CEO Howard Schultz when he returned to the company's helm in 2008. In a leaked company email, Schultz shared his concern that even though the company's stock price was high and business was good, Starbucks was losing sight of its culture and values.[277] In response to what Schultz saw as this loss of focus on what mattered most (amongst other things, the customer experience), he took the unprecedented step of closing all 7,100 Starbucks stores in North America for three hours on the evening of Feb 26, 2010, to retrain about 135,000 in-store employees. It was a shock to the system and a public admission that the business needed to go back to its core.

Even more impressively, Schultz took the step of gathering all Starbucks store managers together in New Orleans for further retraining (at a cost of $7 million). In an effort to model the core values Schultz was hoping to galvanize companywide, every store manager was expected to put in five hours of community service helping Hurricane Katrina victims before the training sessions commenced.

Schultz describes how this focus on community service went to the core of the Starbucks' DNA which was that of a company "attentive to the fragile balance between profitability and social conscience". This masterstroke served to powerfully Re-Calibrate the Starbucks Corporation and was a critical factor in the success the company has enjoyed in the ensuing years.[278]

Similarly, luxury hotel chain Ritz Carlton has developed a business practice over the years designed to ensure that the company's DNA is known and owned at a grassroots level. At the beginning of shifts, all Ritz Carlton staff take part in a 15-minute 'line up' where the company's guest-centered credo and motto are recited and discussed. More than simply giving the company's values lip service however, Ritz has also taken steps to embed their values practically by permitting every employee to spend up to $2000 to make any single guest satisfied.[279]

My own management agency, Ode Management, has a unique way of keeping its purpose "to make a tangible difference in audience members" top of mind. In its offices a giant board features a running tally of 'lives touched' by speakers the agency has booked to present at events around the world. Ode's managing director, Leanne Christie, describes how the running tally keeps her sales team continually aware that what they are doing makes a difference in people's lives. "The screen helps us stay focused on why we are in business," she said.

Probably the best example of taking deliberate steps to ensure a company's DNA stays front-of-mind is that of Facebook.

In late 2012 just as Facebook was celebrating the milestone of having one billion users, a little red book started appearing on the desks of all its employees. The book was full of inspirational quotes and credos including:

- Facebook was not created to be a company, it was built to accomplish a social mission – to make the world more open and connected
- Greatness and comfort rarely coexist
- Remember people don't use Facebook because they like us. They use it because they like their friends.
- If we don't create the thing that kills Facebook, someone else will.[280]

In doing this, I believe Facebook's leadership displayed a wisdom well beyond their years – a wisdom which will hopefully ensure the company's core values and DNA remain top priority regardless of how successful the brand becomes.

Continual Re-Calibration can be unconscious, but more often it is something that requires deliberate effort. In order to stay aligned and on track, enduringly relevant brands and organizations tend to go through alignment checks regularly – either annually or quarterly. However, in addition to more formal and explicit check-ups, staying relevant and ahead of the curve will also require Re-Calibration when the organization finds itself prompted by one of the following three triggers:

TRIGGER 1: CRISIS

'Getting back to basics' is a critical first step to take when crisis hits – as the Ford Corporation did back in the 1980s.

Consider the predicament faced by U.S. fast food giant, Wendy's. In early 2005, Wendy's was a victim of fraud when a customer planted part of a human finger in her meal, 'discovered' it, and then sued the company.

While Wendy's was eventually cleared of any wrongdoing, CEO Jack Scheussler described how Wendy's core values and purpose proved indispensible while the company was in the midst of the crisis. "It might have been expedient to pay off the accuser in an attempt to end the media onslaught... but we never considered this option," said Scheussler. "Instead, we focused on helping the police uncover the truth, while standing behind our employees and protecting our brand. Wendy's founder, Dave Thomas, believed that reputation is earned by the actions you take every day, and that's still our credo."[281]

Pharmaceutical giant Johnson and Johnson also leant heavily on its corporate credo when, in 1982, seven people in the Chicago area died after taking Tylenol tablets which had been tampered with. Guided by its publicly stated core values of social responsibility and a ruthless commitment to quality, the company immediately removed all Tylenol capsules from the entire U.S. market (not just from stores in Chicago) at a cost of roughly $100 million.

"Johnson and Johnson has succeeded in portraying itself as a company willing to do what's right, regardless of the cost," noted the *Washington Post* in the crisis' aftermath.[282]

In a similar vein, former Merck pharmaceutical CEO Raymond Gilmartin drew inspiration from the 'greater than profits' purpose espoused by the company's founder when faced with the Vioxx crisis of 2005. Although recalling the drug came at great expense and embarrassment, it was a step Gilmartin was willing to take because failure to do so would have violated the very principals that had made Merck great in the first place.[283]

The experience of Wendy's, Johnson and Johnson and Merck all prove the old axiom to be true: a *principle isn't a principle until it costs you something.*

A PRINCIPLE ISN'T A PRINCIPLE UNTIL IT COSTS YOU SOMETHING.

TRIGGER 2: CHANGE

A second instance when it is critically important to Re-Calibrate with a brand or organization's DNA is when the fundamentals of an industry or operating environment are shifting.

A number of years ago I was doing some strategic planning work with the *International Award for Young People*. This program, known in some countries as the Duke of Edinburgh's Award, traces its roots back to 1934 when a German educator named Kurt Hahn observed what he called the 'Six Declines in Modern Youth':

1. Decline of Fitness due to modern methods of transportation;
2. Decline of Initiative and Enterprise due to the widespread disease of 'spectatoritis';
3. Decline of Memory and Imagination due to the confused restlessness of modern life;
4. Decline of Skill and Care due to the weakened tradition of craftsmanship;
5. Decline of Self-discipline due to the ever-present availability of stimulants and tranquilizers;
6. Decline of Compassion due to the unseemly haste with which modern life is conducted.

To address these concerns, Hahn created a formal program for young people which included physical training for fitness; challenging expeditions to foster endurance; targeted projects to build practical skills; and community service for instilling empathy. Over the decades, more than seven million youth across 130 countries have participated in the *International Award for Young People*.

Despite its track record however, the program facilitators have found it increasingly difficult to attract new young participants over recent years. In a bid to remain relevant, the organization's leaders have introduced several initiatives including online record keeping for participants, new program design which gives local communities more control, and even dedicated Facebook groups which allow participants to share their experiences.

In the context of my involvement in helping the organization adapt and evolve, I listened with interest to the various strategies being implemented to keep the program up-to-date. As discussions unfolded, however, I expressed concern that there was a lot of focus on *what* to do and *how* things needed to change, but little discussion on *why* the organization existed in the first place. I challenged the organization's leadership to return again to Kurt Hahn's original observations and vision for the program. Although many decades old, Hahn's observations are as true today as they were in the 1930s.

My encouragement to the International Award's executive was to ensure that the program's core DNA and purpose remained front and center amid all the discussions of change and modernization.

It is imperative that when faced with widespread change, organizations return to the essence of what makes them unique. Strategies, approaches, processes can change with time, but core DNA does not - and *must* not.

RELEVANCE ≠ COMPROMISE

Some organizations and brands, in their desire to stay relevant, make the mistake of equating relevance with compromise, assuming core values and purpose need to change in order to keep with the times. On the contrary, one of the defining characteristics of enduring organizations is their commitment to hold unswervingly to the values and principles that created their success in the first place.[284]

Former Hewlett-Packard CEO John Young describes the importance of adhering to principles this way: "Our basic principles have endured intact since our founders conceived them. We distinguish between core values and practices; the core values don't change, but the practices might."[285]

The reality is that organizations and brands that compromise their core DNA in the pursuit of profits, growth or relevance are unlikely to last the distance. As the saying goes, *if you don't stand for something, you'll fall for anything.*

IF YOU DON'T STAND FOR SOMETHING, YOU'LL FALL FOR ANYTHING.

TRIGGER 3: CHOICE

This third instance when Re-Calibrating can be an important exercise is when tough decisions need to be made and the way forward is unclear.

Take the case of a Chicago businessman by the name of Herbert J Taylor who realized the importance of having an objective guide for making decisions based on unchangeable values and principles. Taylor firmly believed that in order to turn around his near-bankrupt company, Club Aluminum, ethically-driven decision-making was necessary: In 'right' there is 'might' was his motto.

Taylor set out to develop an easy-to-memorize and simple-to-understand ethical yardstick that would guide and influence the decisions and actions of everyone in his company. The end result was a Four-Question test that encapsulated the values of both Taylor personally and the company he had founded.

1. Is it the truth?
2. Is it fair to all concerned?
3. Will it build goodwill and better friendships?
4. Will it be beneficial to all concerned?

Almost immediately, Taylor's '4-way test' started to have an impact. The company re-wrote one of its advertising posters which declared that its product was 'the best cookware in the world.' Taylor knew that the company could not prove that this was true and therefore the claim violated Question 1 in the test. The advertisement was rewritten to include only the facts.

In another instance, Club Aluminum awarded a contract to a local printer who had competitively tendered for the job. Soon after the contract was awarded however, the printer realized he had under-estimated the quote by a relatively small amount. Although it would have been well within Club Aluminum's legal rights to force the printer to fulfill his side of the contract, Taylor and his leadership went back to questions 2 and 3 of the 4-way test and decided to pay the additional amount in good faith.

Over time, Club Aluminum became known for its high ethical standards and Taylor's 4-way test began to be adopted by other business leaders and organizations worldwide.

Recalibrating an organization as it navigates change, crisis and choice is critically important if you are to win the battle for relevance. It is not enough to simply repeat the practices and methodologies that have worked in the past without being clear on the principles underpinning them. After all, as times evolve, practices and methodologies need to evolve with them. This evolutionary process, however, must be guided by the compass bearing of values and purpose if you hope to go the distance and remain on course.

PERSONAL RE-CALIBRATION

This chapter has been dedicated to the importance of Re-Calibrating corporately or organizationally as a key strategy for staying relevant. However, Re-Calibrating is as important at a personal level too.

Regardless of whether you are a position of leadership in an organization or not, I would urge you to apply the same principles in this chapter to you personally:

What are your defining values as an individual (the non-negotiables)?

What is your driving purpose in life (more than your profession or earning capacity)?

How can these guide you in the face of crisis, change and choice?

While these questions can be confronting or challenging, they are incredibly powerful. After all, there is nothing as soul-destroying as walking through life on auto-pilot or living a life that is out of alignment with who you are and why you believe you are on the planet.

In contrast, there is nothing as inspiring and invigorating as living each day with a sense of conviction, purpose and intentionality - knowing you are right where you need to be, on the way to where you are going.

CHAPTER 11:
RELEVANCE STRATEGY 2 — RE-FOCUS

This second strategy for staying relevant is critical in counteracting the effects of preservation obsession and apathy within organizations. Re-Focusing is about setting ambitious new goals, casting fresh vision and outlining bold strategies for the future.

In the same way that damaged or inefficient muscles in our bodies will heal naturally when blood flow and movement are restored, so it is with brands and businesses. When a team or organization has become dysfunctional or 'stuck', the best way to restore momentum, energy and vigor is to pump in new life by refocusing on the road ahead.

Re-Focusing on the future does four important things for an organization or brand:

1. RE-FOCUSING RESTORES INSPIRATION

Vision has a unique ability to inspire energy, concentrate effort and garner commitment. The old proverb tells us that 'Where there is no vision, people will perish'.[286] Importantly, however, the reverse of this adage is also true. People and organizations will naturally flourish when a vision is both clear and compelling.

Most businesses and organizations start off with an inspiring vision for the future. In the early stages, aspirations are high, energy is boundless and challenges seem like little more than insignificant obstacles that need to be navigated.

Over time as things settle into a routine, however, sober realism begins to replace naive optimism. Possibility thinking gives way to probability planning. The inspiring 'big picture' gets crowded out as challenges and circumstances become all-consuming. Lethargy, despondency and fatigue creep in ever so slowly until they become the default operating mode.

The best way to break this cycle is by getting people to lift their eyes from the day-to-day and focus on the horizon instead.

IN SIGHT BUT OUT OF REACH

Although the exercise of vision casting and goal setting is inspiring in and of itself, a vision cannot be so big that it seems implausible or impossible. A long-range vision may be energizing but short-range

A TRULY INSPIRING VISION OF THE FUTURE WILL ALWAYS BE OUT OF REACH, BUT STILL WITHIN SIGHT.

strategies are necessary for an organization to believe that the future can be different from the past. In short, a truly inspiring vision of the future will always be out of reach, but still within sight.

In a revealing example of the inspirational power of long-term vision coupled with short-term strategy, Dan and Chip Heath in their book *Adapt* share the story of a group of students in Howard, South Dakota, who set out to revive their dying community. After decades of declining employment in the farming and industrial sector, Howard's median house price had sunk to $26,500 and the population by the mid-1990s stood at 3000 and was falling.

Having read in class about the death of similar regional communities in Iowa, the students started asking, 'What can we do about this?' They dared to envisage a future for their town that saw it thrive and flourish once more – a dream that perhaps only those with the benefit of youthful idealism and naïveté could have imagined.

Idealistic or not, the students' vision sparked a sense of inspiration that had been absent from the community for years. Importantly however, the students' long-range vision was underpinned with an action plan of short-term strategies. These included everything from a community-wide roster for clean-up days, to a simple economic calculation that showed that if residents spent just 10% more of their disposable income in the town, the local economy would grow by $7 million in one year.

Because the plan for turning around Howard's fortunes appeared achievable, the support it garnered was huge. Twelve months later, the local economy had grown by $15.6 million, providing revenue to address other local issues. Within a few years, Howard began to attract new and innovative businesses and before long was a flourishing and vibrant community once more.[287]

2. RE-FOCUSING COMBATS INERTIA

If you think back to when you learned to ride a bicycle as a child, you will recall how you came to realize that speed is your best friend. Naturally, this seemed counterintuitive at first; typically, an unsteady rider will assume that the lowest speed possible is safest. The reality however is that a bike is at its most unsafe and unstable when moving slowly; forward momentum is the key to setting off and staying upright.

It is much the same in collective groups of people. When an organization is idle or simply going through the motions, political power trips and destructive in-fighting bubble to the surface with incredible predictability.

> A BUSINESS OR ORGANIZATION THAT IS ON THE MOVE AND *GOING SOMEWHERE* TENDS TO BE A PLACE OF INCREDIBLE UNITY, HARMONY AND FOCUS.

People lose perspective and small things are blown out of proportion. Just as a rolling stone gathers no moss, a business or organization that is on the move and *going somewhere* tends to be a place of incredible unity, harmony and focus. Further still, the great thing about forward movement is that it is generative:

the more momentum you have, the more you gain. We all know that if you want something done; give it to a busy person. Well, the same principle applies in organizations.

SHAKING THEM FROM THEIR SLUMBER

In order for a future vision to unlock a business or brand from a state of inertia, it must be dramatic enough to create dissatisfaction with the status quo. Effective vision casting always elicits a response – it cannot be ignored.

When John Young was CEO of Hewlett Packard, for instance, he re-invigorated the organization by casting an expansive vision and setting unreasonable goals like:

- Producing laser-jet printers that could retail for less than one-third of the current price;
- Reducing by 50% the time it took for a project to go from idea to market release.

These 'unreasonable' goals, though initially met with resistance, had an electrifying effect on the organization. HP employees were forced to think outside the box and amazingly managed to achieve every one of Young's goals in record time.[288]

THE PERSUASIVE POWER OF VISION

Re-Focusing also has an amazing ability to combat the mental inertia that comes from entrenched paradigms. In the early 1670s, Christopher Wren discovered this when he embarked on an ambitious plan to rebuild St Paul's Cathedral after the devastating Great Fire of London. Inspired by emerging French and Italian architecture, Wren envisioned a new cathedral that departed from London's traditional gothic style – a style Wren believed was outdated and recalled England's dark medieval past.

When Wren submitted his master plan for a reconstructed St Paul's however, it was met with violent resistance from the Royal Council and leading churchmen. Wren's European-inspired design was seen as 'too Catholic' and hence unacceptable to the Church of England hierarchy. Unperturbed, Wren employed an unusual tactic to win over his detractors: he built a model of his proposed vision for the new cathedral. Breathtakingly detailed, extraordinarily intricate and costing more than half a million pounds in today's money, the model could be pulled apart and thus allowed members of the council and the public to get a real vision of how the cathedral would look and feel, externally *and* internally.

While some remained unconvinced, Wren's strategy of bringing his vision to life in a tangible way worked. Once people could get a real sense how bold, impressive and inspiring his design was, public support turned overwhelmingly in his favor. This resulted in the commission for design and construction of St Paul's being awarded to Wren, and the rest is history.

3. RE-FOCUSING SHAPES CULTURE

By the end of the 1980s, Whirlpool had become the world's largest manufacturer and marketer of household appliances. Six years later however, it was quite a different story. As sales began to level off and Whirlpool rapidly lost ground to its competitors, the company's leadership decided to embark on an exercise in cultural transformation by casting a new five-word internal vision: *Innovation comes from everyone, everywhere.*

This dramatically shifted the way that company's employees viewed their role and responsibilities. Creativity and innovation was now everybody's job. Within a few years, Whirlpool had transformed itself from a traditional manufacturer to a customer-focused enterprise producing some of the most innovative products in the industry.[289]

It was a similar story at Apollo Tyres in India. In 2005, the company was a relatively small tire manufacturer turning over $300 million a year in revenue. However, Managing director Neeraj Kanwar described that the company's culture had become small-minded resulted in leaders "...constantly fighting fires and spending all our time on things that probably weren't the best use of our time."

During an offsite meeting with the company's leadership, Kanwar challenged the group to chart out a path that would lead the company to it's full potential. The meeting concluded with a clearly articulated vision: an audacious goal to grow almost 7-fold to $2 billion of revenue placing Apollo as one of the world's top 15 tire companies. This vision inspired the team, saw a shift in focus from maintenance to growth, and renewed a commitment to empowering employees with the skills required to win. In short, the vision-casting exercise re-ignited energy and drive like nothing else could have.[290]

Without doubt, culture change like that seen in Whirlpool and Apollo Tyres would never have occurred without a clear and compelling vision to set it in motion.

4. RE-FOCUSING GUIDES DECISION-MAKING

A strong sense of vision is critical if a company or brand is to stay relevant in the

A CLEAR CONVICTION OF WHERE YOU ARE GOING IS THE BEST WAY TO KNOW WHEN TO SAY YES BUT, MORE IMPORTANTLY, WHEN TO SAY NO TO IDEAS AND OPPORTUNITIES.

long run. After all, a clear conviction of where you are going is the best way to know when to say yes but, more importantly, when to say no to ideas and opportunities.

Re-Focusing a brand or organization on the future is a key way to stay vibrant, relevant and on track. Before we move on, I would urge you to reflect on the questions below and take a few moments to Re-Focus on your own road ahead:

- What would you set out to do if your success was assured?

_____

_____

- If a genie were to grant you three wishes for your organization, what would you ask for?

  1. _____

  2. _____

  3. _____

- What would you want others to be saying about you and your organization in 3-5 years?

  _____

  _____

  _____

- Who is where you would like to be? What is it that you admire about the success they are achieving?

  _____

  _____

  _____

- What would represent a bitter and disappointing failure in five years' time – and what would the opposite look like?

  _____

  _____

  _____

CHAPTER 12:
RELEVANCE STRATEGY 3 — RE-FRESH

Downturns and hard times are often perceived as a curse in business. When market share contracts, sales dry up and nothing seems to be going your way, leaders often long for the former glory days of growth and prosperity. However, in the same way that nature has seasons, industries have cycles that serve an important purpose. The key to surviving, thriving and achieving enduring relevance in the long-term is to *work with* rather than *war against* seasons and cycles – especially the adverse ones.

Speaking to this point, economist Harry S. Dent suggests that the late 2000s great recession was far more than the consequence of poor management by corporate lenders or government regulators; it was an inevitable 'season' that companies and world economies needed to go through.

Economic winters, according to Dent, force companies to pay down debt, adopt new technologies and strive for greater efficiencies — after all, even poorly run companies can experience

> **EVEN POORLY RUN COMPANIES CAN EXPERIENCE ENORMOUS SUCCESS WHEN TIMES ARE GOOD.**

enormous success when times are good.[291] In the words of Warren Buffett, 'It's only when the tide goes out that you realize who's been swimming naked'.[292] Further still, seasons of adversity actually represent an opportunity for organizations to sow seeds for the future. Dent describes how, in the 1930s Depression for instance, smart companies laid the very foundations that would see them prevail and prosper for the remainder of the 20th century.

History is full of cases of people making the most of recessions. Andrew Carnegie and John D Rockefeller took advantage of the 1873 panic following the bust of the railroad bubble and went on to create some of the largest fortunes the U.S. has ever known. In more recent decades, Southwest Airlines grew enormously in the recession of the early 1980s and has since gone on to dominate the low-cost airline market.

A similar pattern is emerging now with many large and successful companies surfacing from the great recession less weighed down by debt. Sung Won Sohn, former chief economist at Wells Fargo Bank suggests that U.S. companies are "leaner, meaner and hungrier" as a result of the downturn.[293] "Bad companies are destroyed by crisis," says former Intel CEO Andy Grove. "Good companies survive them. Great companies are improved by them."[294]

A TERRIBLE THING TO WASTE

The central message of this chapter is that a crisis is a terrible thing to waste. If you realize that you are not as 'hot' as you once were, now is the time to hit the Re-Fresh button and take the steps necessary to prevail. Now is the time for renewal, renovation and transformation. Even if you are not at a point of crisis, the principles of this chapter will help you navigate the seasons and cycles ahead.

Hitting the 'Re-Fresh button' in an organization or brand can tend to take one of three forms:

1. COMBATTING THE TYRANNY OF TRADITION

Growing up in a seaside town on the east coast of Australia, I used to love walking around the wharves and admiring the boats harbored there. I especially loved visiting the dry dock where boats were hauled out of the water for repairs and maintenance.

There I was intrigued to discover how different boats looked above and below water level. Vessels that appeared sleek and polished as they glided through the waves were revealed, below their water line, to be anything but. Hulls were caked with a rough blackish substance and sharp shell-like objects which I learned were called barnacles. The longer a boat is in water, the more barnacles build up over time to the point where they can significantly reduce a boat's speed, agility and efficiency. In order to combat this, boats must have their hulls scoured on a regular basis.

In an organizational context, it is critical that leaders routinely and consciously scrape off traditions and rituals that have become encrusted like barnacles.

Naturally, the challenge when eliminating traditions and rituals is to know which ones to jettison, and which ones to keep. As we

> **IT IS CRITICAL THAT LEADERS ROUTINELY SCRAPE OFF TRADITIONS AND RITUALS THAT HAVE BECOME ENCRUSTED LIKE BARNACLES.**

have already discussed, many traditions have value and provide a foundation on which to build, while others can strangle an organization to death, just like the Curtain Fig.

Leading business author Robert Kriegel offers three helpful diagnostic questions to determine whether a tradition is constructive or constrictive: [295]

1. Does it add value to the customer?
2. Does it increase productivity?
3. Does it improve organizational morale?

If a given tradition or ritual doesn't result in a 'yes' answer to at least two of these questions, it is in all likelihood a 'barnacle' that is slowing you down.

NURSES CAPS

Having consulted to the healthcare sector and specifically with many nursing units over the years, I have always been amazed by how tradition-bound the nursing profession is – often to its own detriment.

Take a nurse's headwear, for example. The tradition of nurses wearing caps has its roots in religion. At the earliest nursing schools in France and Germany, student caps were similar to the veils worn by the nuns who ran these schools. Then the founder of modern nursing, Florence Nightingale, mobilized nurses during the Crimean war in the mid-1800s and expected nurses to wear a uniform with a distinctive cap. Before long, these caps became an inseparable part of a nurse's uniform and identity.

Laura Stokowski, a registered nurse and industry expert, describes how the purpose and role of the cap evolved over the years. "In the early stages, the nurse's cap was for sanitary purposes in that it covered long hair which was fashionable for women in the early 20th century. However, as time went on and fashions changed, so did the cap. Some stylized versions

A TRADITION THAT STARTED OUT AS PRAGMATIC GRADUALLY BECAME FURTHER AND FURTHER REMOVED FROM ITS INITIAL PURPOSE.

started to be worn at the back of the head – scarcely covering any hair at all. So a tradition that started out as pragmatic gradually became further and further removed from its initial purpose."

When hospitals began to phase out the nurse's cap in recent decades, members of the old guard considered such steps sacrilegious. However, there was pressure on the nursing profession to modernize and dispense with traditions that had become impractical and purpose-less – including but not limited to the wearing of caps.

Knowing something of the challenges that the nursing sector still faces in attracting and retaining talented professionals, I can only imagine how much more unattractive and irrelevant the profession would seem to younger generations of nurses had the cap-wearing tradition not been phased out.

If an organization or brand is to embrace the new opportunities and innovations necessary to win the battle for relevance, outdated and outmoded traditions from the past may well need to be done away with. While this process may be unpopular, painful and politically costly, it is absolutely necessary and easiest to do when faced with crisis. Remember again, a crisis is a terrible thing to waste.

2. PRUNING DEAD WOOD

Avid gardeners know how critical pruning is in order for a garden to thrive. Planting, watering and even weeding a garden are not enough - at times more drastic steps need to be taken. Branches, foliage and even entire trees need to be cut away for the good of the garden as a whole.

Broadly speaking, pruning serves four purposes:

1. To remove dead and diseased branches which are potential sources of infection[296]
2. To stimulate fruit growth by not allowing the tree to expend its energies as it would naturally in the production of roots or foliage[297]
3. To maintain balance in the framework of branches[298]
4. To allow light and air to penetrate through thus encouraging new growth[299]

In a very similar way, pruning dead wood in an organization is vitally important in maintaining health and vitality over time.

> PRUNING DEAD WOOD IN AN ORGANIZATION IS VITALLY IMPORTANT IN MAINTAINING HEALTH AND VITALITY OVER TIME.

GETTING SONY OUT OF THE SLOW LANE

Consider the legendary innovator, Sony. In the 1980s and 1990s Sony was responsible for producing wonders like the Trinitron; the Walkman; the world's first CD player; the 3.5 inch floppy disk; the first PlayStation and Blue Ray player.[300] Steve Jobs was so inspired by Sony that he used it as his model in Apple's early days.[301]

Like many successful companies, however, Sony got stuck. Where it had once been at the cutting edge of technology and design, the company grew big and complex at the cost of its agility and responsiveness. Sony was late to embrace LCD televisions; slow to react to the iPhone; and their answer to Apple's iPad reached the market six months after Apple released a second edition of its tablet computer.[302] Ironically, the company that had once inspired Apple was now scrambling to keep up.

By late 2011, things were looking grim at Sony. The company had suffered four consecutive years of losses[303] and finished 2012 $6.4 billion in the red.[304] Adding insult to injury, Sony's stock hit two-decade lows and the company's credit rating was dramatically downgraded.[305]

In April 2012 new Sony CEO Kazuo Hirai identified that the company's number one problem was it's lack of speed in responding to marketplace events.[306] To address this, Hirai got out his pruning shears. His first step was to end Sony's decade-long marriage with Swedish mobile phone company, Ericsson. Next to go were any Sony-owned non-core companies including a chemical-products business and a unit that specialized in producing small and mid-sized LCD displays.[307] Hirai also trimmed Sony's global workforce by roughly 10,000 employees[308] and streamlined manufacturing processes so that Sony's TV business expenses were slashed by half.

Speaking of his resolve to turn Sony around even in the face of stiff opposition, Kazuo Hirai argued, "There is no time but now for Sony to change. We can't turn away from making painful decisions."[309] The posting of a $2.15 billion loss in 2014 (in contrast with the forecasted $300 million profit that year) indicates just how challenging the transformation at Sony will likely be.[310]

While it remains to be seen how successful the steps Sony has taken will be in the long run, history suggests that Kazuo Hirai is on the right track. After all, he is walking a similar path to the one trod by the legendary CEO Lou Gerstner who successfully and dramatically turned around IBM during the mid-1990s.

BIG BLUE BECOMES AS GOOD AS NEW

Although IBM had been one of the great corporate success stories of the 20th century, the 1980s and then early 1990s saw the company stumble spectacularly.

In 1993, Lou Gerstner took the helm and quickly set about turning around IBM's fortunes. He began by pruning any executives who failed to share his sense of urgency for change, or who fell short of delivering on their responsibilities. Gerstner was a stickler for responsibility and accountability. In his book *Who Say's Elephants Can't Dance*, he describes how an IBM culture existed where negative results were typically met with excuses. Confronting this attitude head-on, Gerstner pointed to the profitability of competitors operating under similar circumstances and urged his workforce to quit pointing fingers and laying blame.

Gerstner's management team then had to face just how bad things had become. The company's mainframe computers were not only overpriced and quickly losing market share; IBM was also facing stiffer competition in the marketplace than ever before. Furthermore, a culture of bureaucracy, inefficiency and entitlement had spread throughout the organization.

Following this sobering analysis, Gerstner embarked on ruthless and incredibly effective pruning agenda that included:

- Ceasing production of applications software development;
- Selling the company's Federal Systems division;
- Explicitly linking employee benefits with results and performance;
- Thoroughly re-engineering almost all company processes resulting in an elimination of $14 billion of inefficiencies between 1993 and 2002.[311]

Although IBM has come a long way, recent years have seen the company's leadership re-visit many of the principles that guided Gerstner in the 1990s. In October 2014, the newly appointed CEO Ginni Rometty responded to IBM's 9th consecutive quarter of profit decline with the observation; "We have more to do and we need to do it faster". While IBM is gradually expanding into data analytics, cloud and mobile technology, the problem is that two-thirds of its revenue is derived from legacy assets – many of which need significant pruning.[312]

While organizational pruning is a key element of any turnaround strategy, it is also a powerful way to realize the potential of an already flourishing business. Take the example of Ricardo Semler and his famed transformation of the Brazilian industrial equipment company, Semco.

When Antonio Semler resigned as CEO of Semco in 1980 and handed the reins to his son, Ricardo embarked on an ambitious program of pruning and re-design. Aged 21 at the time, he was one of Harvard Business School's youngest ever graduates and he was determined that under his leadership the company would differ dramatically from the autocratic and bureaucratic business he had inherited.

On his first day as CEO, Ricardo Semler fired 60% of all senior managers and then promptly dismantled what he called the 'tools of corporate oppression' such as time clocks, strict dress codes and rigid security procedures. Semler then set out to empower and mobilize the workforce to manage itself. He instituted 'factory committees' which allowed workers a say in decisions regarding everything from pay levels to work hours. Through the introduction of profit-sharing schemes for employees, Semler encouraged every member of the company to look for ways to increase productivity and efficiency. This allowed employees to debate management issues, even assuming responsibility for hiring and firing their own bosses. As time passed, Semco became more and more decentralized as various factories and specific business units were spun off into self-regulating entities.

During the 1990s, Semler's organizational experiment faced its greatest challenge when financial woes and liquidity restrictions in Brazil caused Semco to go into sharp decline. Responding to this crisis, Semco staff agreed democratically to cut wages by as much as 40% providing employee profit shares increased and the workforce gained greater control over every item of expenditure.

Semco's crisis proved to be a blessing in disguise as crises so often do. As workers rose to the challenge and willingly performed multiple roles in an effort to retain profitability, each employee gained greater understanding of the company's various operations and numerous new ideas for improvement came as a result. During the downturn and the reforms it bought about, Semco's inventories fell by 65%, its delivery times decreased significantly and the rate of product defects fell to below 1%. Semco became leaner, smarter and far more efficient than it had ever been – since 2003, average YOY growth has been a staggering 40%.[313]

WHEN, WHAT AND HOW TO PRUNE

For an entity to remain healthy, growing and relevant, enduring organizations typically take their pruning shears to three key areas:

- The baggage of bureaucracy and red tape
- Underperforming or non-strategic products and initiatives
- People not aligned with the entity's vision

A. PRUNING THE BAGGAGE OF BUREAUCRACY

When German political economist Max Weber first devised the bureaucratic theory of management in the late 19th century, his intention was to combat the nepotism and unproductiveness rife in the family-run businesses of the day. Weber believed that efficient organizations needed to 'have a strict hierarchy or authority, clear rules and regulations, standardized procedures and meticulous record keeping.'[314] Ironically, the very organizational approach that set out to drive efficiency has, over time, resulted in the opposite outcome.

The larger an organization becomes and the longer it exists, the more bureaucratic and inefficient it often becomes. Recalling how this occurred at General Motors, former company board member Ross Perot once

AT GENERAL MOTORS, IF YOU SEE A SNAKE, THE FIRST THING YOU DO IS GO HIRE A CONSULTANT ON SNAKES.

joked, "At General Motors, if you see a snake, the first thing you do is go hire a consultant on snakes. Then you get together a committee on snakes, and you discuss it for a couple of years. And the most likely course of action is: nothing." Reflecting on such an inefficient state of affairs, Perot concluded in 1988 that "the GM system has to be nuked."[315]

While Perot's criticism of GM's culture is applicable to many other companies, at an even broader level, there are entire nations whose systems and processes have become so bureaucratic they need to be nuked – or at least ruthlessly pruned.

In his 2012 *State of the Union* Address, President Obama observed that one of the U.S.'s greatest challenges is its bloated bureaucracy.

"We must clear away red tape because there is no question that some of our regulations are outdated, unnecessary or too costly. I've ordered every federal agency to eliminate rules that don't make sense. We got rid of one rule from 40 years ago that could have forced some dairy farmers to spend $10,000 a year proving that they could contain an oil spill – because somewhere along the line milk had been classified as an oil."[316]

Having worked with clients in both the private and public sector, I have identified five dangers of bureaucracy that wreak havoc on relevance:

DANGER 1: RESPONSIBILITY IS SHARED OR SHIRKED

One of the characteristics of a bureaucratic system is that it shifts the emphasis from the individual to the collective. While this makes organizations less vulnerable to 'key person' risks, it also leads people to hide behind systems and processes rather than take responsibility for action, or inaction. Blame gets spread across the whole organization. When something goes wrong, it is the system's fault.

Anyone who has contacted a customer service call center only to be passed from one department to another because the person on the line lacks the know-how, will or authority to solve your problem, knows how infuriating this aspect of bureaucracy can be.

DANGER 2: CRACKS GET FALLEN THROUGH

The second danger of bureaucracy is that because systems and processes are rigid by nature, anything or anyone that doesn't fit in the boxes on a form or the categories in a database tends to be rejected or fall through the cracks. Large organizations like government agencies are particularly vulnerable to this as countless child protection oversights can attest.

Just as people can fall through the cracks, so can ideas and opportunities. This was largely the case when Xerox's Palo Alto Research Center (PARC) failed to capitalize commercially on many of its innovations due to gaps in communication between its research and marketing divisions.[317]

DANGER 3: THINGS GET OVERLOOKED

Bureaucracy tends to mask underlying weaknesses and can cause the basics to be overlooked. Take the infamous exploding Ford Pinto – a car that became irreverently known as 'the barbeque that seats four'.

An engineer's early assessment and subsequent strong recommendation to buffer the Pinto's fuel tanks disappeared entirely as Pinto reports filtered up Ford's bureaucratic chain. By the time the management committee approved the final specs for the car, no one was aware of the fuel tank recommendation and almost 30 Pinto drivers died as a result of this needless oversight.[318]

This is the problem with bureaucracy: everyone assumes that someone else has 'covered all bases,' 'asked the question,' or 'done the research' when it is entirely possible that no one has, or someone has, and no one had paid any attention!

DANGER 4: RISK IS AVOIDED AND INNOVATION BLOCKED

Highly bureaucratic and process-driven institutions tend to attract certain personality types and temperaments – namely those who like to know where the boundaries are, and who are seldom tempted to 'color outside the lines'. Over time, this tendency can result in a culture of conformity, close-mindedness and risk aversion.

A phenomenon which is common to most if not all bureaucratic organizations is that of the 'clay layer.' This term describes how those in the lower echelons of an organization often have the best ideas for improving performance, productivity or profitability, yet their ideas and insights typically fail to come to the attention of those who could act on them.

Why so? Because a 'clay layer' of middle management gatekeepers stifle such innovation in order to preserve and protect the status quo.

This aspect of bureaucracy played a role in Nokia's demise as leader in the mobile phone business. A full seven years before the iPhone's release, Nokia's research team developed mobile phones with color touch screens, mapping software and e-commerce functionality.

A few years later, Nokia designed a wireless-enabled tablet computer long before the iPad was even imagined. And yet, according to former Nokia chief designer Frank Nuovo, many cutting edge innovations like these never made it to market due to a dysfunctional corporate culture. Nuovo describes how, in addition to being fragmented by internal rivalries, Nokia's research efforts were disconnected from the company's operations departments who were responsible for bringing devices to market – resulting in missed opportunities that cost the company dearly.[319]

Leading business thinker and author John Linkner said it best when he observed "Most large organizations exist to protect old ideas, not create new ones. Many of us punch the clock at large bureaucracies that are more focused on *compliance* than *creativity*. *Obedience* is valued over *imagination*."[320]

DANGER 5: INERTIA AND NON-RESPONSIVENESS

Highly bureaucratic organizations are incredibly resistant to outside influences and lack the ability to respond quickly when shift happens. Like the ill-fated Titanic, bureaucracies often alter their course far too slowly when threats and changes emerge.

In a scathing assessment of the how bureaucracy led software giant Microsoft off-track in the 2000s, one U.S. commentator put it this way: "What began as a lean machine led by young visionaries of unparalleled talent mutated into something bloated and laden, with an internal culture that unintentionally rewarded managers who strangled ideas that might threaten the established order of things."[321]

While Microsoft had once laughed at how bogged down competitors like IBM had become, over time Microsoft itself became the thing it despised: bureaucratic.[322] As Microsoft had expanded during the early 2000s, so did its bureaucracy. More managers led to more

| **MICROSOFT, OVER TIME, BECAME THE THING IT DESPISED: BUREAUCRATIC.**

meetings; more meetings meant more memos; and all this red tape came at the cost of innovation and agility. According to one former Microsoft engineer at the time, things moved at a snail's pace to the point where software was essentially being designed by committee.[323]

A 2012 *Vanity Fair* article describes just how "toxic and dysfunctional" the Microsoft bureaucracy became as the company grew. It describes a management technique of 'stack ranking' where staff were rewarded not only for doing well, but also for ensuring colleagues failed. Endless power plays ensued as a result of this directive - resulting in numerous opportunities including e-books and smartphones being missed almost entirely. The cost of missing the early opportunity of smartphones alone is hard to estimate considering that by the middle of 2012 the iPhone was earning more revenue per quarter than the entirety of Microsoft.[324]

More recent Microsoft initiatives, including the Bing search engine, appear to have also become bogged down in red tape. According to a Microsoft product manager who worked on Bing, an unnecessarily bloated project team resulted in relentless in-fighting and a loss of design momentum. So far, Bing has cost Microsoft in excess of $6 billion.[325]

3 WAYS TO BLUDGEON BUREAUCRACY

In order to combat the baggage of bureaucracy and stay both relevant and agile, enduring organizations must engage in pruning exercises that take one or more of the following forms:

I. REDUCING SIZE

Giving an organization a quick trim is often the first port of call when leaders are looking to get an entity's mojo back. When Meg Whitman took the reins at HP in September 2011 for instance, she made job cuts her first step to reorganizing and reviving the company and she made it clear that no position was beyond scrutiny.[326]

In October 2014, Meg Whitman took this a step further splitting HP in two. Ms. Whitman said the breakup would make the company more nimble and enable it to invest in products and acquisitions necessary to keep pace with the market.[327]

It was a similar story at American Airlines and Japanese carrier, JAL. After filing for bankruptcy protection in November 2011, American Airlines announced that it would cut 13,000 jobs (or roughly 15% of the company's workforce) in order to regain economic viability.[328]

In the case of JAL, a significant 20-year decline resulting in bankruptcy in 2009 forced the company to significantly reduce costs across the board. JAL's pruning saw the airline shed a third of its workforce, dramatically reduce flight routes worldwide and cut its operating costs in half. This has resulted in a stunning resurgence for JAL which posted an impressive 17% profit margin by the end of 2012.

Pruning was also a key strategy employed by U.S. electronics giant, Best Buy. Having posted a $1.7 billion first quarter loss in 2012, the company shed 50 of its flagship big-box stores in a ruthless move to avoid the retail graveyard of its one-time rival, Circuit City.[329] Reflecting on the challenges facing Best Buy, interim chief executive Mike Mikan observed in May 2012 that the company needed to take "bold actions" to turn things around. This would require taking a fresh look at the entirety of Best Buys operation and "sparing no sacred cows."[330]

II. STREAMLINING OPERATIONS

A second way to counteract bureaucracy is to seek greater efficiency through streamlining operations and processes. When 3G Capital Management took

Burger King private in 2012, for example, its first step in reinvigorating the fast food chain was to create a much leaner corporate operating structure.[331]

Streamlining operations within an organization need not only be a reactive step - it can also be done preemptively. Smart leaders set plans and initiatives in place to ensure that operations remain efficient and non-bureaucratic as an organization grows in size.

Geoff Bezos did this at Amazon with the creation of the 'Two Pizza Team' rule. Designed to ensure that teams stayed small, efficient and agile, Bezos set a rule than no work group could grow beyond six to 10 members – or small enough to be adequately fed by two large pizzas.[332]

III. DECENTRALIZING POWER AND CONTROL

A third way to combat bureaucracy is to embrace a decentralized model of power — as Ricardo Semler did at Semco. Rather than having power cascade down from the top, network-based and decentralized organizations tend to be more collaborative and innovative than their hierarchical counterparts.

> **DECENTRALIZED ORGANIZATIONS TEND TO BE MORE COLLABORATIVE AND INNOVATIVE THAN THEIR HIERARCHICAL COUNTERPARTS.**

Excellent examples exist of established companies that have embraced the decentralized model. Consider W.L Gore, the Delaware-based manufacturers of Gore-tex and other market-leading products. The company's founder, Bill Gore, was a pioneer in the decentralized company model. He devised a simple but effective way of ensuring that no single company facility or location had more than 150 people working at it – he never built car parking lots with more than 150 spaces. Once a company facility's car park became close to full, Bill Gore knew it was time to break up the unit or build a new facility entirely.

Today W.L Gore employs over 10,000 people worldwide but by design no facility boasts more than 150 employees – and each location is empowered to make decisions regarding its own projects and operations. This decentralized power structure has been cited as a key reason for the company's impressive track record of 7,500 registered patents to date.[333]

Looking at a different industry entirely, GE Aviation has adopted a similar structure of decentralized power by eliminating shop-floor foremen across their 83 factory sites. GE's 26,000 production employees now work within self-managed teams and the result has been a marked increase in efficiency and effectiveness. Interestingly, GE's experience is in line with the findings of a recent study conducted by the University of Iowa which found that factory workers who supervise themselves tended to outperform workers in more traditional hierarchies.[334]

AN EXCELLENT SERVANT BUT A TERRIBLE MASTER

Naturally, bureaucracy has a place. But like so many things in life, bureaucracy is a fantastic servant, but a dreadful master. Sadly, many organizations, businesses and even nations are being slowly choked to death by the very systems designed to preserve order and efficiency.

In order to stay relevant, leaders may need to press the Re-Fresh button and engage in some ruthless pruning of an organizations red tape and bureaucracy. This may be unpopular with some and uncomfortable for many, but it is necessary for the long-term agility, responsiveness and momentum of any organization or brand.

B. PRUNING NON-STRATEGIC PRODUCTS AND INITIATIVES

If pruning the baggage of bureaucracy is first on the agenda for organizations seeking to endure, the culling of products or initiatives that are underperforming or non-strategic comes a close second.

In the same way that entire branches on trees sometimes need to be pruned because they take away energy that could be better directed toward new growth, every organization or brand has products and initiatives that are unhelpfully diverting focus or attention.

The CEO of engineering and electronics giant Hitachi, Hiroaki Nakanishi, recognized the importance of pruning the old in order to make way for the new. When Nakanishi took the reins of Hitachi in April 2010, the company was in the worst position of its 102-year history having experienced massive losses for four consecutive years. In response to these challenges, Nakanishi set out to turn things around. His first step was to dump Hitachi's mobile phone, computer parts and flat-panel TV businesses. This was done to enable the company to focus on its more profitable infrastructure projects like power plants, rail lines and water treatment facilities. The effects of this pruning exercise were swift and stunning – by the end of 2011, Hitachi was back in the black with a $4.35 billion profit.[335]

Fellow Japanese electronics giant Panasonic recently announced it will no longer tolerate unprofitable units in its sprawling pool of businesses. The company said it will halt losses in businesses such as semiconductors, mobile phones and its oncemighty but nowflagging television operations.[336]

It is a similar story in the banking sector. Following years of nearly unchecked expansion, financial institutions across the U.S. are closing thousands of outlets as pressures mount to cut costs and more customers embrace online and mobile banking.

According to SNL Financial, U.S. banks shut 2,267 branches in 2012, putting the U.S. bank-branch count at 93,000. This figure is expected to drop to below 80,000 by the mid-2020s as banks invest in new technologies rather than physical branches.

Bank of America, the U.S's second-largest, has set a goal to eliminate 12% of branches in the coming years. Rob Aulebach, a senior vice president in Bank of America's consumer unit, says customers just aren't coming to the branch as often as they used to. He cites the "tens of thousands" of customers each week who bank on mobile devices. "Convenience is still very important, but convenience means something different than it used to," he says.[337]

FOCUS ON THE GOOD STUFF

Steve Jobs recognized the importance of pruning underperforming products and non-strategic initiatives. Back in 2006 when Mark Parker assumed the role of CEO at Nike and sought advice from Jobs, the Apple guru was candid. "Nike makes some of the best products in the world, but you also make a lot of crap," he said. "Just get rid of the crappy stuff and focus on the good stuff." Although the advice may have been blunter than Parker had anticipated, he conceded later that Jobs was absolutely correct. "We had to edit," as Parker described it.[338]

Jobs offered similar advice to Larry Page upon his return to the helm at Google. Jobs warned Page that Google was making products that were adequate, but not great, and that he needed to cull some of them.[339] Page took Steve Jobs' advice to heart - within seven months of his return, Google had killed off 25 projects.[340]

DUPONT DUMPS ITS SUCCESS STORY

Although it goes against conventional thinking, sometimes it is actually necessary to prune products and initiatives that are highly profitable. After all, although these products and initiatives may be successful in the marketplace, they may no longer be a strategic fit with the organization – and therefore need to go.

To see a brilliant example of this, look at pioneering science company DuPont. For over two centuries, DuPont has been at the cutting edge of bringing scientific discoveries to market. Although the company's origins were in the manufacture of gunpowder and dynamite, in the early 1900s DuPont began focusing on products and technologies that would lead to the betterment of society.

Over the coming decades, DuPont was responsible for the invention of numerous landmark products such as nylon, Teflon and Lycra. More recently, the company turned its attention to innovation and invention in the areas of food, fuel and people security, each with a strong emphasis on sustainability.

What is impressive about DuPont is not the array of new products it has pioneered, but the long list of old ones it has deliberately left behind.

WHAT IS IMPRESSIVE ABOUT DUPONT IS NOT THE ARRAY OF NEW PRODUCTS IT HAS PIONEERED, BUT THE LONG LIST OF OLD ONES IT HAS DELIBERATELY LEFT BEHIND.

Because the strategic focus of DuPont is to continually bring new science to market, the company has realized the need to divest itself of the very brands and businesses that made it successful in the first place. It is this ruthless commitment to hitting the Re-Fresh button that has allowed DuPont to stay ahead of the curve when many of its rivals have fallen by the wayside.

Procter & Gamble is set to follow DuPont's lead in the coming years with plans to shed more than half its brands in a bold attempt by the world's largest consumer products company to become more nimble and growth-oriented.

The move is a major strategic reversal for a company that has been expanding aggressively for decades amid concerns among investors and top management that P&G has become too bloated to navigate an increasingly competitive marketplace.

Chief Executive A.G. Lafley said P&G will narrow its focus to 70 to 80 of its biggest brands and shed as many as 100 others whose performance has been lagging.[341]

C. PRUNING KEY INDIVIDUALS

This final form of pruning relates not to reducing the general headcount of an organization, but refers instead to the removal of key individuals who are no longer a good fit with the organization's vision and direction.

Winning the battle to stay relevant will always require

WINNING THE BATTLE TO STAY RELEVANT WILL ALWAYS REQUIRE HAVING THE RIGHT PEOPLE IN THE RIGHT ROLES AT THE RIGHT TIME

having the right people in the right roles at the right time – but it's as important to remove those who are the wrong person, in the wrong position, at the wrong time.

Former AOL CEO Tim Armstrong indicated this was a key factor in the departure of a number of senior executives from the company in early 2012. While some described it as a talent drain, Armstrong defended his strategy saying that all he was doing was "removing people from the company who are not performing."[342]

Although non-performance is a clear reason for removing someone from a position, sometimes the same step needs to be taken because the role has out-grown the individual. A person may have had the skills necessary to get things to where they are currently, but he or she lacks the capacity to take the organization to where it needs to go next.

In other instances, executives in certain positions may have grown complacent and closed-minded and as a result have become something of a hand-brake on new initiatives or innovation. In these instances, unless a willingness to change and grow can be fostered in those existing team members, there may be few options left than to prune away the old guard to make way for fresh blood. Circumstances notwithstanding, it is important when pruning individuals to do so in a way that leaves those involved with their dignity intact.

BEWARE OF OVER-PRUNING

Although we have talked at length about the importance of pruning an organization, it is also important to recognize that over-pruning can do an enormous amount of harm.

As any gardener knows, good judgment, common sense and a long-term view are necessary when pruning. Just as over-pruning a tree or shrub can retard growth and flowering, cut away too much too quickly in an

VISIONARY ORGANIZATIONS AND LEADERS ALWAYS EMERGE FROM CHALLENGING TIMES STRONGER AND MORE RELEVANT THAN EVER

organization and you can end up impeding growth and effectiveness.[343]

3. OVERHAULING THE CONTEXT

The third way to Re-Fresh a business or brand is to overhaul the context.

Sometimes all an organization needs to shift its mental state or cultural tone is a fresh context. This could mean revamping the company logo; overhauling product design and marketing; or renovating/relocating office spaces and facilities.

While such a step can seem like little more than window dressing, never underestimate the power of fresh context – after all, a change really can be as good as a holiday.

In the same way that fair weather doesn't produce good sailors, economic challenges and cyclical downturns can be a blessing in disguise as they force organizations to hit the Re-Fresh button and make tough decisions they may otherwise avoid when times are good.

Whether as a result of combatting bureaucracy, pruning dead wood, or streamlining operations, visionary organizations and leaders always emerge from challenging times stronger and more relevant than ever.

However, while smart leaders are willing and ready to hit the Re-Fresh button when adversity strikes, even smarter leaders take proactive steps to re-invigorate their organizations long before their hand is forced by external forces. This is something we will explore further in the pages ahead.

FOR REFLECTION:

Looking below at the various ways to Re-Fresh an organization or brand, which could be applicable or valuable in your context?

1. **Combatting the tyranny of tradition (eliminating outdated 'barnacles' that are slowing you down)**
2. **Pruning dead wood in the form of:**
   - **The Baggage of Bureaucracy (by either reducing size, streamlining operations or decentralizing power & control)**
   - **Non-strategic Products and Initiatives**
   - **Key Individuals**
3. **Overhauling the Context (remembering that a change is as good as a holiday)**

What steps can you take to start Re-Freshing your organization in the next week?

CHAPTER 13:

RELEVANCE STRATEGY 4 — RE-ENGINEER

In chapter 6 we talked about the woes of the Swiss watch making industry during the 1970s and 80s as competitors introduced new quartz movement timepieces. While many watchmakers in Switzerland at the time were decimated, this was far from the end of the story. In the mid-1980s, a man by the name of Nicolas Hayek took over a new amalgamation of faltering Swiss watchmakers under the banner 'SMH' – an entity which would later be renamed Swatch.

Hayek recognized immediately that if this new company was to succeed, it would need to adopt entirely new watch manufacturing approaches. The brief was clear: timepieces needed to be inexpensive enough to compete with Japanese rivals while retaining Swiss quality – all the while offering margins that made the new venture economically viable.

This challenge forced the watchmakers to Re-Engineer every element of a timepiece and its manufacture. Unable to fall back on traditional knowledge and assumptions, the Swiss watchmakers had to adopt an entirely new paradigm in order to produce watches made with far fewer components, significantly greater automation and in much larger quantities.

Hayek set out to position the product with a lifestyle message rather than simply selling time on the cheap. Thus Swatch was born – a company that would be known for creating functional and fashionable timepieces which were high quality, yet affordable. The rest is history. Fifty-five million Swatches were sold in five years, and in 2006 the company celebrated aggregate sales of over 333 million watches.[344]

DOCKSIDE REDESIGN

Looking to a very different industry to see how powerful Re-Engineering can be, consider the world of freight and logistics. In the early 1950s, the ocean-going freight industry was in rapid decline as airfreight became more popular. Adding to the industry's challenges, costs and delivery times of sea freight were increasing sharply due to congestion at docks. This led to significant pilferage as cargo and merchandise piled up at the waterfront waiting to be loaded.

The reason for this predicament was simply that for years the ocean freight industry had focused on building faster and more fuel-efficient ships while giving little thought to the bottle necks that arose when the ships arrived at the destination port. The solution was to entirely Re-Engineer the process of loading and stowing freight stock so that these became separate activities. This new approach meant that stock could be pre-loaded away from the dock into containers which could then be transported to the dock only once the ship was ready to receive the cargo. The results of this process-innovation were dramatic: between 1955 and 1985, freighter traffic increased five-fold while costs decreased by 60% and turnaround time was cut by three-quarters.[345]

Taking a leaf out of the freight container industry's book, Walmart powerfully re-engineered their own supply chain many years ago – a step that was instrumental in taking them from $44 million to $44 billion in revenue over a 20-year period. Prior to their re-engineering efforts, Walmart like all retailers took delivery from suppliers, stored the inventory in a warehouse, and then held it in stock until stores needed the goods. Dissatisfied with the lack of efficiency in this approach, Walmart invented a concept called cross-docking whereby products on trucks from suppliers were loaded directly onto trucks heading for stores, thereby completely eliminating the expense of storing and managing inventory. The cost savings from the new approach were passed on to Walmarts consumers garnering both their gratitude and loyalty.[346]

Re-Engineering internal processes is critically important for those organizations or brands seeking to stay competitive and efficient as times change.

In my consulting work with clients, there is a simple four-step Re-Engineering exercise I work through which has proven to be incredibly effective. As in previous chapters, I encourage you to take this opportunity to apply it in your own context.

STEP 1: DE-CONSTRUCT

The first step in Re-Engineering is itemizing every element of a particular organizational activity. This could be a process for manufacturing, inventory, customer service, quality control or any other feature of an entity's operations.

This may sound simple enough, but can actually be quite difficult to do. One of the key reasons for this is that so much in business and life is done on autopilot as we repeat day-to-day habits without giving them any thought. This becomes more prevalent the longer we have been doing something - known as 'unconscious competence' in the world of psychology. Due to this tendency, the first step of identifying *what we do* and *how we do things* is critically important.

> **SO MUCH IN BUSINESS AND LIFE IS DONE ON AUTOPILOT AS WE REPEAT DAY-TO-DAY HABITS WITHOUT GIVING THEM ANY THOUGHT.**

In a practical sense, the best way to de-construct a process is to chronologically list all the components or steps involved – including even the most mundane and overlooked elements. This can be quite a revealing experience. Typically clients express shock when they realize just how irrational and inefficient some of the things they do every day are.

One company I worked with found this part of the exercise especially enlightening. As we de-constructed the business's product ordering process, the exercise revealed an unconscious habit had formed over the years whereby orders were expected to be placed with head office every week by close of business on a Thursday. When the company's leaders became conscious of this organizational norm, the natural question was 'why.' Interestingly, nobody had any idea why orders had to be placed that day – it was just something that had 'always been done that way'.

As discussion continued, the general consensus in the group, including amongst head office staff, was that this habit served no purpose and, furthermore, it was constricting, disruptive and frustrating to many within the organization. Without doubt, this revelation would not have come about had the group not de-constructed their processes and become aware of the unconscious things they were already doing.

STEP 2: EVALUATE

The next step in Re-Engineering is to evaluate each of the process-elements itemized in step one. In evaluating each individual element, I challenge clients to ask three questions:

1. IS IT EFFECTIVE?

This question is about determining how helpful each activity is in achieving the process' overall outcome. Put simply, if the process has to do with sales, the question to be applied for each activity step is to ask 'how

> **THERE IS NOTHING QUITE SO USELESS AS DOING WITH GREAT EFFICIENCY WHAT SHOULD NOT BE DONE AT ALL.**

effectively does this help us to make more sales?' It is not only revealing to ruthlessly evaluate the various steps and activities performed in a business or organization, it is also sensible. As Peter Drucker once said, "There is nothing quite so useless as doing with great efficiency what should not be done at all."[347]

I encourage clients when they are doing this to look at the de-construction list from step one and *give each process step a rating of between 1 and 5* where 1 is 'highly ineffective' and 5 is 'highly effective'.

2. IS IT NECESSARY?

The second question to ask of each activity itemized in the de-construction list is whether it is *necessary* in order to achieve the desired outcome of the process.

This question tends to be quite valuable, as one U.K.-based print company I came across discovered. After going through and itemizing out all the various elements of their systems and processes and asking the 'is it necessary' question, they discovered that from the point when a new customer enters a store to when their print job is completed, company staff would write out the customer's name and address by hand more than 30 times. Realizing the degree of duplication and wasted time this represented, the company quickly set about changing their processes.

Looking through de-construction list from step one, **place a question mark** next to those process steps that you feel may be unnecessary.

3. IS IT ALIGNED?

This third question to ask of each process element goes back to the theme we discussed in chapter 10. It is important to make sure that each activity is in alignment with the organization's values and DNA. After all, if individuals are being required to take steps or perform actions on a daily basis that

IF INDIVIDUALS ARE BEING REQUIRED TO PERFORM ACTIONS ON A DAILY BASIS THAT ARE INCONSISTENT WITH THE COMPANY'S CORE VALUES, SOMETHING NEEDS TO CHANGE.

are inconsistent with the company's core values, something needs to change.

Former IBM chief executive Thomas J. Watson Jnr. described the importance of consistency and alignment in his 1963 booklet entitled *A business and its beliefs:* "I firmly believe that any organization, in order to survive and achieve success, must have a sound set of beliefs on which it premises all its policies and actions. Beliefs must always come before policies, practices, and goals. The latter must always be altered if they are seen to violate fundamental beliefs."[348]

Beyond safeguarding long-term success, one of the reasons alignment matters so much is that nothing will damage a sense of morale and cohesion as quickly as when an organization claims to value something, but then expects its employees to take actions that contradict those stated values. While this hypocrisy may not be deliberate, it is no less damaging.

So, if there are process elements from your de-construction list that are inconsistent with your brand or organization's core DNA, simply *place a thin red line through them*.

SIZE DOESN'T MATTER

While this second step of evaluating process elements can be time consuming, it is vitally important regardless of the organization's size. A special warning for small organizations: beware of relying on 'gut feel' alone when evaluating processes.[349] A systematized approach like the one above is valuable because it removes subjectivity and personal biases. For instance, big-picture people will naturally devalue and even disdain administrative functions even though these are vitally important.

In larger organizations, Re-Engineering on a regular basis is especially critical. No entity is too big to do this.

Take Quicken Loans as a case in point. Facing industry-wide turmoil in 2007, Quicken founder Dan Gilbert realized the need to Re-Engineer how the company operated. Gilbert and his team conducted a thorough investigation of the entire organization, looking under every rock and challenging every assumption. Bearing in mind that Quicken was already a massive operation and complex business, this was no mean feat.

Over the space of 12-18 months, Gilbert and his leadership team completely redesigned Quicken Loans from top to bottom making the company significantly more streamlined, efficient and customer-focused. By the end of the process, Quicken was light years ahead of its competition without having significantly innovated or changed the company's product offering at all.[350]

The truth is that no organization is too big to Re-Engineer. Consider the fact that the second Vatican council in the early 1960s was essentially a Re-

Engineering of the habits, practices and processes in the Catholic Church. If an organization with more than a billion members worldwide can Re-Engineer how it does things, no organization can claim they are too big to do so!

STEP 3: INNOVATE

Now that you are clear on the various elements of a particular process and have evaluated them individually, the next step is to consider improved ways of doing things.

The journey of embarking on innovation, however, is often easier said than done. Microsoft's *Culturing Success* report released in March 2015 found that 67% of companies lack the internal culture required to drive innovation.[351] The reality is that while we all recognize the need to innovate, often we lack the skills to do so.

To determine which process elements may need to be refashioned, start with those that have an effectiveness rating of 2 or lower; a question mark next to them; or a red line drawn through them, and consider the questions below:

- **Innovation question 1: What would be a better/faster/cheaper/ more efficient approach?**

Consider the example of one bank executive who had grown frustrated by his company's long-winded meetings. People would sit back in soft chairs in no hurry to complete the meeting's agenda and get back to work. In an effort to make the meetings more efficient, the executive took the radical step of removing all chairs from the boardroom for three months. The result? Meetings suddenly took half as long![352]

In a similar way, Queen Victoria famously insisted on Privy Council members standing during royal briefings – simply because council members had a tendency, once seated, to take up more of her time than she could bear. Once the standing-only rule was introduced in the early 1860s, meetings immediately got shorter and more to the point.

Aircraft manufacturer Boeing recently sought to Re-Engineer its production processes after a string of delays and costly overruns. Their strategy has been to take greater control of their supply chain by buying up suppliers and bringing production work back in-house. This is a dramatic reversal of their outsourcing strategy in the early 1990s[353] but is a step that will save the company $1.6 billion over the space of 2 years.[354]

Colleges and universities are also re-thinking the way they do things by adopting new formats for courses and degrees. As tuition costs rise and time pressures on students become greater, some colleges such as Wesleyan University in Middletown, Connecticut, have cut the number of years it takes to complete a degree. By adopting a 12-month academic calendar rather than shutting down for the summer, students are able to complete a degree in three years rather than the customary four. This change will put colleges more in step with current needs. After all, the traditional school calendar was designed around the agricultural cycles of 19th century communities.[355]

- **Innovation question 2: What are our competitors doing?**

Naturally every organization must run its own race and be true to its own DNA. However, that doesn't mean you can't take inspiration from those in the same marketplace or industry – think of it as benchmarking rather than plagiarism!

Apple used this questioning technique when designing its first iPhone. In 2006, Apple design chief Jonathon Ive asked one of his designers a defining question: "If Sony were to make an iPhone, what would it look like?" The designer came back with a skinny black phone that looks remarkably like today's iPhone except that it had volume buttons on the front rather than on the side.[356]

- **Innovation question 3: How have things been done in the past?**

This third innovation question may seem surprising – after all, we are so conditioned to believe that innovation means doing something new. However,

WHILE SOME OF THE BEST INNOVATIONS MAY BE FRESH, THEY ARE NOT NECESSARILY ENTIRELY ORIGINAL.

while some of the best innovations may be fresh,

they are not necessarily entirely original.

By looking back at what people have done in previous eras, often we can learn valuable lessons that don't involve reinventing the wheel. I discovered the value of this when on the board of an industry association a number of years ago. At one particular board meeting, we were brainstorming ideas for improving member events. Stuck for inspiration, one board member suggested we make a list of 20 things that the organization had done in the past. The list revealed a number of valuable activities had fallen by the wayside over the years. We set about reviving them and, funnily enough, these activities were among the best initiatives we put in place that year. Simply because these ideas were not *new* didn't prevent them from being innovative or effective.

BEWARE THE 3 INNOVATION TRAPS

The theme of innovation is something we will explore on in much greater detail in the next chapter. Before we move on however, there are three common mistakes that leaders make when innovating activities or processes in an organization:

INNOVATION TRAP 1: MISDIAGNOSIS

Rather than simply accepting inefficiencies at face value, leaders must take active steps to look beyond symptoms and diagnose the underlying causes. One simple and effective enquiry technique is the 5-why questioning process. In case you are unfamiliar with this approach, it is a process of asking 'why' at least 5 times when a problem arises in an effort to reveal its root cause.

In 2004, Amazon's Jeff Bezos used the 5-why technique in response to a safety incident where an employee working at one of the company's fulfillment centers had injured his thumb. The process that unfolded went something like this:

| **Question 1:** | *Why did the employee damage his thumb?* |
| **Answer:** | *Because his thumb got caught in a conveyor.* |

| **Question 2:** | *Why did his thumb get caught in the conveyor?* |
| **Answer:** | *Because he was chasing his bag which was running on a conveyor.* |

| **Question 3:** | *Why was his bag on the conveyor and why was he chasing it?* |
| **Answer:** | *Because he placed his bag on the conveyor, and then the conveyor was turned on to his surprise.* |

| **Question 4:** | *Why had he put his bag on the conveyor in the first place?* |
| **Answer:** | *Because he used the conveyor as a table.* |

| **Question 5:** | *Why did he use the conveyor as a table for his bag?* |
| **Answer:** | *Because there wasn't any place near his workstation to put a bag or other personal items.* |

As a result of this line of enquiry, Amazon's management team realized that fulfillment center staff had nowhere to store their personal belongings. Once they rectified this, the safety issue was resolved. Had Bezos not engaged in the 5-why process, it is quite possible he may have dealt with symptoms of the problem rather than its cause.[357]

INNOVATION TRAP 2: SUPERFICIALITY

When changing the way things are done, it is important to do more than simply rebadge the current practice without truly altering it. I recently came across a metaphor that described superficial innovations as 'paving the cattle track'.

To unpack the metaphor, cattle have a natural propensity to form a well-worn track over time. As settlers and developers move in to build roads and infrastructure, they tend to unthinkingly pave over the track cleared by the cattle without giving any thought to whether it is a sensible or appropriate route for vehicles to take. This short-sighted and superficial solution then leads to problems later on.

When applying this principle to innovation, it is important to not simply tweak old ways of doing things when a more fundamental re-think is required. To put it differently, avoid the trap of simply

AVOID THE TRAP OF SIMPLY FINDING MORE EFFECTIVE WAYS TO DO INEFFICIENT THINGS.

finding more effective ways to do inefficient things.

INNOVATION TRAP 3: INCONGRUENCE

Before putting in place any change or process innovation, ensure that the new activity is again aligned with your core DNA. Past CEO of Southwest Airlines Herb Kelleher knew the critical importance of this when he gave an employee a famous piece of advice:

"I can teach you the secret to running this airline in 30 seconds. This is it: we are THE low-fare airline. Once you understand that, you can make any decision about this company's future as well as I can. Here's an example. Tracy from marketing comes into your office. She says that her surveys indicate that passengers might enjoy a light entrée on the Houston to Las Vegas flight. All we offer is peanuts, and she thinks a nice chicken Caesar salad would be popular. My response would be 'Will adding that chicken Caesar salad make us THE low-cost airline from Houston to Las Vegas? Because if it doesn't help us stay the unchallenged low-cost airline, we are not serving any damn chicken salad.'"[358]

In contrast to Kelleher's approach, during the early 1990s direct selling cosmetic giant Avon fell into the trap of innovating their business processes in ways that were incongruent with their core DNA. For years, Avon's primary focus had revolved around caring for, motivating and rewarding the company's sales force through prizes, incentives and public recognition of achievement at conferences.

When new CEO James E. Preston took the helm in 1992 however, he introduced direct marketing to consumers through catalogues – thus cutting out Avon's sales force in the process. In addition, the company cut

600 jobs, restructured commissions, and got rid of traditional incentives like birthday presents and anniversary pins. Unsurprisingly, this was perceived by Avon's sales force as evidence that the company didn't care about them – a significant departure from how things had worked in the past. The results were dramatic – Avon's pre-tax profits dropped 10% in the first quarter of 2003; 7% in the second quarter; 36% in the third quarter; and 29% in the fourth.[359]

Having worked extensively with some of the world's biggest companies in the direct sales industry, one of the big 'unaligned innovation' mistakes I am seeing direct sellers make at the moment relates to their adoption of new technologies.

By their very nature, direct selling companies are people businesses. Whether in a networking marketing or party plan model, companies such as Amway, Tupperware, Mary Kay, Arbonne, Usana and others are all based on relationships between associates, their 'downline team' of distributors, and their customers.

Naturally, the evolution of communication technologies like email, Facebook and Twitter has streamlined the administrative functions of direct sales companies. However, the mistake made by many of these companies is to go so far down the high-tech route that they lose sight of the high-touch nature of their industry. In a rush to stay on the cutting edge, these businesses have in some cases removed the people element all together with online virtual meetings, digital product presentations and Facebook teams.

While these moves may be exceptionally innovative, I believe a purely high-tech focus is incongruent with what makes the direct selling business work. The end result is often a lack of community, connection and commitment – all keys to building a successful direct sales empire.

STEP 4: RE-ASSEMBLE

The fourth and final step in Re-Engineering is to take all the process elements and re-assemble them. If you have effectively de-constructed, evaluated and innovated the various activities involved in a certain process, it should be significantly more efficient, competitive and relevant once you put it back together again than it was prior to the exercise.

Many great books deal with the themes of change execution and implementing innovation so we are not going to deal with these topics in any great depth here. Needless to say, however, execution is a critical part of Re-Engineering. Research indicates that as much as 70% of Re-Engineering efforts fail simply because of poor execution – something akin to dropping the ball just shy of the finish line.[360]

REAL-WORLD RE-ENGINEERING

There are numerous examples of companies and organizations who have realized great benefits from Re-Engineering what they do and how they do things on a daily basis.

Consider how the Italian carmaker Fiat came to the realization in 2009 that its production processes were in dire need of Re-Engineering. After some investigation, management discovered that while a Fiat plant in Italy required 22,000 workers, an equivalent manufacturing plant in Poland required just 6,100 workers to produce the same output. In response, Fiat embarked on a dramatic overhaul of its assembly lines in an effort to reduce waste. The changes introduced included a pegging of pay to performance and reducing unnecessary activities that took workers time, but added no value.

Although the changes were hard to make, one Fiat engineer argued that ignoring the inefficiencies would only lead to disaster down the track and that "sooner or later a collapse would occur" if things did not change.[361]

In a similar move, former General Motors Chief Executive Dan Ackerson embarked on an ambitious plan in mid-2012 to Re-Engineer GMs internal processes. His first step was to dismantle GMs four regional arms in an effort to eliminate duplication in the company's manufacturing, purchasing and marketing functions.[362] As evidence of the necessity of this move, GM's Chevrolet division alone had 70 separate contracts with ad agencies in 140 countries that were all signed off by different executives who rarely share resources or coordinate their brand messages.[363]

Despite the challenge this Re-Engineering presented, GM predicted it would save the company an estimated $2 billion in five years. Further still the changes put GM on level pegging with rival carmaker Ford who in November 2012 concluded a six-year widespread overhaul of their production processes aimed at reducing costs and increasing efficiency.[364]

Similarly, Harley-Davidson finalized a thorough Re-Engineering of its production processes in late 2012. Whereas the company's manufacturing activities were spread across over 40 buildings in the past, they have now been consolidated into one ultra-modern facility that makes extensive use of automation and robotic production.

These and other Re-Engineering efforts at Harley-Davidson were largely driven by former chief executive Keith Wandell who was appointed to the role in 2009 in the midst of a severe slump in the company's sales and revenue. As an outsider coming into the role, Wandell immediately identified that manufacturing processes were unsustainable and set about making changes. While these changes were challenging - Wandell referring to them as like "having open-heart surgery while running a marathon" - the Re-Engineering efforts were estimated to have reduced annual running costs at Harley by $275 million.[365]

CHANGE BEFORE YOU ARE FORCED

While we have talked a great deal in the last two chapters about change and innovation, it is important to acknowledge the fact that for many organizations and individuals these two concepts are ones that engender terror.

Leaders are often petrified of making significant changes to internal processes and systems in case these changes fail. In my experience, the vast majority of organizations and leaders don't change until they are forced to - they wait until a point of crisis and then desperately try to find a quick fix in an effort to catch up. On the contrary,

❙ IT IS WISE TO DIG A WELL BEFORE YOU NEED WATER.

embracing change when you are already out in front is the best way to ensure that you stay there.[366] Just as it is wise to dig a well before you need water, the ideal time to embark on change initiatives is before you are forced to.

Brand consultant Tony Camilletti goes as far as to suggest that the golden rule in business is to not "wait until something is broken to fix it."[367]

Pepsi is one brand that exemplifies this pro-active approach to change. In the mid-1990s, Pepsi's leadership took deliberate steps to tweak their brand and improve business processes even when riding high and achieving great success. Pepsi's then chairman Wayne Calloway said: "Some might argue that we should not tamper with our brands in either image or substance. But we don't agree. We know that in a fast-paced world, today's popular brand could be tomorrow's trivia question."

Pepsi applied this philosophy even while the company's Doritos range was the biggest-selling snack food, spending $50 million in 2005 to 'jazz up the brand.'[368] Not happy to rest on its laurels, Pepsi indicated its commitment to not just enjoy success and prominence but to ensure such success was enduring.

Although Re-Engineering an organization's internal systems and processes can be difficult, doing so is critical in order to stay viable and competitive. Speaking to this point, chief executive of electrical retailer GameStop, Paul Raines, said it well: "In order to survive, a company's *internal rate of change has to be greater than the external rate of change.*"[369]

IN ORDER TO SURVIVE, A COMPANY'S *INTERNAL* RATE OF CHANGE HAS TO BE GREATER THAN THE EXTERNAL RATE OF CHANGE.

Of each of the four Re-Engineering steps we have discussed in this chapter, I have found that the one clients struggle with the most is step three: *innovation*. It is one thing to be able to de-construct and evaluate how an organization has done things in the past. However, the real power of Re-Engineering lies in the ability to think of new ways to do old things. Bearing this in mind, in the next chapter we will explore the theme of innovation in greater depth, highlighting strategies for fostering and leveraging it within an organization.

CHAPTER 14:

RELEVANCE STRATEGY 5 — RE-FRAME

In the late 16th century, a medical student in the Italian city of Pisa observed a swinging chandelier with interest. Later, after scrutinizing a collection of chandeliers of all shapes and sizes arcing from left to right the student, one Galileo Galilei, concluded that whatever their form or size, chandeliers take roughly the same time to complete one arc.

Galileo's subsequent experiments led to theories that rocked the prevalent school of thought in Europe at the time, namely that the Earth was the centre of the universe and that the sun, stars and other planets revolved around it – a world view known as Geocentrism.

Six decades earlier, a mathematician and astronomer by the name of Copernicus had proposed a radical new theory that our planet and others revolved around the sun. This view had been seen as threatening to the scientific and religious assumptions of the day and led ultimately to a decree denouncing it as heresy. Despite this, Galileo staunchly defended Copernicus's views until he was placed under house arrest for his heretical stance in the early 1630s – where he remained until his death in 1642.

Although Galileo suffered greatly for his views, the ground-breaking discoveries he made in the fields of mathematics and astronomy laid the foundations for what would later become known as the Scientific Revolution. Today he is even referred to as the father of modern science.

GREAT MINDS THINK… UNALIKE

History is punctuated by great thinkers like Galileo who posed questions others were unwilling to ask - and who saw things that others failed to see. These great men and women were able to think beyond the paradigms of their times – and dramatically change the world as a result. Although conventional wisdom tells us that "great minds think alike," the reality is that many of the greatest minds have thought decidedly *unalike* their peers or the rest of society.

From the scientific and medical through to the organizational or commercial fields, history shows us that continually relying on established paradigms and practices can prevent mankind from taking giant leaps into the future.

Consider the way PayPal founder Elon Musk has disrupted the automotive and space exploration industries in recent years by approaching them with a powerfully new set of assumptions. In the case of Musk's company SpaceX, his radical approach to the design and functionality of rockets have resulted in successful space launches at a fraction of the cost that the bureaucracy-bound NASA could have achieved.[370]

More recently, Musk's automotive company Tesla Motors has turned the car sector on its head.[371] With its revolutionary electronic vehicles and unorthodox distribution model which bypasses traditional dealership channels, Tesla is beginning to undermine the very foundations upon which the automotive business is built.[372] With such a powerful ability to enter, disrupt and re-shape entire industries, it is little wonder Elon Musk was named *Wall Street Journal Magazine's* 2011 Innovator of the Year.

As evidenced in the examples above, the secret to true innovation and creativity is to Re-Frame the realities we see – to actively look to see things from different perspectives or points of view. As

WHEN YOU CHANGE THE WAY YOU LOOK AT THINGS, THE THINGS YOU LOOK AT CHANGE

Dr. Wayne Dyer put it, "When you change the way you look at things, the things you look at change."

Below are five simple but powerful ways organizations and brands can foster innovation by actively Re-Framing:

1. LEVERAGE FRESH EYES

Old information looked at through new perspectives makes new information, said futurist Alvin Toffler, and he's right. Quite simply, leveraging the insights of those who have a fresh perspective is a powerful way **| OLD INFORMATION LOOKED AT THROUGH NEW PERSPECTIVES MAKES NEW INFORMATION** of imagining new opportunities and solutions that may not otherwise have been apparent.

Consider the creative power of fresh eyes:

* In IKEA's early days, a marketing manager was struggling to fit furniture back into a truck at the end of a catalogue photo shoot. Watching as one attempt after another met with failure or frustration, the photographer suggested removing the offending table's legs – a simple but genius idea. Following on from this suggestion, it occurred to IKEA's leadership that if all their furniture could be shipped and sold disassembled that they could save significantly on freight costs.

  This one suggestion from a fresh eyes perspective became the foundation of IKEA's enormously successful flat-pack business model.[373] As one who has assembled my fair share of IKEA furniture, I often wonder how many relationship breakdowns that one photographer has been indirectly responsible for in the years since!

* Having grown up in Kabul, Afghanistan, Massoud Hassani was more than familiar with the scourge of land mines. However, his formative years also offered him a unique perspective that spawned a remarkably innovative way to deal with minefield's dotted around the worlds trouble spots. Without the benefit of advanced studies in

weaponry and disarmament, Hassani's brilliant idea came from an observation of nature – the behavior of a tumbleweed to be exact. Noticing how tumbleweeds would blow freely in the wind rolling gently along the ground, Hassani came up with the design for an artificial tumbleweed made up of 200 bamboo rods and plastic feet. Heavy enough to trigger mines, light enough to be blown by the wind, and flexible enough to withstand multiple blasts per unit, Hassani's ingenious invention became known as a *Mine Kafon* ('mine exploder' in his native language) and has saved countless lives around the world.[374]

• In a similar display of naïve brilliance, take the case of a 14year-old Pittsburgh student by the name of Suvir Mirchandani. Noticing how many printed handouts he was receiving in middle school, the environmentally and economically sensitive Suvir began to wonder if there was a way to minimize the amount of ink being used by his school – especially considering ink is two times more expensive than French perfume by volume.

Collecting random samples of teachers' handouts, Suvir concentrated on the most commonly used characters (e, t, a, o and r). First, he charted how often each character was used in four different typefaces: Garamond, Times New Roman, Century Gothic and Comic Sans. Then he measured how much ink was used for each letter.

Next he enlarged the letters, printed them and cut them out on cardstock paper to weigh them to verify his findings. He did three trials for each letter, graphing the ink usage for each font. No-one could question this 14-year-old's attention to detail!

From this analysis, Suvir figured out that by using Garamond with its thinner strokes, his school district could reduce its ink consumption by 24%, and in turn save as much as $21,000 annually.

Taking his findings one step further, Suvir calculated that if the U.S. federal government used Garamond exclusively, it could save nearly $136 million per year.[375]

Whether it is a new staff member who has just joined the team or a young person who hasn't yet 'learned their place', the beauty of those with fresh eyes is that they have no trouble thinking outside the box because they don't yet know what the box even looks like. More importantly people with fresh eyes are blissfully unaware of how things have

> **SOLUTIONS OFTEN LIE IN UNEXPECTED PLACES WHERE ONLY BEGINNERS MIGHT BOTHER TO LOOK.**

always been done. As *The Forgotten Plague* author Frank Ryan suggests, "Solutions often lie in unexpected places where only beginners might bother to look."[376]

Attesting to this fact, a Harvard Business Review article from November 2014 argued the best ideas often come from outside your industry. Three European economics professors conducted a study of roofers, carpenters, and inline skaters to collect ideas on how to improve the comfort of their respective safety gear. What's fascinating is each group came up with better ideas to improve gear from the other two fields than its own.[377]

THE GENIUS OF THE UNDERGRADUATE

Chairman of software giant SAP, Hasso Plattner, recognized the value of fresh eyes - particularly from younger generations. In the late 2000s Plattner embarked on an unorthodox plan to achieve a competitive edge over SAPs main rival, Oracle.

Rather than using a traditional research and development department staffed by experienced engineers, Plattner recruited a bunch of university students from his home city just outside Berlin who, due to their studies, were in the habit of asking questions and deconstructing the status quo. In no time, the students developed a revolutionary new cloud-based framework called HANA which allows corporations to access and analyze their business data on hand-held devices at lightning speed.

SAP piloted HANA in 2010 with clients Proctor & Gamble and Nestle before releasing the software to the general market. By 2011, the response had been overwhelmingly positive, and sales were well ahead of projections.[378]

Some industry experts even consider HANA to be the biggest innovation in the business software industry in years![379] And yet, if not for the fresh eyes of 20-year-old undergraduates, HANA may never have been invented.

In a similar way, McDonalds' corporate leadership has recognized the valuable perspective of younger generations – particularly within its franchise network. As ownership of McDonald's franchises has passed from older family members to younger in recent years, a raft of changes and new approaches have been ushered in. Having grown up with fast food criticism in the form of the 'Super Size Me' documentaries, younger franchise owners are taking deliberate steps to address the negative public perception of fast food.

In addition to proposing healthier menu items ranging from gluten-free hamburger buns to organic produce, these young franchisees are making a concerted push for greater corporate social responsibility through in-store recycling. They are also making restaurants tech savvy with Wi-Fi connection and store-specific Facebook pages.

On top of these changes, younger franchisees have taken steps to Re-Engineer processes and procedures through innovations like picture-based ordering systems, keeping stores open later, and making credit card facilities non-negotiable.[380]

In my experience of working with clients across a wide range of industries, SAP and McDonald's are far from alone in realizing the benefits of

YOUNG PEOPLE TEND TO HAVE A BOLDNESS, OPTIMISM AND 'NAIVETY' WHICH LEADS THEM TO ASK THE MOST IMPORTANT RE-FRAMING QUESTION OF ALL — *WHY.*

leveraging a younger generation's perspective. Young people tend to have a boldness, optimism and 'naivety' which leads them to ask the most important Re-Framing question of all - *why.*

Sometimes referred to as 'Generation Why', this group will come into an organization, see all the established processes, systems and routines and simply ask *"Why do you do things that way?"*

This is a powerful question because it forces others to stop and ask themselves the same question. Like the monkey experiment described in chapter 7, organizational cultures so often form around habits that are perpetuated long after the reasons for those ways of doing things have been forgotten. Outsiders, unaware of historical rules or expectations, simply ask a question that we should always be asking ourselves in an effort to stay fresh and relevant: *why*.

Organizational theorist James G. March argues that in order for knowledge to develop and grow, there must be a constant influx of the naive and the ignorant. In his book *The Wisdom of Crowds,* James Surowiecki agrees. "Homogenous groups are great at doing what they do well, but they become progressively less able to investigate alternatives,' he points out. 'Bringing new members into the organization, even if they are less experienced and less capable, actually makes a group smarter."[381]

Unfortunately, encouraging fresh perspectives from newcomers is often low on the agenda for many organizations and leaders. More often than not, when a new person comes into the organization, they tend to be implicitly told to sit in the corner and learn 'how things are done around here.' Then only once they know how things are done can they offer any input or suggestions. In essence, new entrants are given their own custom-fitting set of mental blinkers through a process called induction (more appropriately known as indoctrination) and by the time their input or suggestions are sought they no longer have fresh eyes at all.

I strongly urge you to make the most of the people in your organization or business who have fresh eyes – either due to their age or lack of experience. Furthermore, consider *deliberately* bringing people into your organization who have experience in a different context.

This was what carmaker Kia did when it hired legendary auto designer, Peter Schreyer. Kia knew that having achieved great success and innovation at Audi and Volkswagen, Schreyer would bring a fresh approach that would give Kia a competitive edge over its rivals - something it has done with great success.

STEP OUTSIDE OF YOURSELF

Here is a question: when did you last truly look at your organization from an outsider's perspective?

I have often put this challenge to my clients in the retail sector, urging them to walk into one of their stores, or one of their competitor's stores, and make a note of the experience.

WHEN DID YOU LAST TRULY LOOK AT YOUR ORGANIZATION FROM AN OUTSIDER'S PERSPECTIVE?

What does it look, smell, sound like? What doesn't make sense? What seems strange? What questions would you have, but may be too afraid to ask?

Taking this one step further, how could you actively look to leverage the fresh eyes of those outside your organization – such as customers or members of the public? How many of the things that you take for granted as obvious or self-explanatory may seem baffling or alienating to those who don't know your business as well as you do? Actively encourage the input, questions and suggestions of those with fresh perspectives and you may be amazed at the creativity and innovation that comes as a result.

Ford and General Motors have recognized the value of leveraging their customer's ideas and creativity. In early 2013, both automotive giants announced programs encouraging customers to develop apps for their cars. To facilitate this, Ford has even opened up access to a specialized application connection software called AppLink.[382]

While younger generations, new entrants and outsiders can offer powerfully different perspectives, there are other ways to leverage the value of fresh eyes in an organization.

Here are just three:

A. CROSS-POLLINATION

In 2008, Proctor & Gamble and Google embarked on an employee swap program in an effort to spur creativity. Although both companies are known for their innovation, each believed they could learn from the perspectives of the other – especially considering the very different industries they operated in.

Just over 20 human resource and marketing employees from each company spent weeks observing how the other did business – and made suggestions that seemed obvious from their 'outside' perspective.

As one example of how valuable this proved to be, Google observed P&G planning the promotional launch for its new *Pampers* line. The Google team members noticed that P&G hadn't thought to invite any 'mommy bloggers' to attend the product launch even though these bloggers can attract up to six million visitors to their websites. Google's suggestion of this one key element which P&G had overlooked ended up being a critical factor in the product launch's success.[383]

While cross-pollination can occur between vastly different organizations, it can be equally effective with people within the same organization, but from different departments or areas of specialty.

A ski resort operator in Colorado, Keystone, used internal cross-pollination in an effort to bring about innovation. Keystone initiated a program they called 'novice consulting' where individual staff members would spend a number of hours once a week in an area of the business about which they had no knowledge. They were encouraged not to go in with an intention of providing solutions but rather to ask as many 'dumb questions' as possible about the things they didn't understand such as peculiar work routines or operational practices that didn't seem to serve a purpose. Within six weeks, the results were staggering. The asking of hundreds of naïve questions resulted in dozens of new ideas and innovations. One idea alone involving the process of selling tickets has reportedly saved the company tens of thousands of dollars annually.[384]

B. COMPETITION

A second way of harnessing the value of those with fresh perspectives is by using competition to incentivize creativity.

Netflix used this approach in October 2006 when it offered a $1 million prize to anyone who could improve the company's in-house algorithm, Cinematch. Within 12 months, over 2,500 teams from 161 countries had entered the competition and the net result was a significant reduction in

Cinematch's recommendation errors. The corresponding jump in customer satisfaction made the prize money investment more than worthwhile.[385]

In a slightly different way, software provider Citrix used competition to drive 'fresh eyes' innovation. The company recognized that cloud computing and the ever-blurring line between personal and business computing threatened the viability of its established product offering. In an effort to address this threat, Citrix established a startup accelerator in 2011 whereby it invested $250,000 in emerging companies building technology that Citrix thought might offer a strategic advantage in the short- to medium-term. Naturally, each of the companies accepted into the accelerator program realized the competitive stakes were high and the payoff potentially huge if an innovation could be presented that stood apart from the pack.[386]

Along similar lines, cloud computing giant EMC leverages the creative power of competition each year with their annual Innovation Roadmap contest in which they challenge employees to compete in discovering innovative solutions to the company's most pressing business problems.

C. COLLABORATION

This third way to leverage fresh eyes is by using a collaborative or 'open market' approach and here again, Proctor and Gamble offers a good example.

When A.G. Lafley became CEO of the company in 2000, he increased the projected ratio of product innovation from external sources from 10% to 50% and by 2006, had all but realized his goal. Some of the products that were developed using ideas from external sources included Swiffer, WetJet, Olay Daily Facials, Crest Whitestrip and Max Factor *Lipfinity.*

One way P&G has achieved such success with external innovation is by using 3rd party companies like NineSigma and InnoCentive which connect large companies like P&G with a network of designers and inventors.[387] Today P&G is harnessing further external input through an ingenious platform called YouEncore.com which solicits knowledge from retirees.[388]

Reflecting on the power of collaboration and the creativity it can bring about, Frans Johansson coined the term 'Medici Effect' which describes innovation that comes about when people from different backgrounds share insights and ideas. This Medici effect has been credited for both the Islamic and Italian Renaissances and is evidenced today in events like the Aspen Ideas Festival, the *South by Southwest* conference held each year in Austin, Texas, and the many TED events held and broadcast around the world. Each of these is underpinned by the purpose of bringing together intentionally diverse groups of people to share, learn and release a flood of innovation.[389]

While there are numerous ways to leverage the value of fresh eyes, the important thing is that the ideas and input of those 'outside the box' are always encouraged and heard. This is perhaps the best and only way to generate truly revolutionary ideas and get perspectives that those too invested in or close to the status quo will never see.

As Marshall McLuhan once famously said, "I

> **I DON'T KNOW WHO DISCOVERED WATER, BUT I'M PRETTY SURE IT WASN'T A FISH.**

don't know who discovered water, but I'm pretty sure it wasn't a fish."[390]

2. FOSTER A CULTURE OF CURIOSITY

This second strategy for Re-Framing centers on creating an organizational culture where creativity is not just permitted but rewarded.

In the early 1990s Delta airlines, like many major U.S. carriers, was looking to trim costs. Announcing its challenge to employees, management encouraged its workforce to look out for ideas to reduce overheads without affecting the customer experience. One flight steward noticed that whenever he cleared trays at the end of the meal service, the 'lettuce liner' which formed the base of salads and sandwiches served in the economy cabin were typically left untouched. The employee asked his supervisor a simple question. "What is the point of serving lettuce if no-one ever eats it?" His supervisor thought it was a good question and passed it up the chain of command until the question reached someone with sufficient authority.

After some deliberation, Delta's management decided to trial removing the lettuce from meal trays to see what happened. Months passed with customers neither noticing nor missing the lettuce. Eventually, Delta took the step of removing lettuce liners from meal services company-wide and in the first year saved a staggering $1.4 million as a result of the one change![391]

Questioning the status quo is one of the most powerful sources of innovation. In his book *The Practice of Management*, Peter Drucker observed that the most important and difficult job is never to find

THERE ARE FEW THINGS AS USELESS — IF NOT DANGEROUS — AS THE RIGHT ANSWER TO THE WRONG QUESTION

the right answers; it is to find the right questions. "There are few things as useless – if not dangerous – as the right answer to the wrong question," he noted.[392]

QUESTIONS ARE THE ANSWER

Tech giant Intel certainly found that asking the right question was of critical importance. By the early 1980s, it was becoming increasingly clear that Intel's highly successful DRAM memory-chip business was doomed. Confronting this stark reality, the company's then chief operating officer asked his fellow executives a powerful question: *If we were fired right now and new management came in, what would they do?*

After some reflection, the answer was clear – get out of the DRAM business. And that's exactly what Intel did. They shifted their focus to the business of micro processing and within a few years dominated this new emerging technology.[393]

The power of questions was also evidenced in a novel new approach adopted at automaker McLaren. The company's chief designer Frank Stephenson one day noticed that military aircraft weren't fitted with windscreen wipers. Intrigued, Stephenson did some investigating as to how this was practical and what he discovered surprised him.

He was informed that the secret was not a coating on the surface but in fact high-frequency sound waves similar to those used by dentists to remove plaque from patients' teeth.

Impressed by the simplicity and genius of this technology, Stephenson got to work incorporating it into McLaren's P1 Hypercar. [394]

Asking strategic questions is a powerful tool indeed. However, rather than relying only on those with fresh eyes to ask it, smart leaders can take deliberate steps to foster a culture of curiosity throughout their entire organizations.

Consider the resort operator who could not figure out why his state-of-the-art cafeteria was underperforming. After research, it appeared that food quality, location and price were not to blame. Management did everything they could to address the situation – new menus, new color schemes, new managers – but nothing made a quantifiable difference. One day a puzzled member of the resort's management team decided to eat at the cafeteria in an effort to get to the bottom of the issue. As he waited in line, the manager noticed a customer ahead of him trying to squeeze a dish of ice cream onto his tray and knocking off his sandwich in the process. Suspecting that the small size of the trays could be part of the issue, the manager wondered, "What if we simply gave customers larger meal trays?"

Remarkably, this suggestion was met with significant resistance. The tray, as it happened, was precisely the right size for the cafeteria's dishwasher and had been purchased in bulk at a significantly discounted price. But after some persuasion, the company decided to experiment with larger tray sizes and the results were astounding. Within 90 days, the per-person meal spend had increased by $1.50 which equated to an additional $500,000 in annual revenue.[395]

As in the case of the resort cafeteria, a simple way of

A SIMPLE WAY OF FOSTERING A CULTURE OF CURIOSITY IS TO ENCOURAGE LEADERS AND INDIVIDUALS TO ASK 'WHAT IF' QUESTIONS

fostering a culture of curiosity is to encourage leaders and individuals to ask 'what if' questions when an impasse is reached. Consider how powerful 'what if' questions can be:

- Rolls-Royce completely transformed itself from a loss-making British manufacturer to the second biggest provider of large jet engines in the world by asking the question "What if airlines didn't buy engines for their airplanes but instead paid for every hour an engine runs?"[396]

- Car-maker Daimler developed their enormously successful *car2go* car-sharing business as a result of the question "What if manufacturers didn't sell cars but provided mobility services?"[397]

As a mentor of mine once told me, the purpose of a good question is never to get an answer – it is to prompt reflection and open the mind to new ideas. As such, fostering a culture of curiosity is a powerful strategy for driving creativity and innovation in organizations and brands.

3. ACTIVELY ENCOURAGE DISSENSION

Despite its more notable resistance to innovative thinkers as seen in the case of Gallileo, throughout its history the Catholic Church has in other ways championed the cause of critical thinking and analysis. Consider, for instance, the practice developed many centuries ago in the Catholic Church known as 'the devil's advocate'.

Designed as an error-correcting and bias-avoiding technique, the original devil's advocates were key individuals appointed as part of the vetting process for sainthood. Before someone was canonized a saint, the devil's advocate was tasked with adopting a skeptical view - critically assessing all evidence compiled during the investigation of the nominated saint and then laying out every reasonable argument for why canonization should be denied.[398]

While the formal practice of nominating a devil's advocate is well over 400 years old, many work groups, teams and committees would do well to adopt some of the principles that underpin this approach.

IT'S IMPORTANT TO DISAGREE

Peter Drucker went as far as to say that good decisions are always a function of dissenting views being encouraged and heard. "The first rule in decision-making," he suggested, "is that one does not make a decision unless there is disagreement."[399]

Further still, it is important for organizations to be vigilant to what I call the *Galileo Effect*. This concept describes the tendency for individuals within a group to shy away from pointing out the elephants in a room – realities that are patently obvious and fundamentally true, but politically inconvenient.

Unlike Galileo, people in teams or organizations often choose to stay quiet rather than voice realities that may undermine or destabilize all that the organization 'knows to be true' and has based its confidence and identity on.

For organizations to Re-Frame and allow for new perspectives and ideas to emerge, dissension needs to be actively encouraged. Leaders must ensure that those who hold radically different views or bear confronting news are encouraged rather than ignored, shunned or persecuted.

> **FOR ORGANIZATIONS TO RE-FRAME AND ALLOW FOR NEW PERSPECTIVES AND IDEAS TO EMERGE, DISSENSION NEEDS TO BE ACTIVELY ENCOURAGED.**

Iconic animation studio Pixar has a novel way of ensuring this through the development of an internal group called the "Pixar Braintrust." The goal of this initiative is to create a diverse team of people tasked with candidly criticizing the company's current projects.

As co-founder of Pixar, Ed Catmull says, it's amazing what happens when you "put smart, passionate people in a room together, charge them with identifying and solving problems, and encourage them to be candid."[400]

Alfred Sloan, widely regarded as the man who built General Motors, once illustrated the importance of this when he said to a group of his leaders: "Gentlemen, I take it we are all in complete agreement on the decision?" When everyone around the table nodded, Sloan responded, "I propose then that we postpone further discussion on this matter until our next meeting to give ourselves time to develop disagreement."[401]

Naturally, for such an approach to work, a culture has to be created where junior members of staff feel safe and encouraged to 'speak truth to power.'[402]

4. INSTITUTIONALIZE INNOVATION

The United States constitution is a magnificent document. Although it is the fundamental framework on which the American nation was built, it is very much a living document and is as flexible as it is durable. Through its mechanism of amendments, the crafters of the U.S. Constitution have allowed for – and even encouraged – changes and additions to occur over time.[403]

Remaining open to new perspectives and approaches may be difficult to instill in an organization, but there are deliberate steps that leaders can take to institutionalize innovation in the same way that the crafters of the U.S. constitution did.

Below are three simple ways to embed innovation in an organization to ensure that it occurs:

A. EMBEDDING INNOVATION *STRUCTURALLY*

In early 2003, Quicken Loans founder Dan Gilbert realized the need to continually re-invent his business but also recognized the challenges presented in doing so. He knew that team members with direct line responsibility were busy delivering and couldn't be expected to reinvent at the same time – a challenge he likened to asking a pilot to rebuild the plane while flying it.

As a result, Gilbert launched what became known as the company's 'mousetrap team'. This business unit had no direct production responsibilities and was charged solely with 'building a better mousetrap'. They examined every process big or small and, in doing so, propelled the company to new levels of efficiency, growth and client satisfaction through better internal systems.[404]

Similarly, when Sarah Nolan took over as president of Amex Life, she recognized that the pace of change in the marketplace made it necessary not just to anticipate shifts in the industry but to shape them. Consequently she broke off a part of the company and formed a small entrepreneurial unit based off-site called the Pioneer Team. Nolan made it clear that the Pioneer Team's role was to envisage the future saying, "Don't investigate anything we do already. That's the past; assume it's wrong... and re-create this business from scratch."

Within 12 months Nolan's Pioneer Team had generated ideas which brought about a 40% reduction in operating expenses and significantly increased Amex Life's profitability.[405]

The creation of separate innovation-focused groups within organizations is not a new phenomenon. Sometimes known as 'skunk works', these breakaway groups derive their name from an independent unit of engineers created by the Lockheed Corporation in the 1950s who were set up to work in isolation in a circus tent pitched alongside a foul-smelling plastics factory.[406]

Other businesses have also initiated splinter groups to bring about reform over the years. Xerox set up the Palo Alto Research Center or (PARC)[407] and Amazon has developed a 'Web Lab' whose purpose it is to uncover ways to improve the Amazon customer experience.[408]

B. EMBEDDING INNOVATION *PROCEDURALLY*

In their book *The Innovator's DNA,* Dyer, Gregersen and Christensen highlight a number of successful examples of companies who set in place procedures in an effort to foster innovation:

- Proctor & Gamble employees have long been encouraged to spend 75% of their time working 'in the system' and the remaining 25% 'on the system'.[409]

- Geoff Bezos is legendary for insisting on the saving of an 'empty chair' at company meetings explaining that this chair represents the most important person in the room – Amazon's customer. This tangible reminder, according to Bezos, is the key to ensuring that his company remains driven by and focused on constantly improving the customer experience.[410]

- Adobe recently took the creative step of making 'innovation kits' available to any employee within the company. These kits are designed to empower individuals with everything they need to pursue a new idea they're passionate about. This makes the creative process accessible to all, with tangible exercises, suggestions, and checklists to help structure the thought process. The program was recently open-sourced so other companies can consider a similar approach without starting from scratch.[411]

C. EMBEDDING INNOVATION *CULTURALLY*

While tangible changes to procedures and structures can be an effective way of institutionalizing innovation, there are less explicit ways of achieving the same goal in an organization's culture.

In Walter Isaacson's biography of Steve Jobs, Jobs describes how it is often the culture of a mature organization that stymies innovation and ultimately leads to the entity's decline. As Jobs describes it, a business or organization typically starts off as an innovator but as it grows, the culture become so sales-driven that the focus is taken off innovation and this spells doom.[412]

Dyer, Gregersen and Christensen explain it another way. They describe how in the early days of any venture, discovery skills (such as exploration, innovation, creativity) are more highly valued than delivery, execution or management skills. However, as the company flourishes, this priority is reversed. Entrepreneurs are replaced by professional managers who have proven skills in delivering results but are not necessarily good at creating new ideas.[413]

Bearing this in mind, it is critically important that leaders take steps to foster and retain a culture of experimentation and innovation as their organizations grow. Amazon's Geoff Bezos again offers a good example of how this can be achieved. Recognizing that a culture of innovation begins at the hiring stage, Bezos routinely asks potential new employees "tell me something that you have invented." In doing this, Bezos measures the inventive pulse of potential employees and keeps innovation at the forefront of the organizational mind.

One of the keys to embedding innovation culturally in an organization is to deliberately de-stigmatize failure.

I am always amazed and even bewildered when I hear leaders tout that failure is 'not an option.' While I acknowledge the aspirational sentiment behind this statement, the reality is that failure must be an option, even a requirement, if an organization is going to be innovative. In fact, if you haven't failed significantly in the past 12-months, there's every chance you're just not taking enough swings.

Spanx founder Sara Blakely grew up with a keen awareness of the power of failure as her father would often ask, "What have you failed at this week?" Learning early on that the one thing worse than failing was not to try, Blakely developed the perseverance necessary to build the billion-dollar empire she has.[414]

In order to innovate, employees and team members must know that they have permission to fail. Otherwise, they will shirk responsibility when things do go wrong, hide the evidence, or worse still, never attempt anything daring in the first place.

History is full of examples of failures that laid the foundations for future success. Consider WD-40 - the world-famous cure for all things squeaky. While we all know the product's name, far fewer of us realize that it was a name earned through a series of failed trials – 39 to be precise. The name actually stands for 'Water Displacement, Fortieth Experiment'. It could just as easily have been WD-31 except that it took 40 attempts to fine the winning formula.[415]

The reality is that failures are rarely fatal and in fact they are a necessary part of the process of discovery.

I love the story of a young IBM employee shared by Andy Stanley in his fantastic book *Next Generation Leader*. As the story goes, the young employee had made a decision that many of his colleagues warned would be unwise. However, he was convinced that he knew best and went along with his plans. Unfortunately, it turned out that his colleagues' judgment had been right and the decision ended up costing the company $10 million. Needless to say the young man was immediately called to the office of IBM founder Tom Watson Sr. Upon entering Mr. Watson's office the nervous young man looked down and said, "Well I suppose you want my resignation." "You can't be serious!" Mr. Watson exclaimed, "We just spent 10 million dollars educating you! You're not going anywhere!"

What a refreshing attitude – and one that stands in stark contrast to many blame-obsessed organizational cultures today.

All this said, a willingness to take risks is not the same as reckless risk-taking. In their book *Great by Choice*, Jim Collins and Morten Hansen describe the difference between sensible and reckless risk taking using the analogy of a gun battle at sea. Only a foolish soldier, they said, would open fire with his one and only cannonball, thereby taking the chance of missing his target and possibly giving the enemy an advantage. Wily tacticians, on the other hand, will use a smaller amount of gun power firing bullets to calibrate their weapons so they can then use their one cannonball and achieve a direct hit.[416] Collins and Hansen argue that smart risk-taking is always proportionate, incremental and strategic.

5. EXPECT (AND LOOK FOR) THE UNEXPECTED

The fifth and final way that an organization can successfully and consistently Re-Frame is by remaining open to and even anticipating the unexpected.

Honda learned this vital lesson when expanding into the North American motorcycle market during the late 1950s. The company's initial efforts met with frustration and disappointment because its motorbikes were not appropriately designed for North American conditions. Honda's bikes proved ill-suited for cruising down highways thus springing oil leaks and wearing out clutches at an alarming rate.

One Saturday, the Honda executive in charge of the U.S. venture, Kihachiro Kawashima, decided to vent his frustrations by taking his motorbike off-road into the hills behind Los Angeles. Over time, he grew fond of letting off steam this way, but not without drawing attention to himself and his bike. Soon, increasing numbers of bystanders were asking how they could get hold of their own version of Kawashima's bike, the Supercub.

As orders for Honda's off-road bikes began to gradually build, the company's Japanese headquarters remained focused on selling on-road bikes in the U.S. market – despite a marked lack of success. Finally, as demand for dirt bikes became impossible to ignore, the Honda team woke up to the opportunity offered by this 'unexpected success' and started targeting their efforts in the U.S. towards the off-road dirt bike market to great triumph.[417]

NEVER UNDERESTIMATE SHEER LUCK

Some of the greatest business breakthroughs have come about by pure accident or sheer luck. The importance of these two factors in the process of innovation and creativity cannot be underestimated.

> SOME OF THE GREATEST BUSINESS BREAKTHROUGHS HAVE COME ABOUT BY PURE ACCIDENT OR SHEER LUCK.

The list of products and breakthroughs that came about by 'accident' is astounding: cornflakes, microwave ovens, Post-It notes, the Walkman, Teflon, Rogaine, Kitty Litter, Velcro, skateboards, to name a few.[418] Even the consumer snack, Craisens, only came about accidentally when someone at the Ocean Spray Corporation discovered one day that leftover cranberry skins actually tasted quite good.[419]

One of DuPont's many great discoveries is another example of a lucky mistake. One Friday evening in late 1928, a DuPont lab assistant left work for the day unaware that he had left a lab burner switched on. When the assistant returned to work the following week, the material he'd been testing the previous Friday had congealed and changed state due to the prolonged heat. This happy accident gave birth to a brand new product that would become known as Nylon.[420]

DuPont is far from alone in enjoying the fruits of luck and good fortune. The challenge for established businesses is to create systems which allow for the unexpected. In most businesses, unexpected successes usually go unnoticed because traditional reporting mechanisms aren't designed to detect them and feed them back to decision makers.

Such anomalies are 'outside the box' so if organizations and individuals are too busy measuring only what is inside the box, they may well miss opportunities that lie just beyond their frame of view.[421]

Former vice president of Monsanto, S. Allen Heininger, suggested that staying alert to the unexpected is a critical ingredient to business longevity

IF A BUSINESS IS TO SUCCEED IN THE LONG RUN, IT HAS NO OPTION BUT TO REMAIN "ALERT TO SERENDIPITY.

and survival. According to Heininger, if a business is to succeed in the long run, it has no option but to remain "alert to serendipity."[422]

Re-Framing is the key to creativity and innovation. Organizations and brands must be constantly open to new paradigms through which they can view and make sense of a changing world. [423] As Albert Einstein once famously said, "It is impossible to solve problems in life by adopting the same kind of thinking we had when we created them."

Being willing to adopt and embrace new perspectives is critically important if an organization is to evolve with the times. In the words of the futurist Alvin Toffler: "The illiterate of the 21st century will not be those who cannot read and write, but those who cannot learn, unlearn and relearn".

FOR REFLECTION:

In looking at the 5 ways that an organization or brand can Re-Frame their reality, which one stands out as the most applicable to you?

1. **Leverage Fresh Eyes through;**
    - **Seeking input from new entrants or outsiders**
    - **Cross pollination with different organizations or teams**
    - **Using competition for developing new ideas and approaches**
    - **Collaboration**
2. **Foster a Culture of Curiosity where 'what if' questions are encouraged**
3. **Actively Encourage Dissent**
4. **Institutionalize and Embed Innovation Structurally, Procedurally or Culturally**
5. **5. Expect (and look for) the Unexpected**

Reflecting on the above 5 Re-Framing strategies, what can you put in place in the coming week to take advantage of different perspectives and points of view?

CHAPTER 15:

RELEVANCE STRATEGY 6 — RE-POSITION

In the early 1930s, with the world in the grip of economic depression, a Danish widowed father of four had a vision. Despite the grim fiscal outlook, Ole Kirk Christiansen purchased a small woodwork shop in the town of Billand and launched a modest toy business with the name *Leg Godt* which is Danish for 'play well'.

A few years later, as the onset of World War II made the cost of timber skyrocket, Christiansen was forced to consider alternative raw materials for his growing toy empire. He stumbled upon a brand new invention called 'plastic' and in 1947 took the visionary step of purchasing a plastic injection molding machine. With this new technology, Christiansen created a collection of interlocking blocks that could fit together allowing children to create different shapes and forms. His iconic blocks grew in popularity and within a few short years *Lego*, as the company was now affectionately known, was the toy of choice for children worldwide.

From the outset, Lego proved to be an innovative and agile company, keeping its product offering fresh in order to remain popular with new generations – even as competition increased and imitators moved in.

In the mid-1950's, Christiansen's son and successor proposed a way of expanding Lego that involved play sets which allowed users to go beyond merely constructing simple shapes to create entire scenes and scenarios. This strategy cemented the company's reputation as an industry leader. Broadening their product offering even further, Lego released the *Lego Man* figurine in 1974 allowing children to not only build entire play scenes but bring them to life too.

Throughout the 1970s and 80s, Lego enjoyed prominence and popularity worldwide. However, this golden age came to an abrupt end in the mid-1990s when Lego began an 11-year loss-making stretch – with the company losing $435 million in just two years at their worst point. With the growing popularity of video games, new generations of kids were opting for an Atari rather than Lego blocks.

ADAPTING TO THE VIRTUAL REALM

By the late 1990s, it was clear that embracing the digital age was going to be critical for the ongoing success and survival of Lego. The question, of course, was how to do this? How could the Lego play experience be transferred to the virtual realm?

The first step in answer to this question was informed by the old adage, *if you can't beat them, join them.* Lego entered a series of licensing arrangements with well-known movie franchises such as Star Wars, Batman and Indiana Jones to create co-branded play sets and even video games.[424] Buoyed by the success of this new direction, Lego expanded their digital offering with the release of robotic Lego kits. In 2006 the product *Mindstorms NXT* was launched and broke all previous Lego sales records.

Recognizing that entering the digital age was not an 'either or' arrangement, Lego explored ways of using new technology to enhance the user's play experience with its traditional physical product. The release of a specially devised software program in the mid-2000s, *Lego Factory*, allowed users to customize and design their own Lego kits creating everything from the buildings to the cars, themes and characters, even the box in which the kit would be delivered. The program marked a pivotal point of transition for the company as customers went from being passive users to active participants.[425]

As Lego's digital toy market grew, behind the scenes the corporation was working on a product that would represent a daring new direction. Released in 2010, Lego's Massively Multiplayer Online Game *Lego Universe* was designed to tap into the two most fundamental child impulses which had driven so much of the company's success – building and role playing. *Lego Universe* allowed users anywhere in the world to play each other in a virtual environment. Lego also made a significant investment in ensuring that *Lego Universe* users were safe from online predators and threats, upholding the company's core values of safety, reliability and 'playing well'. Although *Lego Universe* never attracted the market the company had hoped, it was nevertheless a bold and admirable endeavor through which the company learned a great deal about succeeding in the digital arena.[426]

In more recent years, Lego have taken their digital ambitions to a smaller scale with the release of a clever app called *Life of George* which allows users to construct simple Lego objects on their smartphone.

Despite investing heavily in digital product offerings in recent years, Lego has continued to expand its physical product range with, among others, the 2010 release of its wildly successful board game.[427] But perhaps the greatest stroke of genius has been Lego's range of play sets designed especially for girls. So successful has the female-focus been that by the middle of 2012, 27% of all Lego play sets sold in the U.S. were purchased by or for girls.[428]

Today, children around the world spend a combined five billion hours playing with Lego's various products each year. Every second, seven Lego sets are sold somewhere on the planet with Lego's extensive network of factories churning out a staggering 22 billion plastic bricks each year – or roughly 500 bricks per second.[429]

Recent years have seen Lego enjoy many hard-earned accolades and triumphs. In September 2014, for instance, they overtook Mattel as the world's biggest toymaker – an enormous accomplishment by any measure.[430] Less than a year later, Lego was named the world's most powerful brand and was recently voted the most popular toy of all time.[431]

Lego is a brilliant example of a company that has constantly re-invented itself – all the while never losing sight of its core purpose of inspiring play, creativity and imagination. In contrast, Lego's one-time rival, Meccano, has all but faded into obscurity.

For any entity wishing to stay relevant, Re-Positioning as Lego did is absolutely vital. Re-Positioning is about developing new products; tapping into new markets; and embracing new approaches when shift happens.

When helping clients Re-Position their organizations and their brands, there are seven questions I typically explore with them in the process. You may wish to ask yourself the following questions too:

1. WHAT MOTIVATES/IMPRESSES OUR MARKET?

This is by far the most important question of all – what represents value or benefit to your target market? It is important to not fall into the trap of making assumptions when answering this question. Simply because you did focus group research seven years ago and got a sense of what your **MAKE IT YOUR BUSINESS TO UNCOVER WHAT TRULY DRIVES YOUR MARKETPLACE AND COME TO GRIPS WITH THEIR UNDERLYING MOTIVATORS.** customers wanted then, you cannot assume that the same applies today. Instead, make it your business to uncover what truly drives your marketplace and come to grips with their underlying motivators.

Cake maker Sara Lee discovered the importance of this a number of years ago. Assuming that modern women desired convenience above all else, Sara Lee released a range of packet mixes that required the user to only 'add water'. While the move should have been a sure winner, it didn't sell. Perplexed, Sara Lee's marketing department embarked on research to find out why their new product had missed the mark. What they discovered was that while customers wanted convenience, they also wanted to feel that making a cake involved love, attention and a little bit more skill than simply adding water.

Realizing their error, Sara Lee quickly overhauled their cake mixes so that customers were required to add milk, eggs and butter. The results were staggering – the new formula literally sold like hot cakes. Women loved the new mixes which afforded them fantastic convenience while not robbing them of the joy of baking for their families.[432]

GET TO KNOW YOUR CUSTOMERS

Iconic motorcycle manufacturer Harley-Davidson also discovered the power and importance of taking the time to really find out what customers want rather than relying on outdated assumptions. When sales of its motorcycles began to decline in the 1970s, Harley-Davidson's then CEO took the unconventional step of requiring his senior management team to attend biker rallies and rub shoulders with the company's customers in person.

Looking around at one of these rallies, one of the executive team noticed that almost every Harley-Davidson bike had been modified and customized – in many cases, at a cost equal to or greater than the bike's original purchase price. As a result of this insight the company incorporated the most popular modifications into their subsequent designs. Within a few years, Harley's motorcycle sales were up by 60% and the company returned to prominence and popularity.[433]

Jean maker Levi-Strauss adopted a similar approach. Observing that their customers purchased jeans and then proceeded to tear, bleach and shrink them, Levi-Strauss started offering ripped, pre-shrunk and pre-faded jeans for sale. While this move confounded their competitors, it was an immediate winner and made the company a market leader for years.[434]

In looking at one ingenious tactic for discovering what customers really want, e-book manufacturers and publishers are now monitoring readers' habits in an effort to make books more engaging. E-Readers now provide feedback data as to when readers give up on a book; the sections that a reader underlines or highlights; and how long it takes readers to get through a chapter or section. While tracking reader habits to this degree may be considered invasive, what it does mean is that books will become increasingly tailored to readers' preferences. Thanks to digital technology publishers can reliably know what their readers want for the first time rather than relying on guesswork.[435]

Beyond gleaning insights from the *way* customers use a device, even the *type* of device a consumer uses can be quite revealing for those looking to understand their market. Online travel agency Orbitz, for instance, has discovered that people who use Apple devices spend as much as 30% more per night on hotels. This insight, gained by analyzing its data, has allowed Orbitz to more effectively predict consumer tastes and spending habits.[436]

Similarly, consumer product companies like Kimberly Clark and Unilever have recently started using retina-tracking cameras when testing the packaging and design of new products with focus groups. Recognizing that participants tend to feign more interest in products during testing than they actually feel, the new retina-tracking technology has dispelled some old myths such as the notion that a bigger picture on the product packaging is better.[437]

2. WHAT CONFUSES, DISAPPOINTS OR FRUSTRATES OUR MARKET?

As a counterbalance to the first Re-Positioning question, it is equally valuable to discern the things that are causing customers irritation or inconvenience, or both.

When at the helm of legendary innovator Proctor and Gamble, A.G. Lafley was famous for beginning meetings with questions designed to get to the heart of a consumer's frustrations.[438] Whether it was a new cleaning product or personal hygiene range, Lafley would ask questions like: *What do we know about our target consumer? What does she believe she is missing today? What is she most unhappy about?*

Lafley knew that the nature of the question was what mattered most. Rather than asking a question like, *How can we help our customers clean their houses faster and easier,* he would pose a question like, *How can we give customers their Saturday mornings back?*[439]

American hardware giant Home Depot learned the hard way how important it is to understand what customers did and did not want when they debuted in the Chinese market in 2006. By September 2012, the company announced that it was closing its last remaining stores in China following significant financial losses. Essentially, the company had failed to grasp the local culture or the needs of its people. A company spokesperson admitted that Home Depot had completely misread China's appetite for do-it-yourself products. Apparently, Chinese people want others to do it for them; they don't want to do it themselves!

A great example of innovation that came about by addressing the key frustrations or friction points of customers is that of dive sensation, SNUBA. In late 1980s, the scuba diving industry worldwide was in crisis amid economic downturn and increased competition. Rather than focusing on strategies to gain a larger slice of a decreasing pie, one operator in Hawaii asked a powerful question: what prevents new customers from trying scuba diving? Put simply, how do we make the pie bigger by attracting customers who would not normally consider paying for a Scuba dive?

The answers to the question were abundantly clear. Scuba diving was a real commitment. It required expensive certification, carrying heavy tanks, restrictions on when you can fly home after underwater explorations, and most significantly, a high cost.

As his competitors engaged in an economic race to the bottom through price discounting, this visionary operator started experimenting with new approaches that address the frustrations of potential customers. The result was a new form of diving called SNUBA.

Unlike traditional scuba diving, SNUBA didn't require the diver to lug heavy tanks as SNUBA keeps tanks on the water's surface in a raft and connects to the diver below via a 20-foot tube. Better still, SNUBA required no certification, training or flight restrictions and is a fraction of cost. This ingenious fusion of snorkeling and scuba was an instant hit with over 5 million people having SNUBA dived worldwide to date. [440]

3. WHO ELSE IS CURRENTLY SOLVING OUR MARKET'S PROBLEMS?

Apart from considering what your market wants, it is equally important to note what other players in the marketplace are doing, in particular those emerging competitors who are still in phase one or two of their own Relevance Curve. Leaders would do well to keep a watchful eye on the strategic moves of new and nimble entrants to the market – keep up with them, or they

| **LEADERS WOULD DO WELL TO KEEP A WATCHFUL EYE ON THE STRATEGIC MOVES OF NEW AND NIMBLE ENTRANTS TO THE MARKET.**

may well take large chunks of your market share in the years to come.

While I do not condone or even recommend that you copy or replicate competitors, I believe there is value in learning from and imitating *elements* of the success formulas used by others. Again, think of it as benchmarking not plagiarism.

Professor of Management and Human Resources at Ohio State University, Oded Shenkar, concurs. He points to the commercial benefits of imitation and goes so far as to suggest that it is imitators - and not innovators - who enjoy the greatest success and profitability in the long term. He cites examples to support his case including:

- Diners Club who pioneered the credit card and yet enjoys only a tiny fraction of the market today;
- IBM who have constantly imitated both in mainframes and personal computers and pushed the first movers out of business;
- Apple, who didn't invent the MP3 player, but instead made it sexy.

Shenkar believes that imitators succeed because they can calibrate their product by learning from others' mistakes. As a result, their overall costs are often 60-75% lower than innovators who have to invest heavily in research and development.[441]

ANYTHING YOU CAN DO, I CAN DO BETTER
Samsung is a fantastic example of a company that has made enormous financial gains by capitalizing on the ideas and innovations of others. While innovative in its own right, Samsung has never coveted the 'design pioneer' mantle the way Apple has. In contrast, it has become

adept at refining the ideas of other companies, and packaging them in new ways.

When Samsung took the top spot in smartphone market share from Apple in late 2012, research analyst at IDC Technology, Kevin Restivo, pointed to Samsung's "copycat" approach as key to their success. "Being a fast follower can be a path to number one, and Samsung is a case study of doing so," he noted.[442]

Even the once-famous innovator, Sony, has shifted gears in recent years to follow other electronics companies into new markets. Sony's chief strategy officer Tadashi Saito gave justification for this approach, saying, "The first runner has to face the wind – sometimes, it's easier to run from behind." This is a startling about-face for a company who became famous for inventing world-changing products[443] and whose founder declared Sony as a pioneer who "never intends to follow others."[444]

RATHER THAN RE-INVENTING THE WHEEL OR FORGING A NEW PATH SIMPLY FOR THE SAKE OF DOING SO, CONSIDER WHAT OTHERS ARE DOING THAT IS WORKING.

Rather than re-inventing the wheel or forging a new path simply for the sake of doing so, consider what others are doing that is working. Ask yourself how you could leverage their experience and incorporate some of their successful strategies into what you are doing.

4. HOW ARE WE CURRENTLY PERCEIVED?

This fourth question can be confronting yet critically important: how are you perceived by those external to the organization, business or brand? What matters is not how you would *like* to be perceived, but how others *actually* see you. After all, perception is reality.

If you are going to ask this question, you must be prepared to hear the answer – even if it is difficult to digest. Too often organizations seek to find out how they are perceived only to become defensive if they don't like what they hear.

Innovation giant 3M have recognized in recent years that the very popularity of the company's iconic products has created a perception challenge in the marketplace. Despite the fact that 3M spends around $1.8 billion a year on research and development and employs 8,500 researchers in its labs world-wide, it is known primarily for household and office products including Scotch tape and Post-it Notes.

Yet 3M CEO Inge Thulin wants to change these perceptions and re-assert the company as a leader in science-based research and innovation. He wants more appreciation for 3M's technological skills – a reputational shift that could help the company win new customers, attract bright young employees and even push the stock price higher.[445]

One simple and inexpensive way to monitor and measure how an organization or brand is perceived in the marketplace is by using web services like Klout, Kred or Sprout Social. Each of these online solutions offers an invaluable insight into the social media buzz around a brand. The reason this can be so valuable is that customers are more likely to Tweet about a brand experience or perception than go to the trouble of writing a letter or email to the customer service department.

5. HOW ARE WE A CATEGORY OF ONE?

What do you do that is so distinct that no-one else could reasonably claim that they do it exactly the way you do? Perhaps you are faster, cheaper, sexier, more trustworthy, convenient, ethical or exclusive. Regardless of your point of difference, it is vitally important that you have one or set out to establish one.

REGARDLESS OF YOUR POINT OF DIFFERENCE, IT IS VITALLY IMPORTANT THAT YOU HAVE ONE OR SET OUT TO ESTABLISH ONE.

Rolls-Royce recognized this in the early 20th century when the automobile industry found itself in a time of transition. While Ford embraced the democratization of the automobile with its popular Model T, Rolls Royce opted to focus on the upper end of the market. The company made the unconventional move of deliberately reverting to obsolete technologies rather than competing with Ford's mass production. Rolls Royce positioned itself as a quality carmaker – boasting that its cars would never wear out owing to the fact that they were hand-crafted "the old-fashioned way".

Further solidifying their uniqueness, Rolls Royce restricted sales to only customers they approved of in an effort to ensure that no 'riff raff' owned a Rolls Royce. This positioning of exclusivity has served Rolls Royce well for over a century.[446]

Finding a point of uniqueness was also a key challenge facing iconic beverage brand Coca-Cola a few short years ago. Facing increased competition and a decade-long decline in soft drink consumption, especially amongst young consumers, Coke realized it needed to once again get cut-through. [447]

The solution came in the form of a novel marketing campaign known as "Share A Coke". First launched in 2011 in Australia following an executive team brainstorming session with the ad agency Ogilvy, this campaign saw cans and bottles feature customer's names in an attempt to personalize the product. The campaign was a huge success with Coke consumption rising 7% among young Australians and a subsequent roll out of the marketing initiative across 80 countries including the U.S. Resulting from the campaign, Coke's soft drink sales in the U.S. alone rose more than 2%.[448]

While Coca-Cola's campaign may appear gimmicky, the reality is that it worked simply because it caused the brand to stand out from the pack. The reality is that in any flooded marketplace, if

IN ANY FLOODED MARKETPLACE, IF YOU ARE NOT REMARKABLE, YOU ARE INVISIBLE

you are not remarkable, you are invisible – a truth Coca-Cola knows well.

For small businesses facing industry consolidation and stiff competition from larger players, finding a point of difference is one of the most powerful weapons you have at your disposal.

When I am working with clients in this position, my advice is simple: you have 3 choices – go **big**, go **boutique**, or go **broke**. Because the third option is not ideal and the first option is rarely practical when you are up against a multinational brand, the only option you have is to find a way of providing a boutique offering that the big players can't compete with. Perhaps it is a level of customized service, a unique or memorable user experience, or simply a tug at the 'support the little guys' heartstrings. Regardless of how you pursue the boutique positioning, it is vital to do so.

6. WHERE ARE THE GAPS?

What segments of the market aren't being served right now? Further still, what products, services or solutions are missing at the moment? What gaps could your organization or business fill?

The Marriott Hotel chain has successfully extended its brand in response to this question by exploiting previously untapped markets. For instance their Courtyard hotels are targeted at business travelers; their Fairfield Inns are designed for families wanting an inexpensive vacation; and their Residence Inn brand is specially designed to cater for travelers who want a 'home away from home'.[449]

Exploiting marketplace gaps was also a core element of News Corporation's launch of the Fox Business Network in 2007. Rather than trying to compete with CNBC who target the serious and sophisticated business viewer, Fox Business decided to pitch it's programming to a more mainstream audience. [450]

Recognizing the economic opportunity offered by younger generation consumers, Target has recently taken deliberate steps to overhaul their grocery range in order to attract Millennials. Their new selection is skewing toward an assortment favored by younger consumers who increasingly prefer a healthy lifestyle and have largely shunned the processed foods that their parents grew up with. Those younger families are making up a greater share of Target's customer base, rivaling the spending power of baby boomers.[451]

7. WHAT ARE OUR MARKET'S UNKNOWN FUTURE NEEDS?

This final question is paradoxical, because it is impossible to know what is unknown, and yet this question is at the heart of Steve Jobs' genius at Apple.

Jobs never waited for customer surveys or focus groups to tell him what to create. Rather, he was always pushing Apple to get out ahead of the market and make products that consumers didn't yet know they wanted or needed.[452] Naturally, to successfully pre-empt the market as effectively as Apple has done requires an extraordinary combination of intuition, courage and creativity. It is rare, yet possible, and incredibly important to ongoing success and longevity. The key question can perhaps be better framed like this:

HOW CAN YOU SOLVE A PROBLEM FOR CUSTOMERS BEFORE THEY EVEN KNOW THAT THE PROBLEM EXISTS?

how can you solve a problem for customers before they even know that the problem exists? Do this, and your market will beat a path to your door.[453]

While the seven questions above are a great place to start, the next step is to consider some of the practical ways you can Re-Position your organization or brand by:

a. Developing new Products and Services
b. Exploiting new Markets
c. Adopting new Messaging
d. Embracing new Formats or Approaches

In the pages ahead, we will look at a wide cross-section of brands and organizations that successfully implemented these four Re-Positioning strategies:

A. DEVELOPING NEW PRODUCTS AND SERVICES

Without a doubt, one of the keys to remaining relevant is to keep your product and service offering fresh. 3M have long recognized the importance of this to the point where the company has a strategic goal of deriving 25% of its annual revenue from products that did not exist five years before.

To see how critical the development of new products and services is to the longevity and success of a brand, look no further than 160-year-old glass manufacturer, Corning.

In 1908, half of Corning's revenue came from making glass light bulbs. Over time, the Corning brand extended beyond these roots and became known for its high quality cook- and kitchen-ware. Today however, many of Corning's most lucrative products are ones that didn't exist 10 years ago. The company now specializes in cathode-ray tubes, fiber optics for high definition TVs, and laser technology that enables mobile phones to be fitted with micro projectors.

Corning is a great example of a company rich in tradition and history that has stayed relevant by not being afraid to embrace new products and services as times have changed.[454]

Consider too how Encyclopedia Britannica have proven that the new product and service approach can work. To their credit, the digital threat did not catch Britannica by surprise. On the contrary, the company started taking steps many years ago to Re-Position their business in anticipation of the day their printed volumes would become obsolete.

As far back as the mid-1990s, Britannica started making moves to limit its dependence on print book sales. In the ensuing years, the company slowly but surely transformed itself from a book printer into an online information provider with 85% of Britannica's revenue by the end of 2011 coming from sales of online subscriptions, instructional programs and electronic books. By early 2012, half a million households were subscribing for full access to Encyclopedia Britannica's online database while more than 100 million people have access to it in schools, libraries and colleges.[455] Further still, Britannica's focus in the coming years will be on selling reference works to subscribers through apps for tablets and smartphones.[456] As the company's President Jorge Cauz described it in late 2012, "we are now a fully digital company."

While there are still doubts as to whether Britannica will achieve longevity in a digital age when competing with free information services like Wikipedia, the preliminary results indicate that Britannica is a tremendous success story of a company that transitioned from the pre-digital era by Re-Positioning itself and it's products.

Similarly, a key element of McDonalds' *Play to Win* turnaround strategy in 2003 was developing new products in the form of a wider range of menu items. While it retained popular traditional items such as the Big Mac, McNuggets and the Quarter Pounder, McDonald's introduced a range of healthier alternatives including salads, bottled water, fruit and yoghurt – all with nutritional information for consumers. In addition, McDonald's introduced premium items such as the Angus burger, specialty coffee and snack wraps.[457] The company's turnaround was dramatic following the introduction of these new menu items. McDonalds' sales increased 40% in the next five years, and average sales-per-restaurant increased 25%.[458]

But it's not all been smooth sailing for McDonald's. The fast food giant reported an 11% decrease in revenue and a 30% drop in profit for the first three months of 2015. Facing competition from new-format rivals, a tough economy in Europe and a food safety scare in Asia, McDonald's leadership was left with little option but to close 700 stores worldwide in an attempt to stem the losses. Admittedly, this figure represents a tiny fraction of the chains 32,500-strong restaurant network worldwide but is nevertheless an indication of how tough things have gotten.[459]

In a pre-emptive step to address the company's woes, McDonald's again introduced several new products and limitedtime offers in 2013 to give customers more variety.

According to former president of McDonald's USA, Jeff Stratton, perhaps these changes were made in haste. "The pace of product introduction in my opinion has been too fast," he said in November 2013 at an investor meeting. He went on to describe how the fast pace of the new product introductions had "created challenges for the restaurants," making their operations more complex and slowing service.[460] Indicative of this, McDonald's clocked its slowest average speed for drive through at 189.49 seconds in October 2013.[461]

Beyond negatively impacting speed and efficiency, McDonald's has also diluted their brand messaging in some dangerous ways over recent years. Howard Penney of Hedgeye Risk Management argues that McDonald's had made the mistake of " trying to be all things to all people, whether it's catering to healthminded consumers with oatmeal or to Millennials with snack wraps. They've gone so far afield from their core menu that they're not really resonating with anyone. They don't have a clear marketing message right now."[462]

To Howard Penney's point, demographics do help shed light on the challenges McDonald's is facing. Data compiled by restaurant consultancy Technomic point to a generational problem for the chain. Customers in their 20s and 30s—long a mainstay of McDonald's business—are defecting to competitors, in particular socalled fastcasual restaurants like Chipotle Mexican Grill and gourmetburger chain Five Guys.[463]

Reflecting on the road ahead for McDonald's, the company's newly appointed U.S. president Mike Andres summed it up well in an October 2014 email to U.S. franchisees and corporate staff: "What has worked for McDonald's U.S. for the past decade is not sufficient to propel the business forward in the future."[464]

This sentiment was echoed by the company's global CEO Don Thompson shortly afterward when he said "The key to our success will be our ability to deliver a more relevant McDonald's experience for all of our customers. Customers want to personalize their meals with locally relevant ingredients. They also want to enjoy eating in a contemporary, inviting atmosphere. And they want choices in how they order, choices in what they order and how they're served."[465]

Of course, the key principle for McDonald's in the road ahead will be to re-position their product offering without diluting their brand message or diminishing convenience and efficiency. This is a road they have been down before and I am confident they will emerge from the recent run of challenges stronger than ever. But there is still much work to do.

UP IN SMOKE

Looking to a very different industry, tobacco giants have also embraced new products to retain relevance following widespread public disdain and the declining popularity of their wares.

In April 2012 the U.S.'s third largest tobacco company, Lorillard, acquired the infrastructure to make electronic cigarettes. An electronic cigarette, also known as an e-cigarette, is an electronic inhaler that vaporizes a liquid solution into an aerosol mist, simulating the act of tobacco smoking. Still only a small market in the U.S., Lorillard's e-cigarettes are becoming highly popular in China, suggesting the company is onto a winner.[466]

Lorillard rival, Altria, meanwhile has announced the release of a new range of nicotine lozenges named *Verve* in an effort to address falling sales of traditional cigarettes.

As evidence of just how necessary this new-product Re-Positioning is, smokeless products such as lozenges and e-cigarettes now

SMOKELESS PRODUCTS SUCH AS LOZENGES AND E-CIGARETTES NOW REPRESENT 10% OF TOBACCO INDUSTRY SALES

represent 10% of tobacco industry sales, with this proportion growing at a rate of 7% annually while traditional cigarette volumes contract by roughly 4% a year.[467]

Tellingly, 2014 saw e-cigarette use triple and hookah use double among U.S. teenagers, even as fewer of them light up traditional cigarettes according to the Centers for Disease Control and Prevention.

The findings may well accelerate federal efforts to increase oversight of alternative nicotine products.[468]

QUENCHING A THIRST

The liquor industry has also been forced to explore and develop new products as customer tastes and preferences have changed.

When the world's largest brewer, Anheuser-Busch, saw sales of its flagship beer brand Budweiser plummet almost 50% in the first 10 years of the 21st century,[469] it announced plans to launch 19 new products in the North American market, including small-batch craft beers, cider and sweeter beer.[470] This followed Anheuser-Busch's successful release in 2008 of products like *Bud Light Lime* in an effort to target consumers who had migrated from beer to flavored vodka drinks.[471]

In a similar move, liquor giant Molson Coors launched a new range of *Coors Light Iced T* – a citrus-like iced tea-flavored beer that has 4% alcohol. This product was the result of confronting the reality that new specialty beverages are steadily eroding the popularity of beer. Indicative of this trend, four decades ago, beer sales accounted for 76% of alcohol consumption while in more recent years it has dropped to roughly 40%.[472]

KEEPING PACE

In the fast-paced technology sector, Re-Positioning through the development of new products and services requires constant attention.

As far back as the 1970s National Cash Register (NCR) learned this lesson when electronic cash registers made the company's traditional product range obsolete almost overnight.

Having dominated the cash register business for years, NCR realized that while they had the competitive advantage of strong brand recognition and an established distribution network, they would have to move quickly in overhauling their product offering if they were to avoid annihilation. NCR subsequently developed its own range of electronic registers and set out to Re-Position itself as 'cutting edge' – a move which proved critical to the company's transformation and survival.[473] In more recent years, NCR have gone on to pioneer self-service checkout technology thus solidifying the company's market leadership position.

Staying fresh by constantly developing new products and services is critical to remaining relevant. As evidence of this, consider the short life span of artists or singers who only release one hit song or album. While they may top the charts for a fleeting moment, such 'one hit wonders' are quickly replaced by a new flavor of the month and are soon forgotten.

In contrast, look at pop star greats like Madonna, Elton John or Santana who have constantly re-invented themselves and replenished their material over time and stayed 'in vogue' as a result.

B. EXPLOITING NEW MARKETS

While developing new products and services is a key way to Re-Position a brand, a second effective strategy centers on identifying new customer groups.

Take British pubs, for example. While many of them have been forced to close their doors, some canny publicans have Re-Positioned the watering holes of old to target specific new markets. In 2008, for instance, new owners bought a run-down West London pub, the Princess Victoria, and restored the building to its former glory replete with a marble-topped bar, gilded mirrors and grand oil paintings. They pitched their menu, branding and facilities to the top end of the market, offering fine wines and gourmet dining, and today the Princess Victoria is the haunt of choice for well-heeled locals.[474]

Adopting a very different but equally effective strategy, the owners of cut-price pub chain JD Wetherspoon have positioned their chain of over 800 pubs across the U.K. for the lower end of the market. Offering cheap food, bargain-priced beer and an informal environment, Wetherspoon pubs are extraordinarily popular with hard-drinking youth, cash-strapped pensioners and old-fashioned beer swillers who have drifted away from expensive, up-market establishments.[475]

The above two cases are good examples of businesses in the same industry that have pursued very different markets and have stayed relevant and profitable as a result. They demonstrate that

THERE IS NO ONE RIGHT OR WRONG WAY TO RE-POSITION AN ORGANIZATION OR BRAND

there is no one right or wrong way to Re-Position an organization or brand — just that doing so is critical for survival when shift happens.

There are numerous examples of companies and brands that have embraced new-market Re-Positioning and reaped the rewards of doing so. Here are just a few:

- **Fuji film.** In the 1980s Japanese giant Fuji made the decision to sell film way below what its main rival Kodak charged. Fuji's lower prices made them incredibly attractive to discount merchandisers like Wal-Mart whose business models centered on a 'high volume, low margin' approach. By the late 1990s, this decision saw Fuji eroding Kodak's market dominance to the tune of roughly $1.2 billion per year.[476]

- **Levi-Strauss.** When Levi-Strauss took on the market leaders in men's pants, Haggar, in the 1980s, rather than trying to beat the incumbents at their own game, Levi's developed the Dockers brand targeted to a new market entirely. In contrast to the drab gear being sold at the time, Dockers were bright, bold and eye-catching. They connected with style-conscious baby boomers who were attracted to Dockers' comfortable, loose and stylish fit. The success of this tactic was breathtaking with Levi's menswear sales rocketing from $1 million to $500 million in the space of four years. Through the Dockers move, Levi's Re-Positioned its brand, changed the game, and came out on top.[477]

- **Cirque du Soleil.** When Guy Laliberte and Daniel Gauthier founded *Cirque du Soleil* in 1984, the circus industry was in a clear and steady decline. Laliberte and Gauthier decided to re-think the whole idea of what a circus is - and reappraised who the ticket buyers might be. They opted for an audience of both children *and* adults, and geared their offering accordingly. Today, building on unprecedented worldwide success, the company has extended the brand to spas, restaurants and resorts.[478]

- **The Nintendo Wii.** Nintendo, long the favorite of hard-core gamers, made the risky decision in 2006 to move away from its established fan base and focus instead on developing gaming experiences for families through the release of its wildly successful Wii product.[479]

- **_Harley-Davidson._** Recognizing the demographic limitations of its core domestic market in the U.S. (white males who are 35 and older), Harley-Davidson has set its sights on new horizons - namely emerging markets. Indicative of how effectively their strategy is working, 57% of the company's motorcycle sales in 2014 came from outside the U.S.[480]

SHIFTING THE CAR

New-market Re-Positioning is a consistent theme in the automotive sector. As far back as the 1950s, Ford realized the value of exploiting un-tapped markets following the spectacular failure of its _Edsel_ model. After analyzing the factors contributing to the flop, Ford's leadership identified a distinct segment of car buyers who were not being serviced by Ford, and set out to create a car specifically for them. The result was Ford's _Thunderbird_ – a car which would prove to be the company's most successful and lucrative model since the _Model T_.[481]

Fast-forward a number of decades and Japanese automotive giant Nissan was on the brink of insolvency in the late 1990s. In an effort to turn things around, Nissan took the step of re-introducing some of its legendary sports models including the _Nissan Z_ and _GT-R_ in order to connect with new consumers. The success of this move was stunning – by the late 2000s, Nissan bounced back and had become Japan's most profitable carmaker.[482]

Buoyed by its success, Nissan has since taken further steps in recent years to connect with new markets – this time in the 'third world'. Even though developing nations make up nearly half of all global vehicle sales, no company has yet figured out how to profitably target the lowest segment of the market.[483] A key element of Nissan's strategy to achieve success in this area is to resurrect its Datsun brand that that has been out of production for over 30 years. Priced at between $3000 and $5000,[484] the new Datsun will be specially designed to attract young consumers in less affluent markets such as India, Indonesia and Russia.[485]

Looking at one final example from the automotive sector, consider the predicament of American carmaker Jeep a few years ago. From its first release in the early 1940s up until the late 1990s, the Jeep brand dominated the sports utility market. By 2006 however, Jeep was struggling. With plummeting sales, it was clear that the rough, tough Jeep of old needed to change. Jeep's manufacturer Daimler-Chrysler responded with the release of the *Jeep Compass* – a car designed to attract a mainstream on-road SUV buyer. Jeep spent a massive $75 million promoting the model and Re-Positioning the brand in consumers' eyes – with great success.[486]

DYING CITIES RESURRECTED

New-market Re-Positioning has also proved invaluable for entire cities as they fight to stay relevant in times of change.

> **NEW-MARKET RE-POSITIONING HAS ALSO PROVED INVALUABLE FOR ENTIRE CITIES AS THEY FIGHT TO STAY RELEVANT IN TIMES OF CHANGE.**

One fantastic example of this would be Australia's seventh largest city, Newcastle. A two-hour drive north of Sydney, Newcastle is a port city that historically survived on heavy industry, coal mining and steel manufacturing – not unlike Pittsburgh in the United States.

In 1999, however, Newcastle's steelworks closed their doors after 84 years of operation. Once the lifeblood of the city and surrounding regions, the closure sent shock waves throughout the community and for a number of years, Newcastle floundered. The city's CBD felt like a ghost town as businesses and individuals fled. To all intents and purposes, it looked like Newcastle was set for a steady, saddening decline.

Then, in the mid-2000's, a committee of passionate locals started taking steps to arrest the city's demise and set in place a quiet revolution that has been inspiring to watch unfold. With the help of government funding, idle and decaying docks were converted into state-of-the-art office complexes; former warehouses were transformed into funky bars; and derelict shops were made available rent-free to artists to showcase their work.

Soon a groundswell of change began to gather pace. Artists and designers from around Australia started flocking to Newcastle drawn by its emphasis on creativity; its laid-back lifestyle; its low cost of living; and its burgeoning café culture. Local tourism authorities picked up on the momentum, promoting the city's colorful history, spectacular beaches and nearby world-class Hunter Valley wine region. In recent years, Newcastle has become a tourist destination of choice, even named in *Lonely Planet's* 2011 list of 'Top 10 cities to visit in the world' – Australia's only city to make the list!

Having come a long way from its industrial roots and dark days of decline, Newcastle is a city revitalized. It offers a shining example for regions and communities elsewhere who find themselves in a similar predicament when shift happens.[487]

C. ADOPTING NEW MESSAGING

As a child growing up in Australia during the 1980s, there was a certain type of sweet that was at the top of every kid's wish list, including mine: a packet of Fags. Essentially solid sticks of sugar, Fags were designed to resemble a cigarette with one end colored orange to resemble the cigarette's filter, and a fake glowing red 'ember' at the other. All us kids would love to buy Fags because they made us feel grown up, engendering a 'coolness' associated with smoking when we were too young to puff on the real thing.

During the early 1990s however, pressure was brought to bear on confectionery companies to cease producing Fags. Anti-smoking lobby groups argued, quite rightly, that they were reinforcing unhelpful stereotypes.

Bowing to the pressure, the manufacturer of Fags decided to overhaul the design and packaging of their iconic sweets and renamed them 'Fads'. Gone was the orange stripe and glowing red tip – all that remained was the white cylindrical design which looked more like a thin lollypop stick than a cigarette. The lobby groups were happy; sales of the re-branded confectionery remained strong; and all us kids continued to puff away on the sweets unperturbed by all the controversy.

The repositioning of the Fags confectionery line was an appropriate and effective response to shift happening. By adopting a new name and look, the product's manufacturer successfully staved off a government ban.

None of this is to say that new-message Re-Positioning is something only done in response to bad publicity or a toxic public perception. On the contrary, brands and organizations often overhaul their messaging simply to appear more fresh and vibrant.

> **BRANDS AND ORGANIZATIONS OFTEN OVERHAUL THEIR MESSAGING SIMPLY TO APPEAR MORE FRESH AND VIBRANT.**

Take for example the face of breakfast cereal brand Quaker Oatmeal, a man known as Larry. In mid-2012 the rosy-cheeked, white-haired man that has smiled across the breakfast table at customers for over 130 years received a makeover in a move deemed necessary to reinvigorate the brand. The new, improved Larry appeared with a haircut, his double chin removed, and more of his upper body physique showing. The changes were consciously subtle, not startling, as the Quaker brand managers were keen to not compromise the product's values of tradition, quality and trust.[488]

VOLVO - BOXY AND BEIGE NO MORE

Many established brands could learn from Volvo's successful efforts in recent years to Re-Position their brand through new messaging.

For decades, the car manufacturer was known for producing solid, sturdy and reliable cars. What Volvo lacked in style or coolness, it more than made up for in safety and 'understated sensibleness'. The company had essentially positioned its cars as the automobile for 'professionals who don't need to demonstrate how successful they are by the car they drive, but who value being known for their good judgment'.[489]

Around the turn of the 21st century, however, Volvo came to realize that demographic shifts were happening in their marketplace. Gen Y were buying a quarter of all new cars and would be purchasing one in every two cars by 2020. Overnight, Volvo's conservative, sensible image looked like marketing suicide.

In a decisive and bold move to connect with the younger demographic, Volvo set about Re-Positioning its brand. This culminated with the 2004 release of the *Volvo S40* – a model that exuded speed, performance, youthfulness and excitement.[490] In an effort to ensure that this new release hit the mark with younger car buyers, one of Volvo's television commercials for the *S40* was in the style of an Xbox video game. Another advertisement featured rap star LL Cool J promoting the car in music-video style. In addition, Volvo promoted the car in non-traditional environments including Virgin megastores and even developed an online mockumentary, *The Mystery of Dalaro*, which attracted over one million hits and led to a 105% jump in *S40* sales within months.[491]

What was perhaps most impressive about Volvo's Re-Positioning was the way their efforts to become sexier never compromised on the 85-year old company's core DNA of safety, quality and reliability. More recent innovations such as Volvo's vision to produce 'accident proof' driverless vehicles by 2020 is further evidence of the company's unwillingness to depart from their core ideology while pursuing new horizons.[492]

Fellow carmaker Hyundai also embarked on an ingenious Re-Positioning exercise when the automotive industry faced another seismic shift a handful of years later in the form of the great recession. While automotive giants GM and Ford were fighting for survival due to the economic downturn, Hyundai took a different tack which saw them beat the odds and the competition.

Recognizing that consumers were deferring new car purchases due to fears about job security, Hyundai released an initiative called the *Hyundai Assurance Program* in January 2009. This first-of-its-kind program allowed people who purchased new Hyundai cars to return their automobile in the first 12 months in the event of 'life altering circumstances' such as layoffs, job transfers or accidental death.[493]

The initiative was a breathtaking success with Hyundai selling a whopping 435,000 vehicles in the program's first year – with less than 100 people taking up the offer to return their car.[494]

BOOSTING TIRED BRANDS

New-message Re-Positioning is highly effective is when a brand's core essence no longer resonates with its target audience. Take Levi-Strauss as an example. As we discussed in previous pages, Levi's were once considered a 'revolutionary' brand that challenged the values of the establishment. As the brand's wearers have grown older however, Levi-Strauss has been forced to change in order to connect with a younger generation and maintain its mantle of 'coolness'.

In this, Levi-Strauss is not alone. According to *The Wall Street Journal*, the key reason behind Billabong's falling popularity in recent years has been that the surf wear company had lost touch with its youthful counter-culture roots.

Managing director of rival surf brand Mambo, Angus Kingsmill, suggests that Billabong's challenge is one that many brands face after they have been around for a while. "It's difficult to maintain coolness and be at the cutting edge for long," he points out. "At some point, a brand has to decide if it wants to stay edgy and cool - or become a mass market brand."[495]

USING TXT 2 GET THRU

New-message Re-Positioning can also involve communicating old messages in different ways. In one successful campaign, trendy American retail chain Charlotte Russe used a short text message with a video component offering customers a $5 shopping pass. The video, starring a handsome male actor, was shared so widely amongst young women that the Charlotte Russe database grew 33% in one weekend![496]

Department store Bloomingdale's, fast food chain Jack in the Box and shoe retailer Vans, have also accepted that teenagers are most easily accessible via text. According to the technology consultancy

CONSUMERS ARE *FIVE TIMES MORE LIKELY* TO OPEN A TEXT THAN AN EMAIL — AND TEND TO RESPOND TO TEXTS WITHIN MINUTES.

Mogreet Inc, consumers are *five times more likely* to open a text than an email - and tend to respond to texts within minutes.[497]

The world's biggest advertiser, Proctor and Gamble, is also changing its messaging approaches in order to connect with new customers. In a shift away from traditional broadcast advertising, P&G is moving towards lower-cost digital placements – by mid-2013 P&G was spending 35% of its marketing budget on digital media.[498] Buoyed by the success of its *Old Spice* commercials which achieved enormous reach and impact on the Internet, P&G's strategy is now leveraging off social media to engage younger consumers. One example of this new approach is its *Shave India* campaign which P&G began running in 2008. This campaign puts questions out to the marketplace for debate like, *'Are clean-shaven men sexier than non-clean shaven men?'* or, *'Are clean-shaven men more likely to get a job?'* These campaigns and others like them have successfully created an enormous buzz around P&G's various brands.[499]

While new-message Re-Positioning may appear gimmicky, it must be more than a superficial stunt. Rather than simply window dressing, new-message Re-Positioning is about ensuring that a brand keeps pace with changing market conditions and needs while still staying true to its core values. Furthermore, it is a key way to set a brand or organization apart from the competition.

Remember the age-old marketing adage: *it is better to be different than better.* Rather than trying to emphasize superiority,

IT IS BETTER TO BE DIFFERENT THAN BETTER. ▮

successful brands seek to stand out through differentiation – whether in reality or perception.

D. EMBRACING NEW FORMATS OR APPROACHES

This final type of Re-Positioning is one that many established institutions are recognizing the need to embrace if they are to remain relevant.

In recent years, libraries worldwide have been forced to re-think whom they serve and how. In 2011, some 2600 libraries across America cut their opening hours in response to declining popularity.[500] In contrast, libraries that are managing to buck this trend are doing so largely because they no longer consider books their *raison d'être.*

The Brooklyn Public Library, for instance, has started making studio and rehearsal space available to local musicians and creative talent. They are also offering new services including language classes; resumé writing workshops for the unemployed; adult literacy courses and counseling services for troubled teens.[501] By keeping pace with changing times, libraries adopting similar approaches are being transformed into vibrant and highly relevant community spaces rather than silent storage facilities for bound volumes of information.[502]

Religious institutions are also realizing that their formats and approaches must change if they are to stay relevant. In an era of declining synagogue membership, many Jewish leaders are embracing new technologies as a way of re-engaging believers in the Seder.

Some Jewish congregations have installed webcams dubbed 'Torahcamms' in their places of worship. Another unorthodox approach to engaging tech-savvy worshippers is an app called eScapegoat which allows users to anonymously upload their 120-charater confessions of sin via text or email. When the user presses submit, the cartoon image of a googly-eyed goat gets pushed off a cliff – mimicking the practice used by 3rd century Rabbis.[503] While some religious exponents fear new media may detract from traditional practices, others believe the changes could ultimately lead to the strengthening of religion.[504]

For evangelical Christian churches too, new approaches are proving invaluable in engaging young church members. In recognition of research that shows church engagement falls away dramatically between the ages of 18 and 29, many denominations are re-thinking church and the way it is done.

A good example is Charlotte ONE - a young adult ministry that doesn't perform baptisms, funerals or offer communion. It doesn't meet on Sundays and there is no one single pastor in charge. Despite all these deviations from the traditional church model, the approach at Charlotte ONE seems to be working. In a recent survey, 89% of attendees said the ONE program had enriched their personal relationship with Jesus Christ and 42% of them said it had helped to connect them to a local church.

Adopting new formats and approaches need not erode the sanctity or the solemnity of the message. The way a church's message is communicated must change as times and needs evolve, but the message itself need not change at all. Consider the rise of the Christian mega churches such as Hillsong, Lakewood and Elevation – each examples of ministries uncompromising in their commitment to biblical truth but equally committed to conveying these truths in relevant and engaging ways. As noted in chapter 10, staying relevant does not mean having to compromise on core values.

PUBLISHING TURNED UPSIDE DOWN

As we discussed in chapter 5, there are few businesses as acutely threatened by the digital age as that of print news media. As news has become available online for free, media outlets have been forced to completely re-think their profit centers, distribution methods and value proposition. According to U.S. newspaper owner Steven Newhouse, the entire industry is waiting for someone to break from the pack, blaze a new trail and find a new revenue model that works.[505]

Guru Warren Buffett believes that offering free news content as a business model is simply unsustainable. He describes how news outlets need to "work out a blend of digital and print that will attract both the audience and the revenue we need."

In an effort to strike this balance, in 2011 the *New York Times* began to charge readers to access its news stories online and attracted almost 500,000 subscribers in 12 months. While income from online subscribers is expected to earn the group roughly $125 million per year,[506] the new format has also led to dramatic declines in advertising revenue.[507] In this predicament, the *New York Times* is far from alone: newspaper print advertising in the United States has fallen by more than 50% overall since 2005.[508]

Other traditional paper-based publications have taken different routes to Re-Position their product offering. In October 2012, *Newsweek* magazine announced that they would be ceasing print editions after 80 years of continuous production. Citing an 80% drop in advertising pages and plummeting circulation figures, *Newsweek's* management were left with little option but to turn the magazine into a digital-only publication.[509]

At National Geographic, CEO John Fahey has taken similar steps to rely less on revenue from traditional magazine subscriptions. His new strategy, with multi-platform formats that include an interactive website, joint ventures with television networks and video games, appears to be working well. More than half the company's revenues are already sourced from its television joint ventures, for example.

Fahey goes as far as to say he believes that the idea of a printed magazine will inevitably cease.[510] In the years ahead, the iconic yellow-bordered publication aims to make its stories and pictures available to customers through flexible subscription offerings for iPad, Kindle and Nook readers.

Interestingly, Re-Positioning by adopting new formats is in some ways nothing new for National Geographic. In the early 1900s when Alexander Graham Bell was the company's president, he made the controversial decision to change the National Geographic's academic-oriented, text-heavy, long-story format to one more accessible and engaging to the general reader. Bell achieved this by shortening stories, simplifying the language, and featuring more photographs and illustrations.[511]

NOT EITHER/OR BUT BOTH

While many paper-based publishers seek to strike a balance between traditional and digital formats, few have done so as effectively as photo book manufacturer, Eastmon Digital.

When demand for printed photos declined due to digital formats, Eastmon Digital shifted its focus to printing digital photo books. Although traditional photo printing had once been Eastmon's bread and butter, today one of its most popular and lucrative products is a $20 service which allows users to create a physical printed photo book with images that can be uploaded from a customer's social networking sites. This is a

NEW-FORMAT RE-POSITIONING NEED NOT BE AN EITHER/OR PROPOSITION.

case in point that digital and analogue formats can co-exist and that new-format Re-Positioning need not be an either/or proposition.

This both/and approach to re-positioning has been something I have had to navigate personally in recent years. My second book was a keepsake journal called *Memento* which was designed to help parents record their memories and stories as a legacy to hand on to the next generation. Despite the book's success worldwide, over time it became apparent that a digital solution would be necessary. After 24 months of putting into practice many of the principals we've explored in the preceding chapters, I took the risk of launching an electronic memoir-writing tool called Histography.com.

Wanting to retain the question-and-answer format that had made *Memento* so popular and unique in the marketplace, Histography.com sends users an emailed question each week over the course of a year. These questions are designed to tap into the defining memories and stories of the users life and they can record them by simply replying to the email, typing their story, and then uploading a photo.

The beta version of Histography.com sold well but I quickly realized something was missing. In my attempt to create a functional and beautiful digital product, I overlooked the fact that users still wanted a tangible representation of their stories. As a result, I went back to the drawing-board and re-built the system from the ground up in order to allow users to automatically produce a hardcover printed book at the end of the process.

My own journey of re-positioning what had been a successful product in order to make it's format relevant in a digital age was by no means an easy one but hearing the stories of delighted users certainly made it a worthwhile one!

HANDS-ON BEAUTY

America's largest cosmetics and skin-care brand, Clinique, has begun experimenting with a range of new in-store formats in an effort to Re-Position themselves and respond to changing customer preferences. Following the lead of rival beauty chain Sephora, Clinique has adopted an approach called '*Service as You Like It*' where consumers are invited to experiment with new products uninhibited by interference from a salesperson. As Clinique's VP of global store design and merchandising Anthony Battaglia said: "It is the end of 'do not touch'. We had to remind the customer that our product is here to play with and experience."

In addition to having accessible drawers full of product samples and iPads on hand to help customers diagnose their skin care needs, Clinique clearly displays its prices in an effort to remove consumer's purchasing blocks. Again, early indicators are that the strategy is working - many stores that have adopted the new approach have since enjoyed double-digit sales growth.[512]

Grocery giant Tesco is another retailer adopting new approaches to give customers what they want. In 2011 it installed a virtual grocery store on a South Korean train station wall so that commuters could purchase their groceries on their way home from work using the QR code readers on their smartphones.[513]

RETAILERS GET APP-Y

A growing list of established retailers are making extensive use of new technologies to complement traditional in-store formats – a trend called 'bricks to clicks.'[514]

Target, for instance, is using customized daily deal alerts and exclusive discount coupons sent directly to customers' smartphones.[515] Other retailers such as Bloomingdales are incorporating 3D scanning machines which identify a customer's proportions in-store and link to customers' smartphones offering intelligent shopping suggestions.[516]

Maximizing on smartphone technology, American women's clothing retailer, Maurices, has started using a technology known as 'geofencing' to attract and engage with its customers. 'Geofencing' allows the store to alert opt-in customers with promotions and coupons as they approach or walk nearby any Maurices store.[517]

In sending discount coupons directly to users' mobile devices, Target, Wal-Mart and Maurices seem to be far from

| MORE THAN 3.4 MILLION MOBILE COUPONS ARE REDEEMED IN THE U.S. ANNUALLY.

alone. According to Juniper Research, more than 3.4 million mobile coupons are redeemed in the U.S. annually.[518]

Kmart and Wal-Mart are also looking to blend traditional retailing with digital technologies by encouraging customers to order online and then visit the store for same-day pickup so as to avoid delivery costs. Known in the retailing world as an omni-channel approach, this option is already being utilized by one in two purchasers on Walmart.com.[519]

Macy's approach to bridging the digital and physical divide is somewhat different from its rivals. By building a network of online sales distribution centers dotted across America, Macy's is looking to rival Amazon's highly efficient network of warehouses which underpin its dominance in online retailing. Similar tactics are being employed by Nordstrom, Toys R Us and Babies R Us.[520]

ONE STEP AHEAD

Despite its rivals' efforts, Amazon appears to be consistently one step ahead of the retail competition when it comes to Re-Positioning. As testament to this fact, Amazon sells more online than its next 12 biggest competitors combined.[521] Not content with having the world's most extensive distribution network, Amazon has turned its attention to improving the customer's delivery experience.

Recognizing that the weakest link in the online retailing process is when purchasers are not home to take delivery of parcels, Amazon teamed up with 7-Eleven to provide password-protected lockers that can be accessed 24/7 by its customers. These lockers allow customers the convenience of picking up parcels delivered during the day at any time they feel like it. Similar approaches are now being adopted by other retailers and even grocery stores through the use of refrigerated lockers.[522]

That said, Amazon faces increasing competition itself in the delivery space. October 2014 saw Google ramp up its Google Express delivery service for same-day or overnight delivery of products ordered from physical stores including Costco, Staples and Walgreens.[523] Then of course there's the question of what happens if and when companies like Uber, Lyft and

Carpooling.com turn their attention from delivering people to delivering parcels. Should this occur, Amazon may well find themselves being the disrupted rather than the disruptor – a position they are certainly not used to being in.

Regardless of the Re-Positioning strategy adopted, the future appears to belong to the retailer who has what the customer wants and who can sell it through every channel – in-store, online and mobile.[524]

Stuart Harker, a global retail and consumer advisor with PriceWaterhouseCoopers argues that multi-channel retailing is here to stay. "Retailers and suppliers must embrace the internet or face closure," he said.[525]

| **RETAILERS AND SUPPLIERS MUST EMBRACE THE INTERNET OR FACE CLOSURE**

Setting a brand or organization up for enduring relevance through Re-Positioning involves a principle that every experienced surfer understands well. In order to catch the perfect wave, a good surfer knows the importance of keeping their eyes firmly on the horizon. While a wave is still forming a long way off in the distance, surfers know that this is the time to move – to paddle out and get in position. Move too late or not at all and you'll simply get washed up as the wave crashes over you.

In much the same way, winning the battle for relevance is about anticipating, preparing for and embracing change - no matter how uncomfortable or confronting it may be.

Whether it is by entering new markets, developing new products and services, adopting new messages or embracing new formats and approaches, Re-Positioning is the key to ensuring an organization or brand can ride the waves of change rather than being engulfed by them.

FOR REFLECTION:

Looking at the 7 brainstorming questions below, what insights do they give you into how you may need to Re-Position your brand or organization in the years to come?

1. What Motivates/Impresses our Market?
2. What Confuses, Frustrates or Disappoints our Market?
3. Who Else is Currently Solving Their Problems?
4. How are we Currently Perceived?
5. How are we a Category of One?
6. Where are The Gaps?
7. What are our Markets Unknown Future Needs?

Building on the responses to these 7 questions, what are some practical ways you could Re-Position your brand or organization in the years ahead by:

a. Developing new Products, Services or Features
b. Exploiting new Markets
c. Adopting new Messaging
d. Embracing new Formats or Approaches

CONCLUSION

Of all the childhood memories that I cherish, one stands out more vividly than most.

It was a Sunday afternoon and my father and I were sailing together on a lake near our house, just the two of us, when suddenly a summer storm whipped up out of nowhere. Dad realized that conditions were swiftly deteriorating and that we needed to head back to shore immediately. The only trouble was that gale force winds were now against us.

My father was one of those dads who believed that every adverse experience represents an opportunity to learn something useful. He turned to me on this particular afternoon and announced that today was the day I would learn to sail into a headwind – a critical skill for any eight-year old!

Being a typical schoolteacher, my dad started off by informing me that there were three rules to sailing into a headwind:

1. ***You can't change the wind***. The first step, he said, was to accept that as adverse and inconvenient as the wind direction was, we had to accept it as 'out of our control';
2. ***You can't fight the wind.*** In an unpowered vessel, my father said, we were at the mercy of the elements and waging war against them was futile;

239

3. ***You can't ignore the wind***. Doing nothing, or pretending the headwind didn't exist, he stressed, is potentially dangerous as we could be blown off-course or dashed against the rocks.

Having worked with clients across a wide range of industries, I believe the same rules apply to businesses, brands and organizations. Disruptive changes in the commercial landscape are often like headwinds.

Sadly however, many businesses and leaders are in denial about the headwinds of change that they face. They choose to ignore the challenges or hope that if they bury their heads in the sand long enough, the changes will go away and things will return to normal. Other business leaders try to fight the winds of change, like those retailing heavyweights waging all-out war on online retailing, or government legislators determined to contain or restrict access to online information and entertainment.

In actual fact, organizations and brands would do well to heed the next piece of advice my father gave me all those years ago: he said the secret to sailing into a headwind is to ***go with the wind rather than against it – to tack.***

Rather than fighting a headwind, experienced sailors know to adjust their course so that the headwind rushes over a boat's sail and propels the boat forward in the way that an aerofoil on a plane's wing creates lift.

ADJUST YOUR SAILS

Applying this philosophy to organizations and leaders, the best and only effective response to the headwinds of change is to go with them rather than rile against them. We must be vigilant and

WE CANNOT CHANGE THE WIND, BUT WE CAN - AND MUST — ADJUST OUR SAILS.

sensitive to the conditions around us, adjust our course accordingly and allow the winds of change to propel us forward. We cannot change the wind, but we can - and must - adjust our sails.

My sincere hope is that the preceding chapters have gone some way to highlighting the headwinds you are likely to face in the years ahead – or by which you are being buffeted already. More importantly, my goal is that you have gained more than simply an understanding of the path to irrelevance, but that you leave our time together armed with a game plan to stay relevant.

Charles Darwin said it best when once observed, "It's not the strongest that survives, nor the most intelligent, but those most responsive to change."

As you go forth now and engage in the battle for relevance, as we all must, I wish you the very best.

ABOUT THE AUTHOR

Michael McQueen is a multi award-winning speaker, trends forecaster and business strategist.

Coming from a background in marketing and research, in 2004 Michael founded an international consultancy called The Nexgen Group which specialized in tracking demographic shifts and social change.

Widely recognized for having his finger on the pulse of business and culture, Michael has helped some of the world's best-known brands navigate change and stay ahead of the curve.

In addition to featuring regularly as a commentator on TV and radio, Michael is a familiar face on the international conference circuit having shared the stage with the likes of Bill Gates, Whoopi Goldberg and Larry King. He has spoken to hundreds of thousands of people across 5 continents since 2004 and is known for his high-impact, research-rich and entertaining conference presentations.

Michael was the inaugural president of Professional Speakers Australia in 2015 and is a member of the Speakers Hall of Fame.

For more information or to book Michael to speak at your next conference or training event, please visit **www.michaelmcqueen.net**.

ENDNOTES

1   Collins, J. 2009, *How the Mighty Fall*, Random House Business Books, London, p. 2

2   Obama, B. 2012, 'State of the Union Address Transcript', *Washington Post,* 24 January

3   Zhong, R. 2012, 'The Emperor of Vanished Kingdoms', *The Wall Street Journal*, 25 February

4   Putnam, R. 2000, *Bowling Alone*, Simon and Schuster, New York, p. 55

5   Ibid, p 55

6   Ibid, p 55

7   Ibid, p 56

8   Ibid, p 16

9   Hartcher, P. 2011, 'Game over, comrade', *Sydney Morning Herald,* 10 September

10   Ibid

11   Putnam, R. 2000, *Bowling Alone*, Simon and Schuster, New York, p. 82

12   Ibid, p. 83

13   Ibid, p. 69

14   Ibid, p. 71

15   Ibid, p. 70

16 Aikman, D. 2012, 'America's religious past fades in a secular age', *The Wall Street Journal*, 25 October

17 2012, 'Rise of the nones', *Pittsburgh Post Gazette*, 31 October

18 Cowell, A. 2013, 'A church divided by sexuality', *International Herald Tribune*, 15 January

19 Hughes P & Reid S. 2009, 'All Melbourne Matters', *The Christian Research Association*, February

20 Bendavid, N. 2015, 'Europe's empty churches go on sale', *The Wall Street Journal*, 2 January

21 Johnson, K. 2013, 'Montreal: where the churches convert', *The Wall Street Journal*, 5 November

22 Bendavid, N. 2015, 'Europe's empty churches go on sale', *The Wall Street Journal*, 2 January

23 Harford, T. 2011, *Adapt*, Farrar, Straus and Giroux, New York, pp. 9, 10

24 Ibid, p. 8

25 Christensen, C. 2000, *The Innovator's Dilemma*, Harper Collins, New York, p. xiv

26 Phillips, T. 2011, *Fit to Bust*, Kogan, Philadelphia, p. 2

27 Allen, F. 2012, 'That's all folks: why the writing is on the wall at Microsoft', *Forbes*, 19 June

28 Linkner, J. 2014, *The Road to Reinvention*, Jossey-Bass, San Francisco, p. 14

29 2011, 'Howard Schultz on what's brewing at Starbucks', *Bloomberg Businessweek*, 31 March

30 Efrati, A. 2012, 'A makeover made in Google's image', *The Wall Street Journal*, 9 August

31 Rigby, R. 2011, *Business Thinkers who Changed the World*, Kogan Page, London, p. 157

32 Ecclesiastes 3:3, *The Holy Bible – New Living Translation*, Tyndale House, Wheaton IL, 1996

33 Gettler, L. 2012, 'Focused on the negatives', *Management Today*, April

34 Swartz, J. 2012, 'How high can Apple fly?', *USA Today*, October 5-7

35   Wingfield, N. 2012, 'Apple profit rises 24% on sales of iPhone 5', *The New York Times*, 25 October

36   Arends, B. 2012, 'Why Microsoft beats Apple', *The Wall Street Journal*, 16 November

37   2015, 'Picking the next disruption', *Business Spectator*, 27 July

38   Bort, J. 2015, 'Retiring Cisco CEO delivers dire prediction: 40% of companies will be dead in 10 years', *Business Insider*, 9 June

39   Collins, J. 2009, *How the Mighty Fall*, Random House Business Books, London, p. 8

40   Carroll, P & Mui, C. 2008, *Billion Dollar Lessons*, Penguin, New York, p. 3

41   Collins, J. 2009, *How the Mighty Fall*, Random House Business Books, London, pp. 119, 120

42   Goldsmith, M. 2009, *Succession: Are you Ready?*, Harvard Business School Publishing, p. 50

43   Porter, M. 2012, 'How to save the British pub', *Business Life*, October

44   Surowiecki, J. 2004, *The Wisdom of Crowds*, Anchor Books, New York, p. 243

45   Howard, S. 2012, 'Resurrection on sea', *Australian Way*, March

46   Berry, I & Gee, K. 2012, 'America's milk business in a 'crisis'', *The Wall Street Journal*, 11 December

47   Bowsky, W. 1971. *The Black Death: A Turning Point in History?*, Holt, Rinehart and Winston.

48   Coorey, P. 2012, 'Labor has lost its purpose – and soul', *Sydney Morning Herald,* 26 September

49   Efrati, A. 2012, 'Google founder call U.S. a 'bonfire of partisanship'', *The Wall Street Journal*, 6 November

50   Obama, B. 2012, 'State of the Union Address Transcript', *Washington Post,* 24 January

51   Dent, H. 2009, *The Great Depression Ahead*, Simon and Schuster, New York, p. 9

52   Ibid, p. 43

53 Banjo, S. 2012, 'Shopping's great age divide', *The Wall Street Journal*, 26 November

54 Daniels, S. 2007, 'Gen Y considerations for the retail industry', *Australian Centre for Retail Studies Thought Leadership Series,* June

55 Germano, S. 2014, 'A game of golf? Not for many millennials', *The Wall Street Journal* 1 August

56 Chaykowski, K. 2015, 'Add this to Twitter's growth woes: a flock of younger social apps threatens to eclipse it', *Forbes*, 15 June

57 Putnam, R. 2000, *Bowling Alone*, Simon and Schuster, New York, p. 72

58 Ibid, p. 73

59 Hughes P & Reid S. 2009, 'All Melbourne Matters', *The Christian Research Association*, February

60 Ramsay, M. 2012, 'Old Mustang is put out to pasture', *The Wall Street Journal*, 16 April

61 Ibid.

62 Van den Bergh, J & Behrer, M. 2011, *How Cool Brands Stay Hot*, Kogan, Philadelphia, pp. 131, 132

63 Kash, R & Calhoun, D. 2010, *How Companies Win*, HarperCollins, New York, pp. 15-17

64 Drucker, P. 1985, *Innovation and Entrepreneurship*, HarperCollins, New York, p. 92

65 Ibid, p. 90

66 Turner, M. 2003, *Kmart's 10 Deadly Sins*, Wiley and Sons, New Jersey, p. 84

67 Drucker, P. 1985, *Innovation and Entrepreneurship*, HarperCollins, New York, p. 90

68 Ibid, p. 121

69 Ibid, pp. 121-122

70 Sull, D. 2003, *Why Good Companies Go Bad*, Harvard Business School, pp. 33, 34

71 Ovide, S. 2012, 'Microsoft hits back as Google muscles in', *The Wall Street Journal*, 16 July

72 Kash, R & Calhoun, D. 2010, *How Companies Win*, HarperCollins, New York, pp. 6-7

73 Troianovski, A & Moen, A. 2012, 'Nokia crisis deepens, shares plunge', *The Wall Street Journal*, 11 April

74 2013, 'Suitors circle Blackberry as losses blow out', *The New York Times*, 23 September

75 Dummet, B. 2014, 'Time for Blackberry to find revenue', *The Wall Street Journal*, 15 June

76 Vara, V. 2013, 'How Blackberry Fell', *The New Yorker*, 12 August

77 Connors, W. 2012, 'Blackberry maker in turmoil', *The Wall Street Journal*, 30 March

78 Dou, E. 2013, "HTC's profit drops 83%', *The Wall Street Journal*, 5 July

79 Luk, L. 2012, 'HTC profit falls 79% amid competition', *The Wall Street Journal*, 8 October

80 Dou, E. 2013, 'How HTC lost its way with smartphones', *The Wall Street Journal*, 23 June

81 Carroll, P & Mui, C. 2008, *Billion Dollar Lessons*, Penguin, New York, pp. 109-111

82 Ziobro, P. 2014, 'Barbie's Smile Fails to Mask Sagging Results at Mattel', *The Wall Street Journal*, 16 October

83 Rigby, R. 2011, *Business Thinkers who Changed the World*, Kogan Page, London, p. 194

84 DeGeorge, G. 1996, *The Making of a Blockbuster*, Wiley and Sons, New Jersey

85 Ramachandran, S. 2013, 'Dish to shut 300 Blockbuster sites; 3,000 layoffs loom', *The Wall Street Journal*, 22 January

86 Peers, M. 2013, 'Dish network to close its remaining US Blockbuster stores', *The Wall Street Journal*, 6 November

87 Barnes, T. 2012, 'A little of our culture dies with the printed Britannica', *The Age,* 23 March

88 Bingham, A. 2011, 'U.S. postal service may close 3,700 post offices – is yours on the list?', *ABC News*, 26 July

89 2012, 'Australia Post builds on online shopping', *Sydney Morning Herald,* 14 February

90 Donnell, H. 2012, 'NZPost considers mail cutbacks', *The New Zealand Herald*, 26 April

91 Fowler, G & Loten, A. 2012, 'Old watchdog learns new web tricks', *The Wall Street Journal*, 7 March

92 Corrigan, T. 2015, 'SkyMall files for bankruptcy', *The Wall Street Journal*, 23 January

93 Christensen, P & Raynor, M. 2003, *The Innovators Solution*, Harvard Business School, pp. 103-105

94 Meade, A. 2012, 'After 80 years, ABC rules itself out of plays', *The Australian*, 26 September

95 Carroll, P & Mui, C. 2008, *Billion Dollar Lessons*, Penguin, New York, pp. 106-108

96 Sabbagh, D. 2011, 'Nintendo in crisis: death by iPhone', *Sydney Morning Herald,* 7 November

97 Winkler, R. 2012, 'HP's Facebook challenge', *The Wall Street Journal*, 24 February

98 Hirschauge, O. 2015, 'Are driverless cars safer cars?', *The Wall Street Journal*, 14 August

99 Genziuk, S. 2015, 'Don't blame me – blame the car', *ANZIIF Journal*, Vol 38, Issue 2

100 Kanter, Z. 2015, 'Autonomous cars will destroy millions of jobs and reshape US economy by 2025', *Quartz*, 13 May

101 Ibid.

102 Ibid.

103 Ibid.

104 Ibid.

105 Ramsey, M. 2014, 'Tesla CEO Musk sees full autonomous cars ready in five or six years', *The Wall Street Journal*, 17 September

106 Kanter, Z. 2015, 'Autonomous cars will destroy millions of jobs and reshape US economy by 2025', *Quartz*, 13 May

107 2011, 'The Well Connected Traveller', *Travelport and The Futures Company.*

108 Ibid.

109 Kash, R & Calhoun, D. 2010, *How Companies Win*, HarperCollins, New York, pp. 2-3

110 Bustillo, M. 2012, 'Best Buy forced to rethink big box', *The Wall Street Journal*, 29 March

111 Zimmerman, A. 2012, 'Best Buy to match online prices', *The Wall Street Journal*, 12 October

112 Zimmerman, A. 2012, 'Can retailers halt 'showrooming'?', *The Wall Street Journal*, 11 April

113 Duck, S & Jacob, P. 2011, 'Retailers' try-on fee a fitting response to net losses', *The Herald Sun*, 24 September

114 Gara, T. 2013, 'Has Best Buy turned the tide on Amazon?', *The Wall Street Journal*, 5 April

115 Fitzgerald, D. 2013, 'Fear of showrooming fades', *The Wall Street Journal*, 3 November

116 Tutty, J. 2015, 'Smart shoppers researching online before hitting bricks and mortar stores', *The Courier-Mail*, 18 July

117 Carroll, P & Mui, C. 2008, *Billion Dollar Lessons*, Penguin, New York, p. 102

118 Scott, M. 2012, *Disruptions and Dividends – A presentation delivered to the Institute for a Broadband-Enabled Society at the University of Melbourne*, 30 September

119 Cullinane, S. 2013, 'What's behind collapse of veteran record store HMV?', *CNN*, 16 January

120 2013, 'There's still money in music', *The Sydney Morning Herald*, 27 February

121 Gosden, E. 2013, 'Thousands of jobs in the balance as music stops at HMV', *The Telegraph*, 16 January

122 Cullinane, S. 2013, 'What's behind collapse of veteran record store HMV?', *CNN*, 16 January

123 Smith, E. 2012, 'Forget CDs. Teens are tuning into YouTube', *The Wall Street Journal*, 14 August

124 Breach, J. 2012, 'Digital publishing: different different but same', *The Big Issue*, 11-24 September

125 Price, L. 2012, 'Dead again', *The New York Times*, 10 August

126 Trachtenberg, J. 2012, 'HarperCollins closes last warehouses', *The Wall Street Journal*, 5 November

127 Scott, M. 2012, *Disruptions and Dividends – A presentation delivered to the Institute for a Broadband-Enabled Society at the University of Melbourne*, 30 September

128 Putnam, R. 2000, *Bowling Alone*, Simon and Schuster, New York, p. 218

129 Osterwalder, A & Pigneur, Y. 2010, *Business Model Generation*, Wiley and Sons, New Jersey, p. 93

130 Rusbridger, A. 2010, *The Splintering of the Fourth Estate – Andrew Olle Media Lecture*, 20 November

131 Ibid.

132 Price, L. 2012, 'Dead again', *The New York Times*, 10 August

133 Worthen, B & Sherr, I. 2012, 'Dell still struggling amid shift in computer market', *The Wall Street Journal*, 15 November

134 Worthen, B & Sherr, I. 2012, 'PC sales go into a tailspin', *The Wall Street Journal*, 11 October

135 Jakab, S. 2012, 'Microsoft fate tied to more than earnings', *The Wall Street Journal*, 18 October

136 Liedtke, M. 2014, 'PCs cap off worst-ever sales year with holiday slump', *The Sydney Morning Herald*, 10 January

137 Scott, M. 2012, *Disruptions and Dividends – A presentation delivered to the Institute for a Broadband-Enabled Society at the University of Melbourne*, 30 September

138 Sterngold, J. 2015, 'Uber's rise has taxi lender taking new route', *The Wall Street Journal,* 7 January

139 Karmin, C. 2013, 'Airbnb finds little hospitality in New York market', *The Wall Street Journal*, 20 October

140 Ramsay, M. 2012, 'Ford's trade-in: truck to use aluminum in place of steel', *The Wall Street Journal*, 26 July

141 Sull, D. 2003, *Why Good Companies Go Bad*, Harvard Business School, p. 32

142 Rigby, R. 2011, *Business Thinkers who Changed the World*, Kogan Page, London, p. 1

143 Landes, D. 2000, *Revolution in Time*, Harvard University Press

144 Thompson, J. 2009, '1969: Seiko's breakout year', *Watchtime*, 20 December

145 Ibid.

146 Linkner, J. 2014, *The Road to Reinvention*, Jossey-Bass, San Francisco, p. 28

147 Drucker, P. 1985, *Innovation and Entrepreneurship*, HarperCollins, New York, pp. 71-72

148 Carroll, P & Mui, C. 2008, *Billion Dollar Lessons*, Penguin, New York, p. 91

149 Spector, M & Mattioli, D. 2012, 'Kodak teeters on the brink', *The Wall Street Journal*, 20 January

150 Neate, R. 2012, 'Kodak files for bankruptcy protection', *Sydney Morning Herald,* 7 November

151 Carroll, P & Mui, C. 2008, *Billion Dollar Lessons*, Penguin, New York, p. 88

152 Ibid, pp. 92-93

153 Gettler, L. 2012, 'Focused on the negatives', *Management Today*, April

154 Carroll, P & Mui, C. 2008, *Billion Dollar Lessons*, Penguin, New York, p. 93

155 Ibid, p. 94

156 Neate, R. 2012, 'Kodak files for bankruptcy protection', *Sydney Morning Herald,* 7 November

157 Gettler, L. 2012, 'Focused on the negatives', *Management Today*, April

158 Carroll, P & Mui, C. 2008, *Billion Dollar Lessons*, Penguin, New York, p. 103

159 Ibid, p. 93

160 Ibid, p. 88

161 Ibid, p. 98

162 Neate, R. 2012, 'Kodak files for bankruptcy protection', *Sydney Morning Herald,* 7 November

163 Kriegel, R. 1991, *If it ain't broke... break it!*, Time Warner, New York, p. 74

164 Harford, T. 2011, *Adapt*, Farrar, Straus and Giroux, New York, p. 242

165 Kriegel, R. 1991, *If it ain't broke... break it!*, Time Warner, New York, pp. 64-65

166 Ibid, pp. 67-68

167 Ibid, pp. 66-67

168 Kriegel, R & Brandt, D. 1997, *Sacred Cows Make the Best Burgers*, Time Warner, New York, pp. 46-48

169 Harford, T. 2011, *Adapt*, Farrar, Straus and Giroux, New York, p. 242

170 Gasparro, A. 2015, 'A&P bankruptcy filing indicates likely demise', *The Wall Street Journal*, 20 July

171 Proverbs 16:18, *The Holy Bible – New Living Translation*, Tyndale House, Wheaton IL, 1996

172 Collins, J. 2009, *How the Mighty Fall*, Random House Business Books, London, pp. 28, 29

173 Drucker, P. 1985, *Innovation and Entrepreneurship*, HarperCollins, New York, p. 85

174 Eichenwald, K. 2012, 'Microsoft's lost decade', *Vanity Fair,* August

175 Ibid.

176 Wakabayashi, D. 2012, 'How Japan lost its electronics crown', *The Wall Street Journal*, 15 August

177 MacKay, H. 2011, 'Where there's faith, so too doubt', *Sydney Morning Herald,* 26 December

178 Kriegel, R. 1991, *If it ain't broke... break it!*, Time Warner, New York, p. 4

179 Daley, P. 2011, 'Back to the front', *Australian Way*, November

180 Sull, D. 2003, *Why Good Companies Go Bad*, Harvard Business School, pp. 29-32

181 Turner, M. 2003, *Kmart's 10 Deadly Sins*, Wiley and Sons, New Jersey, pp. 100-101

182 Ibid, pp. 100-101

183 Ibid, p. 8

184 Sull, D. 2003, *Why Good Companies Go Bad*, Harvard Business School, pp. 44-57

185 Krupp, S. 2015, '6 strategies great leaders use for long-term success', *Business Insider*, 19 May

186 Surowiecki, J. 2004, *The Wisdom of Crowds*, Anchor Books, New York, pp. 36-37

187 Sull, D. 2003, *Why Good Companies Go Bad*, Harvard Business School, pp. 44-57

188 Ibid, pp. 44-57

189 Lublin, J. 2015, 'Study links diverse leadership with firms' financial gains', *The Wall Street Journal*, 20 January

190 Drucker, P. 1985, *Innovation and Entrepreneurship*, HarperCollins, New York, p. 126

191 Kriegel, R. 1991, *If it ain't broke… break it!*, Time Warner, New York, pp. 2, 69

192 Collins, J & Porras, J. 1994, *Built to Last*, HarperCollins, New York, p. 81

193 Kriegel, R & Brandt, D. 1997, *Sacred Cows Make the Best Burgers*, Time Warner, New York, pp. 5-6

194 Sull, D. 2003, *Why Good Companies Go Bad*, Harvard Business School, pp. 25-29, 35

195 Kriegel, R & Brandt, D. 1997, *Sacred Cows Make the Best Burgers*, Time Warner, New York, p. 1

196 Collins, J & Porras, J. 1994, *Built to Last*, HarperCollins, New York, p. 83

197 Christensen, C. 2000, *The Innovator's Dilemma*, Harper Collins, New York, pp. 101-103

198 Drucker, P. 1985, *Innovation and Entrepreneurship*, HarperCollins, New York, pp. 59-60

199   Ibid, pp. 38-39

200   Ackerman, P. 2011, 'Senior cop apologises for affidavit shortcuts in Melbourne's gangland war', *The Australian*, 20 December

201   2011, From 60 Minutes feature *The Mad World of '70s Tupperware Parties*, CBS, 20 February

202   Penner, J. 1992. *Goliath,* New Hope Publishing, Los Angeles, p. 106

203   Schuller, R. 2005, *A Place of Beauty, a Joy Forever*, Crystal Cathedral Creative Services, Los Angeles, pp. 19, 22, 26

204   Ibid, pp. 42, 45

205   Ibid, p. 48

206   Santa Cruz, N. 2010, 'Crystal Cathedral stays optimistic amid declining revenue', *Los Angeles Times*, 15 February

207   Linkner, J. 2014, *The Road to Reinvention*, Jossey-Bass, San Francisco, p. 77

208   Kwoh, L. 2012, 'You call that innovation?', *The Wall Street Journal*, 23 May

209   Collins, J. 2009, *How the Mighty Fall*, Random House Business Books, London, p. 55

210   Gallo, C. 2011, 'Steve Jobs: get rid of all the crappy stuff', *Forbes*, 16 May

211   Collins, J. 2009, *How the Mighty Fall*, Random House Business Books, London, p. 47

212   Turner, M. 2003, *Kmart's 10 Deadly Sins*, Wiley and Sons, New Jersey, pp. 165-166

213   Ibid, p. 103

214   Carroll, P & Mui, C. 2008, *Billion Dollar Lessons*, Penguin, New York, p. 171

215   Sonne, P. 2012, 'At Tesco, expansion takes a back seat', *The Wall Street Journal*, 7 November

216   Kash, R & Calhoun, D. 2010, *How Companies Win*, HarperCollins, New York, pp. 15-17

217   Ibid, p. 16

218 Collins, J. 2009, *How the Mighty Fall*, Random House Business Books, London, pp. 48, 49

219 Osati, S. 2011, 'Steve Jobs wanted Apple to be like Sony', *www.sonyrumors.net*, 11 October

220 Collins, J. 2009, *How the Mighty Fall*, Random House Business Books, London, p. 54

221 Burns, M. 2011, 'Its official at HP: Apotheker is out, Meg Whitman named president and CEO', *Tech Crunch*, 22 September

222 Bookman, S. 2011, 'Mike Zafirovski, Nortel networks', *FierceTelecom*, 22 November

223 Dawson, C. 2012, 'For Datsun revival, Nissan gambles on $3,000 model', *The Wall Street Journal*, 1 October

224 Carroll, P & Mui, C. 2008, *Billion Dollar Lessons*, Penguin, New York, p. 117

225 Cohan, P. 2011, 'How success killed Eastman Kodak', *Forbes*, 1 October

226 Carroll, P & Mui, C. 2008, *Billion Dollar Lessons*, Penguin, New York, p. 138

227 Koziol, M. 2015, '10 product flops that outdo Coke life', *The Sydney Morning Herald*, 26 May

228 Collins, J. 2009, *How the Mighty Fall*, Random House Business Books, London, p. 55

229 Andreessen, M. 2011, 'Why software is eating the world', *The Wall Street Journal*, 20 August

230 Carroll, P & Mui, C. 2008, *Billion Dollar Lessons*, Penguin, New York, pp. 143-153

231 Smith, A. 2012, 'Is it bye, bye Blackberry?', *Sydney Morning Herald*, 14 July

232 Connors, W. 2012, 'Multiple missteps led to RIM's fall', *The Wall Street Journal*, 28 June

233 Sharot, T, Korn C & Dolan R. 2011, 'How unrealistic optimism is maintained in the face of reality', *Nature Neuroscience*, 9 October

234 Harford, T. 2011, *Adapt*, Farrar, Straus and Giroux, New York, p. 251

235 Carroll, P & Mui, C. 2008, *Billion Dollar Lessons*, Penguin, New York, p. 87

236 Kriegel, R & Brandt, D. 1997, *Sacred Cows Make the Best Burgers*, Time Warner, New York, p. 6

237 Collins, J. 2009, *How the Mighty Fall*, Random House Business Books, London, p. 78

238 Osati, S. 2011, 'Steve Jobs wanted Apple to be like Sony', *www.sonyrumors.net*, 11 October

239 Harford, T. 2011, *Adapt*, Farrar, Straus and Giroux, New York, p. 250

240 Munsey, P. 2008, *Legacy Now*, Charisma House, Florida, pp. 159-160

241 Kouzes, J & Posner, B. 2006, *A Leader's Legacy*, Jossey-Bass, San Francisco, pp. 99-102.

242 Kriegel, R. 1991, *If it ain't broke… break it!*, Time Warner, New York, p. 33

243 Eichenwald, K. 2012, 'Microsoft's lost decade', *Vanity Fair,* August

244 Ibid.

245 2012, 'Curse of the skyscrapers', *Sydney Morning Herald,* 17 January

246 Echenberg, M. 2002, 'Pestis Redux: The Initial Years of the Third Bubonic Plague Pandemic, 1894-1901', *Journal of World History,* Vol 13, 2

247 Collins, J. 2009, *How the Mighty Fall*, Random House Business Books, London, p. 25

248 Lublin, N. 2010, 'Why charities should have an expiration date', *Fast Company,* 8 December

249 Nagourney, A. 2011, 'Pearl Harbor still a day for the ages, but a memory almost gone', *The New York Times,* 6 December

250 Collins, J & Porras, J. 1994, *Built to Last*, HarperCollins, New York, pp. 52, 53

251 Gettler, L. 2012, 'Focused on the negatives', *Management Today,* April

252 Kriegel, R & Brandt, D. 1997, *Sacred Cows Make the Best Burgers*, Time Warner, New York, p. 51

253 Zschech, D. 2009, *The Great Generational Transition*, EWI, Sydney, p. 25

254 Ashton, J. 2011, 'Google's search for its future', *The Australian*, 4 April

255 Collins, J & Porras, J. 1994, *Built to Last*, HarperCollins, New York, p. 51

256 Ibid, pp. 68, 69

257 Ibid, p. 74

258 Ibid, p. 228

259 Ibid, p. 87

260 Ibid, p. 222

261 Ibid, p. xviii

262 Ibid, p. 74

263 Ibid, p. 73

264 Ibid, p. 225

265 Ibid, pp. 225-226

266 Ibid, p. 81

267 Collins, J. 2009, *How the Mighty Fall*, Random House Business Books, London, p. 164

268 Collins, J & Porras, J. 1994, *Built to Last*, HarperCollins, New York, pp. 81, 82

269 Ibid, pp. 81, 82

270 Ibid, p. 77

271 Ibid, p. 55

272 Ibid, p. 8

273 Ibid, p. 47

274 Ibid, p. 65

275 Ibid, p. 56

276 Ibid, p. 77

277 *This is an excerpt from a presentation delivered by Howard Schultz on April 21, 2011 as part of a publicity tour for his new book 'Onward'*

278 Ibid.

279 Reiss, R. 2009, 'How Ritz-Carlton stays on top', *Forbes*, 30 October

280 England, L. 2015, 'Here's what's inside the little red book that is placed on the desk of every Facebook employee', *Business Insider*, 29 May

281 Galford, R & Maruca, R. 2006, *Your Leadership Legacy*, Harvard Business School, pp. 10-11

282 Collins, J & Porras, J. 1994, *Built to Last*, HarperCollins, New York, p. 80

283 Collins, J. 2009, *How the Mighty Fall*, Random House Business Books, London, p. 53

284 Collins, J. 1995, 'Change is good – but first, know what should never change', *Fortune*, November

285 Collins, J & Porras, J. 1994, *Built to Last*, HarperCollins, New York, p. 46

286 Proverbs 29:18, *The Holy Bible – New Living Translation*, Tyndale House, Wheaton IL, 1996

287 Heath, C & Heath, D. 2010, *Switch*, Broadway Books, New York, pp. 67-71

288 Kriegel, R. 1991, *If it ain't broke... break it!*, Time Warner, New York, p. 101

289 'Case studies on innovation', *IBS Case Development Centre*, p. 20

290 Linkner, J. 2014, *The Road to Reinvention*, Jossey-Bass, San Francisco, p. 134

291 Kash, R & Calhoun, D. 2010, *How Companies Win*, HarperCollins, New York, p. 223

292 Rigby, R. 2011, *Business Thinkers who Changed the World*, Kogan Page, London, p. 23

293 Thurm, S. 2012, 'For big companies, life is good', *The Wall Street Journal*, 9 April

294 Carroll, P & Mui, C. 2008, *Billion Dollar Lessons*, Penguin, New York, pp. xviii-xix

295 Kriegel, R & Brandt, D. 1997, *Sacred Cows Make the Best Burgers*, Time Warner, New York, p. 17

296 Muller, J. 2004, *Plant Pruning A to Z*, Lothian, Melbourne, pp. 10, 11

297 1997, *Pruning Made Easy*, Ward Lock, London, p. 6

298 Stowar, J. 1998, *The Garden Adviser*, Bookman Press, Melbourne, pp. 451-452

299 Muller, J. 2004, *Plant Pruning A to Z*, Lothian, Melbourne, p. 11

300 Wakabayashi, D. 2012, 'New Sony chief executive reveals fast-forward plans', *The Wall Street Journal*, 2 February

301 Osati, S. 2011, 'Steve Jobs wanted Apple to be like Sony', *www.sonyrumors.net*, 11 October

302 Wakabayashi, D & Takahashi, Y. 2012, 'Sony's new CEO vows to 'revive' company', *The Wall Street Journal*, 12 April

303 Ibid.

304 Pascoe, M. 2012, 'What to learn from Sony's greatest mistake', *Sydney Morning Herald*, 29 June

305 Wakabayashi, D. 2012, 'New Sony chief executive reveals fast-forward plans', *The Wall Street Journal*, 2 February

306 Wakabayashi, D. 2012, 'Live blog: Sony CEO Kazuo Hirai', *The Wall Street Journal*, 12 April

307 Wakabayashi, D & Takahashi, Y. 2012, 'New Sony CEO to cut 10,000 jobs', *The Wall Street Journal*, 9 April

308 Ibid.

309 Wakabayashi, D & Takahashi, Y. 2012, 'Sony's new CEO vows to 'revive' company', *The Wall Street Journal*, 12 April

310 Mochizuki, T. 2014, 'Sony turnaround effort falters, expects $2.15 billion yearly loss', *The Wall Street Journal*, 17 September

311 Collins, J. 2009, *How the Mighty Fall*, Random House Business Books, London, pp. 163-166

312 Kehoe, J. 2014, 'IBM struggles in new world', *The Australian Financial Review*, 22 October

313 Morgan, G & Zohar, A. "Ricardo Semler's Transformation at Semco", www.imaginiz.com/provocative/change/semco.html (accessed February 2013)

314 Birchall, A. 2012, 'The brains behind bureaucracy', *Management Today*, May

315 Kriegel, R. 1991, *If it ain't broke… break it!*, Time Warner, New York, p. 117

316 Obama, B. 2012, 'State of the Union Address Transcript', *Washington Post,* 24 January

317 'Case studies on innovation', *IBS Case Development Centre*, p. 21

318 Carroll, P & Mui, C. 2008, *Billion Dollar Lessons*, Penguin, New York, p. 226

319 Troianovski, A & Grundenberg, S. 2012, 'Nokia's bad call on smartphones', *The Wall Street Journal*, 18 July

320 Linkner, J. 2014, *The Road to Reinvention*, Jossey-Bass, San Francisco, p. 58

321 Eichenwald, K. 2012, 'Microsoft's lost decade', *Vanity Fair,* August

322 Ibid.

323 Ibid.

324 Ibid.

325 Ibid.

326 Worthen, B & Sherr, I. 2012, 'CEO Whitman tells HPs workers 'everything is on table' in overhaul', *The Wall Street Journal*, 21 March

327 Ovide, S. 2014, 'Hewlett-Packard: will slimmer make stronger?', *The Wall Street Journal*, 6 October

328 Carey, S. 2012, 'American Air says quick cuts needed', *The Wall Street Journal*, 27 February

329 Bustillo, M. 2012, 'Best Buy forced to rethink big box', *The Wall Street Journal*, 29 March

330 Zimmerman, A. 2012, 'At Best Buy, all eyes are on the boss', *The Wall Street Journal*, 17 June

331 Ziobro, P. 2012, 'Quick changes at Burger King', *The Wall Street Journal*, 4 April

332 Dyer, J, Gregersen, H & Christensen, C. 2011, *The Innovator's DNA*, Harvard Business School, p. 169

333 Fisher, G. 2009, 'Cut the chaos to grow your business', *Entrepreneur,* 25 October

334 Silverman, R. 2012, 'Who's the boss? There isn't one', *The Wall Street Journal*, 19 June

335   Wakabayashi, D. 2012, 'Hitachi President Prods Turnaround', *The Wall Street Journal*, 10 May

336   Wakabayashi, D. 2013, 'Panasonic to Pare Unprofitable Units', *The Wall Street Journal*, 28 March

337   Sidel, R. 2013, 'After years of growth, banks are pruning their branches', *The Wall Street Journal*, 31 March

338   Gallo, C. 2011, 'Steve Jobs: get rid of all the crappy stuff', *Forbes*, 16 May

339   Rosenthall, J. 2012, 'Steve Jobs' advice to Larry Page', *Digg*, 22 October

340   LeClaire, J. 2011, 'Larry Page-Run Google shutters 7 more projects', *NewsFactor*, 23 November

341   Ng, S. 2014, 'P&G to shed more than half of its brands', *The Wall Street Journal,* 1 August

342   Adams, R. 2012, 'AOL's CEO defends strategy', *The Wall Street Journal*, 13 March

343   Stowar, J. 1998, *The Garden Adviser*, Bookman Press, Melbourne, p. 451

344   Osterwalder, A & Pigneur, Y. 2010, *Business Model Generation*, Wiley and Sons, New Jersey, p. 234

345   Drucker, P. 1985, *Innovation and Entrepreneurship*, HarperCollins, New York, pp. 62-63

346   Linkner, J. 2014, *The Road to Reinvention*, Jossey-Bass, San Francisco, p. 83

347   Ries, E. 2011, *The Lean Startup*, Crown Publishing Group, New York, p. 274

348   Collins, J & Porras, J. 1994, *Built to Last*, HarperCollins, New York, pp. 73, 74.

349   Drucker, P. 1985, *Innovation and Entrepreneurship*, HarperCollins, New York, p. 50

350   Linkner, J. 2014, *The Road to Reinvention*, Jossey-Bass, San Francisco, p. 76

351   Jacks, T. 2015, 'Australian SMEs failing the innovation test, says Microsoft', *The Australian Financial Review,* 17 March

352   Kriegel, R. 1991, *If it ain't broke... break it!,* Time Warner, New York, pp. 127-128

353   Michaels, D. 2012, 'Hit by delays, Airbus tries new way of building planes', *The Wall Street Journal,* 11 July

354   Ostrower, J. 2012, 'Boeing says cuts save $1.6 billion', *The Wall Street Journal,* 7 November

355   Vincent, F. 2012, 'How about a three-year B.A.?', *The Wall Street Journal,* 27 June

356   Manjoo, F. 2012, 'How Apple really invented the iPhone', *Sydney Morning Herald,* 12 September

357   Dyer, J, Gregersen, H & Christensen, C. 2011, *The Innovator's DNA,* Harvard Business School, pp. 199, 200

358   Heath, C & Heath, D. 2007, *Made to Stick,* Random House, New York, pp. 29, 30

359   Kriegel, R & Brandt, D. 1997, *Sacred Cows Make the Best Burgers,* Time Warner, New York, pp. 171, 172

360   Ibid, pp. 3, 4

361   Meichtry, S. 2012, 'Fiat chief retools Italian car maker', *The Wall Street Journal,* 8 July

362   Terlep, S. 2012, 'GM's chief labors to get car rebuilt car maker into gear', *The Wall Street Journal,* 11 June

363   Ibid.

364   Ramsay, M. 2012, 'Ford caps turnaround effort', *The Wall Street Journal,* 29 October

365   Hagerty, J. 2012, 'Harley goes lean to build hogs', *The Wall Street Journal,* 21 September

366   Kriegel, R. 1991, *If it ain't broke... break it!,* Time Warner, New York, p. 76

367   Turner, M. 2003, *Kmart's 10 Deadly Sins,* Wiley and Sons, New Jersey, p. 13

368 Kriegel, R & Brandt, D. 1997, *Sacred Cows Make the Best Burgers*, Time Warner, New York, pp. 54, 55

369 Zimmerman, A. 2012, 'Can electronics stores survive?', *The Wall Street Journal*, 30 August

370 Hoffman, C. 2011, 'Shooting for the stars', *The Wall Street Journal*, 27 October

371 Valdes-Dapena, P. 2012, 'Shop at the mall for your $100,000 Tesla', *CNN Money*, 8 June

372 Lee, M. 2012, 'Tesla stores challenges auto dealerships', *Union-Tribune San Diego*, 26 October

373 Dyer, J, Gregersen, H & Christensen, C. 2011, *The Innovator's DNA*, Harvard Business School, p. 150

374 Linkner, J. 2014, *The Road to Reinvention*, Jossey-Bass, San Francisco, p. 66

375 Stix, M. 2014, 'Teen to government: change your typeface, save millions', *CNN digital*, 29 March

376 Ibid, pp. 42, 43

377 Chandra, A. 2015, 'How to help innovation grow up at your organisation', *Fast Company*, 18 May

378 Lawton, C. 2012, 'Inside SAP's skunkworks as it takes aim at Oracle', *The Wall Street Journal*, 26 January

379 Ibid.

380 Jargon, J. 2012, ''Super Size Me' generation takes over at McDonald's', *The Wall Street Journal*, 8 March

381 Surowiecki, J. 2004, *The Wisdom of Crowds*, Anchor Books, New York, pp. 30, 31

382 Sherr, I. 2012, 'Rivals Ford, GM Rev Up With New War on Apps', *The Wall Street Journal*, 7 January

383 Dyer, J, Gregersen, H & Christensen, C. 2011, *The Innovator's DNA*, Harvard Business School, pp. 202, 203

384 Kriegel, R. 1991, *If it ain't broke... break it!*, Time Warner, New York, p. 137

385 Harford, T. 2011, *Adapt*, Farrar, Straus and Giroux, New York, pp. 108, 109

386 Denne, S. 2012, 'Citrix turns to start-ups to stay hip', *The Wall Street Journal*, 22 June

387 Dyer, J, Gregersen, H & Christensen, C. 2011, *The Innovator's DNA*, Harvard Business School, pp. 205, 206

388 Osterwalder, A & Pigneur, Y. 2010, *Business Model Generation*, Wiley and Sons, New Jersey, p. 112

389 Dyer, J, Gregersen, H & Christensen, C. 2011, *The Innovator's DNA*, Harvard Business School, pp. 46, 47

390 Carroll, P & Mui, C. 2008, *Billion Dollar Lessons*, Penguin, New York, p. xvi

391 1993, 'To Delta, that's a lot of lettuce', *The Chicago Tribune*, 28 February

392 Dyer, J, Gregersen, H & Christensen, C. 2011, *The Innovator's DNA*, Harvard Business School, p. 68

393 Collins, J & Hansen, M. 2011, *Great by Choice*, HarperCollins, New York, pp. 139, 140

394 Hall, S. 2013, 'McLaren to axe windscreen wipers: report', *The Sydney Morning Herald*, 19 December

395 Kriegel, R. 1991, *If it ain't broke... break it!*, Time Warner, New York, p. 140

396 Osterwalder, A & Pigneur, Y. 2010, *Business Model Generation*, Wiley and Sons, New Jersey, p. 141

397 Ibid, p. 141

398 Carroll, P & Mui, C. 2008, *Billion Dollar Lessons*, Penguin, New York, p. 232

399 Ibid, p. 233

400 Krupp, S. 2015, '6 strategies great leaders use for long-term success', *Business Insider*, 19 May

401 Carroll, P & Mui, C. 2008, *Billion Dollar Lessons*, Penguin, New York, p. 231

402 Ibid, p. 236

403 Collins, J & Hansen, M. 2011, *Great by Choice*, HarperCollins, New York, pp. 144, 145

404 Linkner, J. 2014, *The Road to Reinvention*, Jossey-Bass, San Francisco, p. 75

405 Kriegel, R. 1991, *If it ain't broke… break it!*, Time Warner, New York, pp. 106-107

406 Harford, T. 2011, *Adapt*, Farrar, Straus and Giroux, New York, p. 242

407 Ibid, p. 11

408 Dyer, J, Gregersen, H & Christensen, C. 2011, *The Innovator's DNA*, Harvard Business School, p. 166

409 Ibid, pp. 221, 222

410 Anders, G. 2012, 'Jeff Bezos gets it', *Forbes*, 7 May

411 Chandra, A. 2015, 'How to help innovation grow up at your organisation', *Fast Company*, 18 May

412 Noonan, P. 2011, 'A caveman won't beat a salesman', *The Wall Street Journal*, 18 November

413 Dyer, J, Gregersen, H & Christensen, C. 2011, *The Innovator's DNA*, Harvard Business School, pp. 32-37

414 Krupp, S. 2015, '6 strategies great leaders use for long-term success', *Business Insider*, 19 May

415 Linkner, J. 2014, *The Road to Reinvention*, Jossey-Bass, San Francisco, p. 34

416 Collins, J & Hansen, M. 2011, *Great by Choice*, HarperCollins, New York, pp. 78-80

417 Christensen, C. 2000, *The Innovator's Dilemma*, Harper Collins, New York, pp. 174, 175

418 Kriegel, R. 1991, *If it ain't broke… break it!*, Time Warner, New York, pp. 155, 156

419 Kwoh, L. 2012, 'You call that innovation?', *The Wall Street Journal*, 23 May

420 Drucker, P. 1985, *Innovation and Entrepreneurship*, HarperCollins, New York, pp. 42, 43

421 Ibid, p. 41

422 Kriegel, R. 1991, *If it ain't broke... break it!*, Time Warner, New York, pp. 155, 156

423 Kash, R & Calhoun, D. 2010, *How Companies Win*, HarperCollins, New York, pp. 224, 225

424 Osterwalder, A & Pigneur, Y. 2010, *Business Model Generation*, Wiley and Sons, New Jersey, p. 72

425 Ibid.

426 Robertson, D. 2013, *Brick by Brick*, Crown Business, New York, p. 231

427 Ibid, p. 259

428 Wilcox, K. 2012, 'The block's answer to Barbie is a hit for Lego', *Sydney Morning Herald,* 14 September

429 Min-Jung, K. 2012, 'Feature of the Months: Lego', *Beyond Magazine,* August

430 Ibid.

431 Robertson, D. 2013, *Brick by Brick*, Crown Business, New York, p. 3

432 Extract taken from www.thinkprogress.org/climate/2012/08/17/705421/how-to-market-efficiency-what-clean-energy-can-learn-from-the-sara-lee-baking-company/ (accessed Feb 2013)

433 Krlegel, R. 1991, *If it ain't broke... break it!*, Time Warner, New York, p. 145

434 Ibid, p. 146

435 Alter, A. 2012, 'Your e-book is reading you', *The Wall Street Journal,* 19 July

436 Mattioli, D. 2012, 'On Orbitz, Mac users steered to pricier hotels', *The Wall Street Journal*, 23 August

437 Glazer, E. 2012, 'The eyes have it: Marketers now track shoppers' retinas', *The Wall Street Journal*, 12 July

438 Dyer, J, Gregersen, H & Christensen, C. 2011, *The Innovator's DNA*, Harvard Business School, pp. 69, 70

439 Ibid.

440 Linkner, J. 2014, *The Road to Reinvention*, Jossey-Bass, San Francisco, pp. 52-53

441 Shenkar, O. 2011, 'The challenge of imovation', *Ivey Business Journal*, March/April

442 Hewitt, G. 2012, ''Uncool' Samsung Muscles ahead of Apple', *Sydney Morning Herald,* 5 November

443 Wakabayashi, D. 2012, 'How Japan lost its electronics crown', *The Wall Street Journal*, 15 August

444 Collins, J & Porras, J. 1994, *Built to Last*, HarperCollins, New York, p. 51

445 Hagerty, J. 2015, '3M's image problem: its products are everywhere, but often overlooked', *The Wall Street Journal*, 10 March

446 Drucker, P. 1985, *Innovation and Entrepreneurship*, HarperCollins, New York, p. 77

447 Mitchell, S. 2015, 'Coca-Cola, Pepsi under pressure as millennials ditch sugar', *The Sydney Morning Herald*, 23 July

448 Esterl, M. 2014, 'Share a Coke credited with pop in sales', *The Wall Street Journal*, 25 September

449 Christensen, P & Raynor, M. 2003, *The Innovators Solution*, Harvard Business School, p. 92

450 'Case studies on innovation', *IBS Case Development Centre*, p. 2

451 Ziobro, P. 2015, 'Target revamps groceries for millennials', *The Wall Street Journal*, 2 March

452 Dyer, J, Gregersen, H & Christensen, C. 2011, *The Innovator's DNA*, Harvard Business School, p. 201

453 Osati, S. 2011, 'Steve Jobs wanted Apple to be like Sony', *www.sonyrumors.net*, 11 October

454 Gettler, L. 2012, 'Focused on the negatives', *Management Today*, April

455 Ramachandran, S & Trachtenberg, J. 2012, 'End of era for Encyclopedia Britannica', *The Wall Street Journal*, 14 March

456 Ibid.

457 Kash, R & Calhoun, D. 2010, *How Companies Win*, HarperCollins, New York, p. 19

458 Ibid, pp. 22, 23

459 Wahba, P. 2015, 'McDonald's is closing hundreds of stores this year', *Fortune*, 22 April

460 Jargon, J. 2013, 'McDonald's acknowledges service has suffered', *The Wall Street Journal*, 14 November

461 Jargon, J. 2013, 'At McDonald's, salads just don't sell', *The Wall Street Journal*, 18 October

462 Ibid.

463 Jargon, J. 2014, 'McDonald's faces millennial challenge', *The Wall Street Journal*, 24 August

464 Jargon, J. 2014, 'McDonald's decline in US sales accelerates', *The Wall Street Journal*, 8 December

465 Jargon, J. 2014, 'McDonald's vows fresh thinking', *The Wall Street Journal*, 21 October

466 Esterl, M. 2012, 'Got a light-er charger? Big tobacco's latest buzz', *The Wall Street Journal*, 25 April

467 Esterl, M. 2012, 'New from Altria: A nicotine lozenge', *The Wall Street Journal*, 21 May

468 Esterl, M, 2015, 'E-cigarette, hookah uses rises among US teens as cigarette use falls', *The Wall Street Journal*, 16 April

469 Esterl, M. 2012, 'Sudsy American dream sells abroad', *The Wall Street Journal*, 8 March

470 Esterl, M. 2012, 'How to build buzz for Bud: More alcohol, Lime-a-Rita', *The Wall Street Journal*, 29 March

471 Kash, R & Calhoun, D. 2010, *How Companies Win*, HarperCollins, New York, pp. 118, 119

472 de Brito, S. 2012, 'Let's hop back to beer, in the spirit of good health', *Sydney Morning Herald,* 20 May

473 Christensen, P & Raynor, M. 2003, *The Innovators Solution*, Harvard Business School, pp. 40, 41

474 Porter, M. 2012, 'How to save the British pub', *Business Life*, October

475 Ibid.

476 Cohan, P. 2011, 'How success killed Eastman Kodak', *Forbes*, 1 October

477 Kriegel, R. 1991, *If it ain't broke… break it!*, Time Warner, New York, pp. 95, 96

478 'Case studies on innovation', *IBS Case Development Centre*, p. 20

479 Simpson, D. 2004, 'Five philosophies for delivering innovative products', www.realinnovation.com/content/c100104.asp (accessed February 2013)

480 Jakab, S. 2015, 'Harley-Davidson's profitable road trip', *The Wall Street Journal*, 20 April

481 Drucker, P. 1985, *Innovation and Entrepreneurship*, HarperCollins, New York, p. 51

482 Dawson, C & Boudette, N. 2012, 'Nissan may revive Datsun', *The Wall Street Journal*, 2 March

483 Dawson, C. 2012, 'For Datsun revival, Nissan gambles on $3000 model', *The Wall Street Journal*, 1 October

484 Ibid.

485 Bellman, E & Dawson. 2012, 'Nissan to resurrect Datsun after 30 years', *The Wall Street Journal*, 20 March

486 'Case studies on innovation', *IBS Case Development Centre*, p. 5

487 2011, 'Newcastle… rediscovered', *Qantaslink Spirit Magazine*, Summer edition

488 Nassauer, S. 2012, ''Larry', Quaker of oatmeal fame, gets a makeover', *The Wall Street Journal*, 29 March

489 Drucker, P. 1985, *Innovation and Entrepreneurship*, HarperCollins, New York, p. 80

490 Van den Bergh, J & Behrer, M. 2011, *How Cool Brands Stay Hot*, Kogan, Philadelphia, pp. 131, 132

491 Ibid.

492 Duxbury, C & Stoll, J. 2012, 'Volvo stakes its claim to driverless vehicles', *The Wall Street Journal*, 3 December

493 2009, 'Lose your job? You can return your new Hyundai', *MSNBC*, 5 January

494 Niedermeyer, E. 2010, 'Fewer than 100 vehicles returned under Hyundai Assurance', *NPR*, 12 January

495 Lower, G. 2012, 'Billabong seeks new cool', *The Wall Street Journal*, 9 July

496 Binkley, C. 2012, 'Teen stores try texts as gr8 nu way to reach out', *The Wall Street Journal*, 1 August

497 Ibid.

498 Ng, S. 2013. 'P&G shifts marketing dollars online, mobile', *The Wall Street Journal*, 1 August

499 Glazer, E. 2012, 'P&G's marketing chief looks to go digital', *The Wall Street Journal*, 13 March

500 Price, L. 2012, 'Dead again', *The New York Times*, 10 August

501 Maloney, J. 2012, 'Libraries rethink their role in the city', *The New York Times*, 9 April

502 Maloney, J. 2013, 'Library eyes new page', *The New York Times*, 14 January

503 Meiser, R. 2013, 'Atoning for Yom Kippur – there's an app for that', *The Wall Street Journal*, 12 September

504 Lagnado, L. 2012, 'Matzo ball soup, check. iPad, check. For Passover, Jews try techie Seders', *The New York Times*, 7 April

505 Hagey, K. 2012, 'Readers vent anger as New Orleans loses daily paper', *The Wall Street Journal*, 11 September

506 Tracer, Z. 2012, 'Buffett says free news is unsustainable, may add more papers', *Bloomberg*, 25 May

507 Hagey, K. 2012, 'New York Times profit sinks 85%', *The Wall Street Journal*, 25 October

508 Hagey, K. 2012, 'Paywalls giving newspapers chance at a comeback', *The Wall Street Journal*, 14 October

509 Daniel, R & Hagey, K. 2012, 'Turning a page: Newsweek ends print run', *The Wall Street Journal*, 14 October

510 Kwoh, L. 2012, 'National Geographic explores digital future', *The Wall Street Journal*, 3 April

511 Ibid.

512 Holmes, E. 2012, 'Leave me alone, I'm shopping', *The Wall Street Journal*, 28 June

513 Smith, A. 2012, 'Just popping by to phone in some window shopping', *Sydney Morning Herald,* 18 February

514 2013, 'It sounds like a scene straight from a science fiction film', *Traveller Magazine,* January

515 Zimmerman, A. 2012, 'Can retailers halt 'showrooming'?', *The Wall Street Journal*, 11 April

516 Papdakis, M. 2013, 'Shopping Channels', *Business Review Weekly,* 28 March

517 Mattioli, D & Bustillo, M. 2012, 'Can texting save stores?', *The Wall Street Journal*, 8 May

518 Ibid.

519 Zimmerman, A. 2012, 'Can retailers halt 'showrooming'?', *The Wall Street Journal*, 11 April

520 Mattioli, D. 2012, 'Macy's regroups in warehouse wars', *The Wall Street Journal*, 14 May

521 Hall, M. 2014, 'Australian company targets online behemoth Amazon', *The Sydney Morning Herald*, 8 April

522 Cummins, C. 2012, 'Nobody home? Postie to leave parcels for pick-up at a locker near you', *Sydney Morning Herald,* 28 May

523 Barr, A. 2014, 'Google adopts delivery-service model, targets Amazon', *The Wall Street Journal*, 14 October

524 Zimmerman, A. 2012, 'Best Buy to match online prices', *The Wall Street Journal*, 12 October

525 Cummins, C. 2012, 'Nobody home? Postie to leave parcels for pick-up at a locker near you', *Sydney Morning Herald,* 28 May